TRANSFERENTIAL POETICS,
FROM POE TO WARHOL

Transferential Poetics, from Poe to Warhol

ADAM FRANK

Fordham University Press
NEW YORK   2015

Copyright © 2015 Fordham University Press

All rights reserved. No part of this publication may be reproduced, stored in a retrieval system, or transmitted in any form or by any means—electronic, mechanical, photocopy, recording, or any other—except for brief quotations in printed reviews, without the prior permission of the publisher.

Fordham University Press has no responsibility for the persistence or accuracy of URLs for external or third-party Internet websites referred to in this publication and does not guarantee that any content on such websites is, or will remain, accurate or appropriate.

Fordham University Press also publishes its books in a variety of electronic formats. Some content that appears in print may not be available in electronic books.

Visit us online at www.fordhampress.com.

Library of Congress Cataloging-in-Publication Data is available from the publisher.

Printed in the United States of America

17 16 15   5 4 3 2 1

First edition

A book in the American Literatures Initiative (ALI), a collaborative publishing project of NYU Press, Fordham University Press, Rutgers University Press, Temple University Press, and the University of Virginia Press. The Initiative is supported by The Andrew W. Mellon Foundation. For more information, please visit www.americanliteratures.org.

To my Ms

Contents

	Introduction: Affect in the Scene of Writing	1
1	Thinking Confusion: On the Compositional Aspect of Affect	24
2	Expression and Theatricality, or Medium Poe	47
3	Maisie's Spasms: Transferential Poetics in Henry James and Wilfred Bion	72
4	Loose Coordinations: Theater and Thinking in Gertrude Stein	96
5	Vis-à-vis Television: Andy Warhol's Therapeutics	119
	Out and Across	150
	Notes	153
	Bibliography	167
	Index	179
	Acknowledgments	187

Introduction: Affect in the Scene of Writing

This book explores the poetics elaborated from the 1840s to the 1980s by four American writers, thinkers, and artists: Edgar Allan Poe, Henry James, Gertrude Stein, and Andy Warhol. I have discerned in the work of these artists an acutely receptive and reflexive attention to the movement of feeling across and between text and reader, or composition and audience, and have therefore named the object of my study *transferential poetics*. To help me describe and understand these transferential movements, I turn to several theories of affect that have entered literary criticism and the theoretical humanities in the past two decades, especially Silvan Tomkins's affect theory and the object-relations theory of Melanie Klein and Wilfred Bion. These theories have permitted me to develop techniques of attention to and a vocabulary to describe compositional force and audience response (my own, in the first instance). By offering new interpretations of a handful of challenging major artists, this book aims to demonstrate how theories of affect may be used to improve the practice of criticism in a specific focus on poetics.

At the same time that it seeks to contribute to practical criticism and to the study of feeling in the humanities, *Transferential Poetics, from Poe to Warhol* advances a set of concepts that may carry over into other critical domains, in particular to studies of media and performance. The work and poetics of each of the artists I study is crucially informed either by technological media contexts (Poe, Warhol) or contexts of performance (James, Stein) or both. While scholars have usually focused on one or the other of these significant contexts, this book brings together questions of affect, media, and performance by way of the concept of theatricality. As I will show, the writing and poetics of these four artists are peculiarly, if differently, theatricalizing. What might it mean for their writing, or writing in general, to be theatricalizing? What relation does this theatricalization of writing have to the transferential movements of affect I have noticed? And how do these in turn relate to the context of technological media? I will answer these questions through a reading of the theatrical metaphor in Jacques Derrida's essay "Freud and the Scene of Writing." The transferential poetics of my study can come into focus only because affect in this period has been reframed and become distinctively, and distinctly, available to writing, perception, and thinking. The name that this book proposes for the remarkable twentieth-century availability of affect to perception is *television*. I will turn to Derrida's essay later in this introduction to explore the roles of affect, theatricality, and technology in a changing scene of writing; at that point I will explain the privileged place of television in this book's historical trajectory.

First, I would like to introduce and offer preliminary discussions of some of the key terms for this project: *poetics*, *affect*, and *transference*. I begin with the term *poetics*, by which I mean those guiding ideas, theories, or phantasies of how writing (and other aesthetic work) may touch or make contact with an audience. My use of the term *poetics* differs from the received definition's emphasis, as the *OED* has it, on form: "The creative principles informing any literary, social or cultural construction, or the theoretical study of these; a theory of form." I define poetics more in terms of compositional force, as consisting of powerful wishes about and images of how an audience will respond to a work; in this way poetics always embed ideas about emotional connection and disconnection. But my use of the term shares with the dictionary definition the sense that poetics may either reside in a given work (as its "creative principles") or appear as a separate theoretical study that aims to understand that work. Poetics as theoretical study may take the shape of a critical essay such as Aristotle's *Poetics* or Poe's "The Philosophy of Composition," a lecture such as Stein's "Composition as Explanation," or a book of criticism such as this one. At the same time poetics may inhabit a work as at once motivated and motivating, a guiding theory nearer the compositional bone, as closely imbricated in the practice of composition as possible without becoming collapsed into it or entirely identified with it. For example, Poe offered allegories of writer-reader relations in many of his short stories, which, I suggest in chapter 2, serve as wishful proposals or guides to his readers' responses and a key aspect of his famous poetics of effect. Poetics can sometimes appear as explicit study and implicit guide simultaneously: the sentences of Stein's "Composition as Explanation," I observe in chapter 1, at once explain her poetic strategies and enact them. In my understanding, then, poetics offers a kind of theory of how poesy or composition gets across—an uncanny theory that may be verbally announced as such but need not be.

The notion of theory that defines my approach to poetics comes from the writing of Silvan Tomkins, a twentieth-century U.S. psychologist whose work Eve Kosofsky Sedgwick and I helped to introduce into the humanities almost twenty years ago.[1] An affect theory, according to Tomkins, is "a simplified and powerful summary of a larger set of affect experiences" that organizes and helps to navigate one's emotional life by selecting and magnifying specific affects and combinations of affect and by offering strategies for dealing with them.[2] An individual may have different theories of, say, what it means to have an angry argument with a loved one: a quarrel can be a discouraging obstacle to shared experience or an exciting sign of intimacy or both. Affect theories tend to be both determined (they have histories) and determining (they create the situations to which they apply); at the same time, they are changeable (they can be overwritten or altered) and operate at various scales and degrees of reflection. Sedgwick puts it this way: "By Tomkins's account, which is strongly marked by early cybernetics' interest in feedback processes, all people's cognitive/affective lives are organized according to alternative, changing, strategic, and hypothetical affect theories. As a result, there would be from the start no ontological difference between the theorizing acts of a Freud and those of, say, one of his analysands."[3] Like poetics, affect theories may be explicit attempts to explain the workings of affect from the outside, or they may serve to guide or navigate experiences of affect themselves. I define poetics in terms of affect theory to acknowledge several things: that composition is always motivated (consciously and unconsciously); that compositions always seek to touch a reader or audience in some manner; and that such contact can take many forms. To put this last point another way, different poetics offer distinct sets of affect theories, with some poetics emphasizing the withholding of emotion or the rejection of readers to the point of a wished-for destruction. The work of each of the writers and artists I explore in this book has been characterized in terms of such negative or perverse contact, whether Poe's shameless, excessive manipulations, James's frustrating circumlocutions, Stein's confusing opacities, or Warhol's seemingly affectless deflections.

That the tools of affect theory can improve the practice of criticism in the specific study of poetics: this is one of the main contentions of

Transferential Poetics, from Poe to Warhol. In this way it clearly participates in the ongoing "affective turn" in the humanities.[4] My goal in this introduction is not to survey the large field of affect studies but to return to the usefulness for criticism of Tomkins's understanding of affect (especially in conjunction with that of object-relations theory). For as often as Tomkins's work has been cited and used to authorize an interest in affect or feeling, it does not appear to have made much of a dent in day-to-day critical practice. In fact it has been difficult to know just how literary criticism can take up and use Tomkins's lively, complex work, in part, it would seem, because his writing does not appear to be very literary. The pointed contrast here is with Freud, whose classical education and use of Greek tragedy to legitimate and give evidence for his theories, as Sarah Winter has shown, helped to establish his writing as part of the literary critical canon of the twentieth-century university; psychoanalysis and literature appear to implicate one another from their inceptions.[5] Tomkins's work, more informed by mid-twentieth-century cybernetics, systems theory, and modern drama than by Greek tragedy, no doubt sounds significantly stranger to many humanities professors than Freud's. At this point in the twenty-first century, however, Tomkins's writing, if it has yet to sound like critical common sense, nevertheless fits (although not quite squarely) with the emerging place of biology and the neurosciences in contemporary attempts to understand the enmeshings of psyches and somas in technological and media landscapes. His writing, my book suggests, continues to offer vocabulary and tools for a broader affective approach to the criticism of works across mediums.[6]

This book is somewhat unusual in that most scholars concerned with an affective approach to media have taken up the writing of Gilles Deleuze.[7] Those of us working in the field have noted the divergence between followers of Deleuze and followers of Tomkins, the incompatibilities of their vocabulary and theoretical disposition, so in this context it is worth pointing out that both camps or schools would appear to disagree more substantively with cognitive theories of emotion popular in analytic philosophy than with one another. The differences between Tomkins and Deleuze strike me as overdetermined by the mutual antagonism between French theoretical and Anglo-American empirical writing (as if Tomkins were an unproblematic empiricist!). It would be the work of another project to assess the real similarities and differences between their conceptualizations of affect. To introduce this book I have chosen to describe the reasons why I continue to prefer Tomkins's thinking about affect over others, especially for the purposes of criticism: his particular emendation of Freud's drive theory, his structuralist emphasis on gaps, and his phenomenologically rich, differentiated account of the affects. These characteristics of Tomkins's approach offer an unusual perspective on twentieth-century psychoanalytic theory and, accompanying this, a hard-won critical traction on the category of (what critics used to call) "the body" that I do not see in other approaches to affect.

In his critique and emendation of Freud's drive theory Tomkins offers the most sophisticated and least pathologizing theory of motivation that I have encountered. Both Freud and Tomkins understood the value of motivational error for learning, that is, the productive possibility that we can be wrong about our desires, wishes, or wants. But where Freud located the possibility of motivational error in the relations between and among conscious and unconscious processes that record and realize the struggle between our base, biological drives (especially the sex drive) and the mechanisms of repression that create civilization, Tomkins located motivational error in the structure of a biologically based affect system and its independence from both the drives and cognition. "The distinction," as he puts it near the start of his four-volume *Affect Imagery Consciousness* (1962–63, 1991–92), "is not between higher and lower, between spiritual and biological, but between *more general* and *more specific biological motives*" (1: 29, emphasis in the original). Tomkins proposed eight or nine innate affects as the more general biological motives in humans: the negative ones, fear-terror, distress-grief, anger-rage, shame-humiliation, and contempt-disgust (which he later divided into two: disgust and dissmell); the positive ones, interest-excitement and enjoyment-joy; and the reorienting affect of surprise-startle. These constitute the affect system, which is distinguished from the drive system by way of a variety of freedoms—of time, of intensity, of density, of combination, and, most significantly, of object. "Had Freud not smuggled some of the properties of the affect system into his conception of the drives," suggests Tomkins, "his system would have been of much less interest than it was" (1: 127).[8]

Any affect may have any object, whereas few objects will satisfy the drives of hunger, thirst, or respiration. This freedom of object opens out onto worlds of motivational possibility but makes it difficult for us to know just what our affects are about: we always know that our thirst is about the lack of water, but we can't always tell what is making us afraid or excited. This gap (or lack of proprietary relation) between motive and object is one of several productive gaps in Tomkins's structuralist model of the affects, a model that is nonpathologizing in part because of his tendency, both dispositional and a result of his midcentury historical context, to think in terms of organized complexity. By contrast with the more linear determinations of both drive theory and the behaviorist emphasis on stimulus-response, Tomkins sought explanations that take account of circular feedback relations, the interleaving of analog with digital difference, and both over- and underdetermination. Consider something as simple as his choice to hyphenate the names of the basic affects so as to index ranges of intensity. This choice effectively multiplies possible experiences of a single affect. For example, the low-level irritation of waiting in line at the grocery store and the intense fury of witnessing an act of police brutality can both be found on the spectrum of anger-rage. If these feel like very different emotional experiences (impatience vs. indignation), it is because affects are experienced in co-assemblies with other affects, cognitions, or drive signals. That is, affects are almost always embedded in feelings, emotions, attitudes, beliefs, perceptions, and other psychic states and events, core elements that Tomkins's theory offers an analytical tool for understanding.[9]

Because Tomkins offers a qualitatively differentiated space of affective response, as well as ways of assembling these responses with other psychophysiological states, his work invites careful phenomenological accounts of feeling. Such accounts ground the critical method that I develop in this book, one that begins with a deceptively simple question: what information does subjective, emotional response give us? Answering this question requires, first, my careful introspective attention to what happens in aesthetic experience, whether that of reading a text, looking at a visual artwork, listening to music, viewing a film, or watching a television program. An act of introspection almost always yields some facts about my feelings, although I would not characterize these facts as value-free since affect theories inevitably operate in the process of self-examination. These theories select some feelings against others and weight the vocabulary that I use to describe my experience; informed by Tomkins's writing, my descriptions tend to reinforce a Tomkinsian way of perceiving affect. Still, this vocabulary has helped me to make sense of the difference between being gripped, embarrassed, or nauseated when reading a Poe story. My excitement, shame, or disgust can lead to very different understandings of what a given composition might want from me. I use this method, for example, in chapter 2, where I follow the peculiar shamelessness of much of Poe's writing to develop an account of expression that does not rely on idealized self-presence and interiority. There I read the rhythmic beating of "The Tell-Tale Heart" as a sonic medium for projecting shame-humiliation out toward the reader, a transferential moment that tells me something about a particular affect theory that the composition is using (and that I may share). My method in this book consists of identifying such transferential moments, describing and analyzing them in some detail, and trying to specify what I am learning from them.

Transferential moment: here is one of this book's key methodological ideas. This idea is clearly indebted to the psychoanalytic concept of transference (more on which below) and, at the same time, is closely related to the method that Tomkins calls "inverse archaeology," an attention to how "affect is at once individual and private and social and shared nonverbal communication."[10] The method of inverse archaeology is based on Tomkins's understanding of affect as a hinge mechanism directed both outward and inward, which acts both on and between bodies and operates at the interface of physiology and psychology. Affect as hinge is, at least in part, a consequence of its location: "Affect is primarily facial behaviour" (*AIC* 1: 205–6), taking place on the skin and muscles of the face as well as in the tones of voice. This emphasis on faciality is one way that Tomkins distinguishes his understanding of affect from expressivist theories for which emotion is, in the first instance, internal to the body. For example, the James-Lange theory defines emotion in terms of the secondary awareness of organic changes within the body. (I discuss the similarities and differences between these theories in more detail in chapter 4.) While Tomkins agrees with such a physiological emphasis, he locates affective responses primarily on the face rather than within the bodily organs; he sometimes calls the face the primary organ of affect, just as the lungs are the primary organ of respiration and the heart the primary organ of the circulation of the blood. He puts it this way: "We regard the relationship between the face and the viscera as analogous to that between the fingers, forearm, upper arm, shoulders and body. The finger does not 'express' what is in the forearm, or shoulder or trunk. It rather leads than follows the movements in these organs to which it is an extension" (1: 205).[11] Affects participate in complex feedback loops that move rapidly both inward and outward, to the self and to others, and sometimes to the self as an other, serving as a hinge mechanism between individual and group.

What I find most appealing about Tomkins's approach to affect is this understanding of its hinge nature. The figure of a hinge strikes me as both more useful and more accurate than the metaphor of "blurring the boundaries" that has been prevalent in cultural studies for so long. Rather than collapsing any number of key binary oppositions (individual/group, form/content, the aesthetic/the political, and many others), Tomkins's systems theoretical approach can assist in thinking the simultaneous dependence, interdependence, and independence of the opposed elements. For example, in his own writing he neither excludes ideological considerations nor makes ideology an explanatory ground or condition for all affective experience. Instead he offers a vocabulary for phenomenological analysis that links individual, bodily experiences with larger social and political dynamics.¹² This book's method suggests that paying close attention to transferential moments, as well as to the poetics that aim for such moments, can be particularly telling of the hinges between levels of experience, a method that I describe in chapter 1 as compositional.

In addition to Tomkins's affect theory this book engages in considerable detail with the work of Melanie Klein and her followers in the school of object-relations theory, work that I have found to be at least as helpful as Tomkins's for my thinking. Klein also focused on the qualitative aspects of affective experience, albeit from within a fundamentally psychoanalytic orientation toward the drive or instinct of sexuality. Klein differed from Freud in her approach to sexuality, however, focusing less on its sources (the erogenous zones) and aims (discharge or sublimation), than on the objects of the sexual instinct. In focusing on good and bad object relations, those qualitative relations that initiate in the earliest exchanges between infant and mother (and which can be roughly translated in terms of Tomkins's positive and negative affects), Klein offered a substantial reorientation of psychoanalytic theory, a movement away from thermodynamic models (libido and the economics of sexual energy) and toward models of information exchange and performativity. The notion of transferential poetics that I develop in this book comes in large part from Klein's elaboration of Freud's theory of the transference, which was due to her emphasis on infantile experience and her understanding of the constant movement of part-objects in projective and introjective identification.

Freud first remarked transference phenomena in the context of psychoanalytic treatment: the displacement of the analysand's feelings of love and hate for a parent onto the analyst. Initially cast as an awkward event (patients falling in love with their doctors), Freud came to understand the transference as it offers material necessary for the analysis and treatment, eventually specifying this material in terms of repetitions, reenactments, or reanimations: "A whole series of earlier psychical experiences is brought to life not as something in the past, but as a current relationship with the doctor."¹³ Transference phenomena would appear, in Tomkins's terms, to derive from the affect system's freedom of object, and Klein would develop the notion in this more general direction, suggesting that, "in some form or other, transference operates throughout life and influences all human relations."¹⁴ Klein's theory of the transference emerged from her clinical experience using play technique to analyze children. Most other analysts followed Freud in assuming that young children could not be properly analyzed precisely because of their inability to undergo the displacements of transference. Against this theory Klein proposed that transference phenomena were based on yet earlier infantile experience. As she put it, "My use of the term 'object-relations' is based on my contention that the infant has from the beginning of post-natal life a relation to the mother (although focusing primarily on her breast) which is imbued with the fundamental elements of an object-relation, i.e. love, hatred, phantasies, anxieties, and defences" (49). She goes on to draw the logical inference a few pages later: "I hold that transference originates in the same processes which in the earliest stages determine object-relations" (53).

While displaced affect remained an important element in Klein's understanding of transference, her focus shifted away from the idea of reenactment of a past relation and toward the present of unconscious phantasy. As Robert Hinshelwood puts it, "The practice of Kleinian psychoanalysis has become an understanding of the transference as an expression of unconscious phantasy, active right here and now in the moment of the analysis."[15] Reenactments of the past become negotiations, through phantasy, of present difficulties in the analytic session. Because phantasy, for Klein, makes use of the infantile defenses that she called projective and introjective identification, a large part of Kleinian psychoanalysis depends on the analyst's attention to the constant movements of identification taking place between analyst and analysand. These movements of projective and introjective identification constitute the ground for object relations and create a rich and shifting topography, more dynamic and complex than that offered by Freud's structural model of the psyche. For the critical purposes of this book, the movements of identification offer an approach to describing and understanding the relations between aesthetic objects and audiences. I introduce and explore Klein's idea of unconscious phantasy in chapter 1 in discussing Stein's poetics of mistake and confusion. Confusion, I argue, comes with the territory of infantile phantasy, for, as Klein puts it, "altogether, in the young infant's mind every external experience is interwoven with his phantasies and on the other hand every phantasy contains elements of actual experience, and it is only by analyzing the transference situation to its depth that we are able to discover the past both in its realistic and phantastic aspects."[16]

Klein's notion of phantasy shares something basic with Tomkins's notion of theory: both organize feelings and wishes into scenarios that serve to guide or navigate experience, and they are both omnipresent in our thinking and feeling lives. But Kleinian phantasy, based on very early experience, is less cognitive than Tomkins's notion of theory, especially insofar as phantasy deals with those intense feelings of destructiveness that Klein called envy. In chapter 1 I describe Klein's understanding of envy, which is based on Freud's controversial concept of the death instinct, and its inevitable role in creating confusion; at the same time I offer a tentative revision of Freud's idea of the death instinct by way of Tomkins's theory of the negative affects. In that chapter, and elsewhere in this book, I try to integrate Tomkins's and Klein's ideas, which strike me as (for the most part) compatible approaches to thinking about affective and emotional experience.[17] I take up as well the work of Klein's most influential follower, Wilfred Bion. Bion is known for his development of Klein's idea of projective identification as a defense against envy, his innovative theories of group phenomena (he coined the phrase *group therapy*), and a remarkable theory of thinking. He eventually brought these theories together in his writing on the fundamental, reversible relation of container and contained. Chapter 3 brings Bion's writing on groups to a reading of James's *What Maisie Knew*, and chapter 4 brings his theory of the container-contained relation to a reading of Stein's lecture "Plays," where I suggest that her theatrical works aim to create reciprocal emotional relations that, according to Bion, condition the activity of thinking itself. My final chapter proposes that Warhol takes up Stein's landscape poetics as particularly suitable for engaging with an American theatrical culture transformed by mass media.

These preliminary discussions of poetics, affect, and transference will, I hope, serve to introduce the reader to the theoretical approaches to affect that I take in this book. More nuanced discussions follow. I turn now to the contexts of media and performance that motivate this book's chronological and national focus and to the idea of theatricality that brings these contexts together. There is some substantial conceptual intimacy between theatricality and affect, based, I suspect, on a fundamental fact: that theatrical performance almost inevitably foregrounds expressive bodies, in particular framing the face and the voice—the primary physiological mediums of affective communication—as aesthetic experience. For this reason theater has often been exemplary or figural in the classic studies of emotion, from Descartes's encounter with mechanical puppets or theatrical automata in the royal gardens of Saint-Germain-en-Laye (one context for *Les passions de l'âme* [1649]) to Adam Smith's several uses of the figure of theater in *The Theory of Moral Sentiments* (1759) and Charles Darwin's inclusion of photographs of actors in *The Expression of the Emotions in Man and Animals* (1872).[18] Tomkins too turns to theatrical concepts in elaborating what he calls "a dramaturgic model for the study of personality" (*AIC* 3: 83) in his later writing on scenes and scripts, which amends and specifies what he had earlier termed "affect theory."

I would like to unfold this conceptual intimacy between theatricality and affect through a selective reading of Derrida's essay "Freud and the Scene of Writing." While this essay does not represent itself as a study of affect—if anything, Derrida claims to seek what he elsewhere calls "a way out of affectivity"—it makes use of theatrical metaphor throughout.[19] I will track and unfold the significance of this metaphor, and in this way repeat or reenact Derrida's own method of tracking the metaphor of writing and inscription in several of Freud's works. Of course, this pursuit of metaphor is a standard critical practice, no more Derrida's than mine, even while it has become powerfully inflected by deconstructive style. As Christopher Johnson suggests in a reading that I have found helpful, "'deconstruction,' as it has come to be called, is inseparable from Derrida's general theory of writing," aspects of which he convincingly compares with basic principles from systems theory.[20] In unfolding Derrida's use of the metaphor of scene/stage, especially in relation to the idea of system, I will begin to locate a role for affect in his general theory. While the notion of affect does not often appear as such in his writing, Derrida does summon or evoke it at crucial junctures. Consider, for example, a famous passage in *Of Grammatology* that seeks a history of writing based on "an adventure of relationships between the face and the hand" (this refers to André Leroi-Gourhan's argument in *Gesture and Speech*) and proposes a difficult, perhaps impossible methodological imperative: "We must attempt to recapture the unity of gesture and speech, of body and language, of tool and thought, before the originality of the one and the other is articulated and without letting this profound unity give rise to confusionism."[21] Affect as hinge, as I described it earlier (or *brisure*, as Derrida would put it), is precisely what connects and divides these binary pairs, what creates confusion and thereby gives rise to the need to articulate or differentiate them. That affect is fundamentally compositional and confusing but can nonetheless be thought, indeed that affect both motivates and obstructs thinking, is the argument of my next chapter.[22]

The title of Derrida's essay immediately signals the importance of the theatrical metaphor: "Freud et la scène de l'écriture," which could also be translated as "Freud and the Stage of Writing." Throughout this piece Derrida makes full use of the semantic resources of the French phrase *mise-en-scène* in both its specifically theatrical definition as, literally, a putting on stage—of stage properties, lighting, music, and other aspects of setting—and its more general sense as environment or milieu. (Stein's approach to plays as landscapes captures a similar set of meanings.) In the background of Derrida's essay (with occasional intrusions into the foreground) is Antonin Artaud's writing on the theater of cruelty and its insistence on mise-en-scène "as the point of departure for all theatrical relation."[23] The word *scène* (scene/stage) first appears in Derrida's discussion of Freud's account of verbal representation in dreams. Here, as Johnson points out, "the already theatrical overtones of Freud's use of the word *Darstellbarkeit* are emphasized and extended by Derrida's play on the terms 'représentation' (performance) and 'répétition [générale]' (rehearsal)."[24] Derrida assimilates the way words work in dreams with the way they work on stage, emphasizing how in both cases (alphabetic) words signify in a manner similar to other visual and aural forms, describing "the Freudian break" this way: "Freud doubtless conceives of the dream as a displacement similar to an original form of writing which puts words on stage without becoming subservient to them; and he is thinking here, no doubt, of a model of writing irreducible to speech which would include, like hieroglyphics, pictographic, ideogrammatic, and phonetic elements" (209). In "The Theater of Cruelty and the Closure of Representation" Derrida makes the point more clearly and with explicit reference to Artaud: "On the stage of the dream, as described by Freud, speech has the same status [as that assigned to it in Artaud's theater of cruelty]. . . . Present in dreams, speech can only behave as an element among others, sometimes like a 'thing' which the primary process manipulates according to its own economy" (241).

The first use that Derrida makes of the theatrical metaphor, then, is in the service of a non-logocentric theory of speech in which words are material entities that no longer serve as representatives of ideas according to a linear code. In the dream and on the stage—that of Artaud's theater but also, as I will argue below, in theatricality more generally—multiple meanings emerge from a complex set of mutually contextualizing systems that are not solely linguistic and do not depend on a "radical" break between signifier and signified (209). In these pages Derrida tracks Freud's insistence on the inadequacy of translation as a way to understand dream interpretation because, in the dream, verbal expression, "its sonority, the materiality of the expression, does not disappear before the signified, or at least cannot be traversed and transgressed as it is in conscious speech. It acts as such, with the efficacy Artaud assigned it on the stage of cruelty. The materiality of a word cannot be translated or carried over into another language" (210). In addition, Derrida explains, the metaphor of translation works on a model of transcription and mistakenly "presupposes a text which would already be there, immobile"

(211); as he puts it later in the same paragraph, "The text is not conceivable in an originary or modified form of presence. The unconscious text is already a weave of pure traces, differences in which meaning and force are united—a text nowhere present" (211).

Derrida's argument concerning the topographical model that Freud ambivalently sketches in *The Interpretation of Dreams* resembles the critique of structuralism he makes elsewhere in *Writing and Difference*, a critique that seeks to supplement ideas of static structure with those of force, play, and duration. He does not reject structuralist models, insisting on "the necessity not of abandoning but of rethinking the space or topology of this [nontranscriptive] writing" (212). The second use that Derrida makes of the theatrical metaphor, then, is as a way to rethink the space of writing in terms of a complex, dynamic, differentiated space in which the binaries of presence/absence, origin/copy, thing/representation can be displaced by a rather different distinction: onstage/offstage. This distinction, implied by the notion of mise-en-scène (since what is put on stage must come from somewhere, and what leaves it must go somewhere), captures various aspects of the space of writing as Derrida wishes to rethink it. For example, on stage and off are functional divisions rather than materially different spaces, especially in Artaud's theater, which seeks to replace the stage and auditorium "by a single site, without partition or barrier of any kind, which will become the theatre of the action."[25] To use Anthony Wilden's helpful terminology, theater and stage become spaces of analog difference rather than digital opposition.[26] Necessarily perspectival (in Artaud's theater as well as more generally), the distinction between on and off stage depends on structural considerations that can be altered (the curtain, the proscenium arch, the configuration of the hall and arrangement of the audience), considerations that are fundamentally social, at once effects and reciprocal causes of group behavior and decision.[27] If actors, props, words, music, lights, and other theatrical elements belong both on stage and off, then what makes meaning are the relations between them as they move among the many spaces on and off the stage. These are the movements of writing in Derrida's general sense.

That the scene/stage becomes Derrida's primary metaphor for rethinking the space of writing becomes more explicit in his discussion of the "Note on the 'Mystic Writing Pad.'" In this essay Freud returns to the fundamental problem of the much earlier *Project for a Scientific Psychology*, that of producing a physical theory of the brain that can accommodate at once the newness of perception and the storage capacities of memory, or, as Derrida puts it, the "potential for indefinite preservation and an unlimited capacity for reception" (222). Thirty years after writing the *Project* Freud discovered a mechanical model that satisfies these requirements in the form of a toy. The Mystic Writing Pad famously consists of a transparent sheet laid over a wax slab receptive to impressions from a stylus, which disappear from the sheet as soon as it is lifted but remain in the wax perpetually. Derrida argues that this model conveys both the spatiality and the temporality of psychic writing, what he calls spacing: "Temporality as spacing will be not only the horizontal discontinuity of a chain of signs, but also will be writing as the interruption and restoration of contact between the various depths of psychical levels.... We find neither the continuity of a line nor the homogeneity of a volume; only the differentiated duration and depth of a stage, and its spacing" (225). Spacing invokes the stage dynamics I described earlier, the movements of elements on stage and off, and especially the timing of these movements. Here is the *Nachträglich* nature of perception in which what appears on the stage of awareness is always a consequence of a set of relations between what is off stage, remembered or forgotten. Derrida puts it this way: "Writing supplements perception before perception even appears to itself [is conscious of itself].... The 'perceived' may be read only in the past, beneath perception and after it" (224).

Both Tomkins's notion of theory and Klein's of unconscious phantasy aim to capture this dynamic between perception and memory and seek to understand the role of affect or object relations in this dynamic. From the perspective of my reading, it is no accident that in this discussion of temporality and spacing Derrida evokes the notion of affect without naming it. In a difficult set of passages he emphasizes the fact that "at least two hands are needed to make the apparatus [the Mystic Writing Pad] function, as well as a system of gestures" (226), and after pointing to "a multiplicity of agencies or origins" (226) for psychical writing, poses a rhetorical question: "Is this not the original relation to the other and the original temporality of writing, its 'primary' complication: an originary spacing, deferring, and erasure of the simple origin, and polemics on the very threshold of what we persist in calling perception? The stage of dreams, 'which follow old facilitations,' was a stage of writing. But this is because 'perception,' the first relationship of life to its other, the origin of life, had always already prepared representation" (226). One form of this "original relation to the other," I suggest, is affect or (otherwise put) object relations, especially when understood as motivational system.[28] Derrida offers "perception" as the name for "the first relationship of life to its other," but missing from this account is what motivates the dynamic relations between perception and memory/forgetting. This is why he turns immediately to Freud's theory of motivation in terms of repression of the drives. "Writing is unthinkable without repression" (226), Derrida asserts, and proposes that "the condition for writing is that there be neither a permanent contact nor an absolute break between strata: the vigilance and failure of censorship" (226). As I remarked earlier, Tomkins's affect theory offers an alternative to Freud's understanding of motivation, and in chapter 2 I explicitly recast repression in terms of Tomkins's description of the inhibiting and amplifying qualities of the affect system. I would rewrite Derrida's assertion as follows: writing is unthinkable without the inhibiting and amplifying relations between and among the affects and the other systems of the psyche. It is less "the vigilance and failure of censorship" per se that acts to create the intermittencies that condition writing than it is the multiple inhibitions as well as amplifications emergent from a complex affect system.

I am arguing that Derrida makes room for affect in his general theory of writing through the metaphor of the stage as it serves to foreground the materiality of verbal expression and to rethink the space of writing. The stage and its movements (on and off) set out a complex, differentiated spatiality and temporality that offer a way to reimagine the interacting, multiple agencies or systems of psychic writing without requiring a single, sovereign subject: "The 'subject' of writing does not exist if we mean by that some sovereign solitude of the author. The subject of writing is a *system* of relations between strata: the Mystic Pad, the psyche, society, the world. Within that scene, on that stage, the punctual simplicity of the classical subject is not to be found" (226–27, emphasis in the original). Instead of sociological approaches that use communication models to describe the relations between subject and society (or subject and structure), relying on only the simplest accounts of motivation, Derrida turns to what he calls "the *sociality* of writing as *drama*": "In order to describe the structure, it is not enough to recall that one always writes for someone; and the oppositions sender-receiver, code-message, etc., always remain extremely coarse instruments. We would search the 'public' in vain for the first reader: i.e., the first author of a work. And the 'sociology of literature' is blind to the war and the ruses perpetrated by the author who reads and by the first reader who dictates, for at stake here is the origin of the work itself. The *sociality* of writing as *drama* requires an entirely different discipline" (226–27, emphasis in the original). In invoking "the author who reads" and "the first reader who dictates" Derrida draws out the close coincidence of writing, reading, and performance, the fundamental multiplicity and circuitousness even of individual subjectivity. (I return to this point in chapter 3 in a discussion of Henry James's scenic method and group psychology.) Drama, here, is Derrida's shorthand for the staging of multiple agencies or systems in complex interaction across levels or "strata," a staging that does not begin from the subject/structure opposition so central to mid-twentieth-century critical and philosophical projects.

While it is tempting to take up Derrida's (characteristically extravagant) gesture toward "an entirely different discipline" in the passage above and that he makes again at the end of the essay, it is no longer necessary to oppose his general theory of writing to sociological approaches. Rather than returning to an old debate that casts deconstructive and Marxist-materialist analyses as antagonistic or mutually exclusive, I would simply point out that these approaches, while distinct, can and have been powerfully brought together, for example, in Jonathan Goldberg's *Writing Matter* (1990). Goldberg reads sixteenth-century English handwriting manuals as they implemented, extended, and regulated access to the italic hand or "hand of power" (from which descends our cursive writing), pursuing an episode in the history of writing precisely along Derridean lines, "a history of technology that is also the history of 'man,' the programmed/programming machine: the human written."[29] Goldberg's attention to the role of graphic technologies in the writing or scripting of the human and in historical institutions of governance navigates between deconstructive insight and materialist criticism, and his final chapter, "The Hand in Theory," demonstrates that "Marxist materialism can communicate with deconstructive protocols once the hand of Engels is relocated within a graphic discourse" (314). In that same chapter Goldberg turns to "Freud and the Scene of Writing" and Derrida's brief sketches of "a new psychoanalytic graphology." "Here, Melanie Klein perhaps opens the way," Derrida writes, for Klein's "entire thematic, her analysis of the constitution of good and bad objects, her genealogy of morals could doubtless begin to illuminate, if followed prudently, the entire problem of the archi-trace . . . in terms of valuation and devaluation" (231). Goldberg queries the privilege Derrida accords this "psychoanalytic graphology," worrying that psychoanalysis aims always to "reveal that sexuality is the truth of the path we are said to tread on the way to Being."[30] But Goldberg sees in Klein's analyses of children's phantasies about writing that "the sexual way is also, and always already, graphic" (310), reading Derrida's gesture toward Klein this way: "The 'privilege' of a psychoanalytic graphology, therefore, does not privilege the psyche or the discipline of psychoanalysis. It leads, rather, to a recognition of the ways in which being (human, material) is scripted. Within the logocentric script of the West, it leads to the hand" (311).

I have found Goldberg's work and its emphasis on graphic technologies helpful for conceptualizing the relations between the historical and affect theoretical aspects of my project. To explain this I should first note that the importance of historical context for my research has shifted: an earlier version of this project focused on poetics by way of the history of technologies of graphic reproduction and their role in the emergence of mass media.[31] A number of years ago I realized that the technologies I was most drawn to were those that transformed specifically affective communication: the graphic technologies, emerging from the 1840s on (telegraphy, photography, phonography, film, wireless), that could reproduce at a distance, and distribute to great numbers, the face and the voice. These technologies, institutionalized in the forms of radio and cinema in the first half of the twentieth century and television in the second half, became the basis for mass media. It would be possible to describe the historical changes that took place in the environment of these technologies during this time in sociological terms: the institutions that intensively developed and captured the new graphic technologies industrialized or modernized affective communication, with the immersive twentieth-century experiences of mass media a consequence of such social processes. This sociological description would complement Max Horkheimer and Theodor Adorno's analysis of the culture industry in *The Dialectic of Enlightenment* (1947) or Raymond Williams's somewhat different account of the emergence of broadcasting in *Television: Technology and Cultural Form* (1974). Some version of this sociological description might also complement the more formalist approaches of Marshall McLuhan, Friedrich Kittler, and Niklas Luhmann. None of these accounts describes the shifts in technology or the emergence of mass media in terms of a change in specifically affective communication. One contribution this project makes to media studies is to emphasize affect as the key category for conceptualizing the historical emergence and significance of mass media. Tomkins's systems theoretical approach offers a promising way to address the fraught question of the causal relations between technologies, institutions, and subjectivities, a question that I pursue in my final chapter, on Warhol and television.

In its current form, however, this book inflects a sociological idiom with a Derridean emphasis on writing in its description of technological change and what Goldberg calls the scripting of human, material being. After all, the nineteenth-century technologies of graphic reproduction are part of a longer history of writing: telegraphy, photography, and phonography are all graphic *techne* that create inscriptions or marks on a surface or in a medium. My attention to inscription in this book is everywhere accompanied by an attention to the circuits of perception and performance that, for Derrida, accompany the scene of writing and that define what I call the theatricalization of writing. Consider that, just as the act of reading aloud transforms marks on parchment or paper into verbal, vocal performance, phonograph playback and film projection transform inscription (whether on wax, vinyl, or celluloid) into visible or audible performance. In this context broadcasting technologies such as radio and television, which do not initially appear to be inscriptive in the same sense as the earlier graphic technologies, similarly coordinate writing, reading, and performance: in broadcasting, writing (with camera or microphone) creates performances that can be seen and heard at a distance. To what degree can the large-scale changes that took place between the 1840s and the 1980s be understood as transformations in the technical and institutional means for reading, playing back, or theatricalizing writing? This is the largest historical-theoretical context for my book: the theatricalization of writing that takes place through technologies of graphic reproduction, and what follows, a new role for affect in the scene of writing.[32]

Especially insofar as they reproduce the face and the voice, the graphic technologies and institutions that capture them are fundamentally theatricalizing: they offer new means for framing or foregrounding expressive bodies. Any analysis of the scripting of human, material being from the nineteenth century on, then, leads not only to the hand but to "an adventure of relationships between the face and the hand," or otherwise put, to the relationships between motivation and thinking in the context of technological media. While I agree with Goldberg's reading of "psychoanalytic graphology," I would suggest that Derrida turns to Klein and her "genealogy of morals" because he is missing some (materialist) account of valuation or motivation in his general theory. I remarked earlier that affect inhabits the scene of writing as a system that motivates the relations between perception and memory/forgetting. Here I would add that the historical advent of graphic technology theatricalizes writing to reframe affect and motivation anew. Indeed there is a strange reciprocity between theatricality and affect, and this is the gist of the conceptual intimacy that I have been pursuing. Affect is theatricalized in (and by) writing at the same time that it serves as an agent of theatricality; to put this another way, affect is at once framed by technologies of graphic reproduction and frames verbal communications more generally.

The notion of theatricality that I have developed in this book is based not only on Derrida's metaphor of the stage and its role in his general theory of writing but also on Gregory Bateson's writing on play and the role of metacommunicative frames in his essay "A Theory of Play and Fantasy."[33] According to Bateson, play dynamics (as well as related phenomena, including psychoanalytic transference) rely on psychological or perceptual frames that function to delimit logical types. Such frames direct the recipient of a communication how to receive it or, more significantly, how not to receive it: "The playful nip denotes the bite, but it does not denote what would be denoted by the bite."[34] Consider a couple of examples of metacommunicative frames. I may read something aloud (say, a set of instructions) or frown to communicate my distress, but once framed, this communication changes: if I frown excessively or ironically, this at once communicates and negates my distress, and if I read instructions in a funny voice, then I detract from their authority. Affect often serves to communicate about whatever verbal (or other) communication is happening concurrently; affect, I suggest, plays a primary role in metacommunication of all kinds.[35]

Any medium of communication necessarily invokes metacommunicative frames. The page, stage, movie screen, and television are technologies that offer distinct frames for communication, including the communication and expression of affect. At the same time, the affects themselves serve to introduce labile frames that guide interpretation and response. The deconstructive and anthropological approach to theatricality that I take in this study defines it in terms of a reciprocal framing relation between affect and writing, one that transforms communication into more complex metacommunication. When I observe that the work of Poe, James, Stein, and Warhol are each peculiarly, if differently, theatricalizing, I mean the following: that their compositions and poetics pay careful attention to the metacommunicative force of affect in the historical context of the emergence and institutionalizing of those graphic technologies that form the basis of twentieth-century mass media in the United States. The trajectory from Poe to Warhol traced by this book offers a route that culminates in television, that technology and cultural form that most powerfully realizes a twentieth-century theatricalization of writing. In its various, insistent returns to television—as technology, as institution, as writing, as theater—this book seeks to discover a loose, integrated approach to criticism across mediums of composition and performance.

If my attention in this book has gone specifically to American writers and artists, it is because of the peculiar manner in which U.S. (democratic, market) culture took hold of, developed, and became identified with the technologies and institutions that created modern mass media and the spectacular, theatricalized, metacommunicative environment of the twentieth century. An earlier title of my study, "American Telepoetics," evoked the historical affinity between the ideas of "America" and "modern media" as these began reciprocally to define one another in the first half of the twentieth century, then to expand their domains during the years of the dissemination of U.S. political ideals after World War II. As a (Canadian) child who learned how to read by watching early 1970s American television (the PBS show *The Electric Company*, a product of Richard Nixon's literacy campaigns), I was acutely aware of the educative role that television played as the primary sociopolitical affective guidance system in late twentieth-century North America (supplanting newspapers and Hollywood film in this role, as the Internet would seem to be supplanting television today). Raymond Williams has observed that cinema, radio, and television have created an astonishing quantitative difference in the sheer amount of drama we experience ("for the first time a majority of the population has regular and constant access to drama, beyond occasion or season") and therefore a qualitative difference in what he calls "drama as habitual experience."[36] A desire to understand the ubiquitous place and emotional roles of television in my lifetime has motivated the genealogical aspects of this project and has driven me to approach sociological questions from the unusual perspective of the theatricalization of writing.

The chapters that follow explore the theatricalization of writing in Poe, James, Stein, and Warhol, and unfold the roles for affect dynamics in fundamental experiences of composition, expression, group phenomena, thinking and learning, and self-care. I have discussed my method, which begins with the question of subjective, emotional response and moves to identify telling transferential moments. I would now add that this method consists less of the application of affect theory to literary and other aesthetic work than of juxtaposition: I set a variety of theoretical, literary, filmic, and graphic works side by side to discover what kinds of readings and knowledges emerge. This choice of juxtaposition has been partly motivated by Sedgwick's discussion in her introduction to *Touching Feeling* (2003) of a project "to explore some ways around the topos of depth or hiddenness, typically followed by the drama of exposure, that has been such a staple of critical work of the past four decades."[37] Sedgwick's writing is particularly concerned to avoid what Foucault called the ruses of the repressive hypothesis; she initially turned to Tomkins because his work offered tools for theorizing motivation in a manner that did not reintroduce the category of repression, which, in Foucault's famous critique, leads to an inevitable focus on prohibition. Rather than those critical practices that in attending to prohibition always look behind, beneath, or beyond a given text, Sedgwick proposes *beside* as a critical heuristic that steps away from the dualisms of binary opposition and toward the more complex spatialization of systems or ecologies.

I take up this heuristic in my first chapter, which reads Stein's poetics of mistake (as she elaborates them in *Lectures in America* [1935]) side by side with Tomkins's understanding of the role of affects in perception and Klein's notion of unconscious phantasy. These thinkers help me to describe what I call the compositional aspect of affect in perception, by which I mean the ways that affect and emotion help to compose psychic objects. Stein's writing invites (or demands) a reader's attention to the intricacies of grammar and to physiological response, that is, to the movements of feeling and thinking that take place here and now in the act of reading. I describe Stein's and Tomkins's shared intellectual and historical affiliation with William James, and their willingness to acknowledge the place of confusion in perception. In the second half of the chapter I read parts of *Tender Buttons* to show how Stein and Klein participated in similar modernist projects to become acquainted with and give verbal form to elements of experience that are difficult to access and entertain in consciousness. I unfold Klein's notion of phantasy and conclude by arguing that confusion is both an expression of what she called envy and a defense against it.

My next chapter reads those of Poe's short stories that offer careful, fragmented depictions of faces next to Tomkins's writing on what he calls the General Images of the affect system. Tomkins proposes a set of basic goals for the affects—maximize positive affect, minimize negative affect, minimize affect inhibition, and the goal of power—the conflicts between which generate much of the complexity of affective experience. I read these conflicts in Poe's stories in order to develop an account of expression that does not oppose repression and that does not rely on idealized self-presence and interiority. The peculiar shamelessness of Poe's writing grounds the notion of expression that I develop, and in the second half of the chapter I offer a reading of one of Poe's most shameless tales, "The Tell-Tale Heart." This reading, which uses Tomkins's understanding of the taboos on looking, leads me to speculate about one affective source for theater: the lifting of the taboos on looking in theatrical experience. I argue that Poe's writing conveys the shamelessness of looking in theatrical experience and that this forms the basis of the appeal of his writing to both high modernists and mass culture workers.

I return to fundamental questions about theatricality in my next chapter, "Maisie's Spasms," which offers a reading of Henry James's midcareer novel *What Maisie Knew* as a study in group psychology. Maisie, James's child heroine, is at the center of an expanding and transforming family group that includes various governesses as well as her divorced parents' multiple new partners. I set James's novel beside Bion's *Experiences in Groups* (1961) and its Kleinian approach to the continuities and discontinuities between individual and group experience. Rather than insisting (as Freud tends to) only on a narrative of individuation and adaptation, Bion emphasizes the necessity and difficulty an individual inevitably experiences in making contact with the emotional life of the group in which she lives. James casts the frustrating necessity of group experience in entirely theatrical terms, figuring Maisie from the start as a spectator to, and eventually an active participant in, the affective circuits of those around her. In my reading the transferential poetics of James and Bion make available the affective, transindividual nature of knowing as a contingent activity that takes place between persons and other objects. I conclude the chapter by unfolding some of the surprising televisual aspects of James's late style.

My next chapter, "Loose Coordinations," returns to Bion and Stein in a new interpretation of Stein's lecture "Plays." The chapter begins by using William James's definition of emotion to analyze what Stein considers to be the main problem of theater: its triggering of audience "nervousness." I turn to Tomkins's writing on excitement to read Stein's meditation on varieties of excitement both in and out of the theater. I then make use of Bion's *Learning from Experience* (1962), in which he elaborates a theory of thinking as a reciprocal relation between container and contained, in order to understand Stein's landscape poetics, that is, her manner of writing plays, which aims for experiences of new knowledge. The chapter concludes by proposing that one crucial context for Stein's phenomenological investigation of plays is the technologies and institutions of mass media (film and broadcasting) that both helped to establish her fame and serve as technical models for her experimental methods. The problem of theater, I suggest, is the problem of how to make emotional contact with groups in the environment of such technologies of affective communication.

My final chapter takes up this problem in the work of Warhol. I argue that by identifying with television itself (as both technology and institution) Warhol finds a powerful solution to the problem of how to make emotional contact with the group. This chapter offers a way to move from a study of poetics to a study of therapeutics. The first half of the chapter brings the affect theories of Klein and Tomkins to readings of some of Warhol's early film and video work and argues that Warhol takes a televisual perspective on emotion. I go on to show that he adopted a televisual perspective in developing his celebrated self, and turn to Foucault's late lectures on ancient therapeutics to read *The Philosophy of Andy Warhol (From A to B and Back Again)*. Here Warhol figures television as a therapeutic device that offers him the technical means to become himself, Andy Warhol, by regulating or tuning emotional perspective and distance. The chapter argues that both Foucault and Warhol share an underexamined set of relations to midcentury cybernetics: the ancient idea of "conversion to self" that Foucault discusses is a figure for cybernetic control central to his notion of governmentality. I read "from A to B and back again," the overarching thematic of Warhol's *Philosophy*, as a version of this ancient figure of conversion and control. I conclude by suggesting that Warhol may be read by way of Foucault's meditations on the Cynics, as an extension to an antitheoretical line of ancient ethics that persists in contemporary culture.

The book ends with a brief epilogue or "outro" that summarizes the central aspects of transferential poetics by meditating on the meanings of *out*, or *out there*, in the work of the American composer Morton Feldman.

1 / Thinking Confusion: On the Compositional Aspect of Affect

In this first chapter I will unfold the meanings of a phrase that I have found useful, *the compositional aspect of affect in perception*. This phrase combines a practical, everyday insight—that feelings matter for how we perceive things, people, ideas, other feelings—with the more technical insights of two theories of emotion: Silvan Tomkins's affect theory and the object-relations theory of Melanie Klein and those who follow her. Writing on different sides of the Atlantic from within very different institutional, disciplinary, national, and continental contexts, Tomkins and Klein were nonetheless both influenced by and crucially departed from Freud's writing, in particular his emphasis on the drives in explaining psychic dynamics and motivation. Where Freud (or rather a certain Freud) offered mainly economic understandings of the transformation of instinct or drive into affect (as Laplanche and Pontalis put it, "The affect is defined as the subjective transposition of the quantity of instinctual energy"),[1] Klein and Tomkins emphasized the phenomenological qualities of affective or emotional experience and the place of phantasy and everyday theory in moment-to-moment living and thinking. As widely different as they may be, both object-relations and Tomkins's theory share this focus on affect qua affect (or emotion qua emotion) for understanding motivation and experience.

The term *compositional* in the phrase above, however, does not come from either of these domains of twentieth-century psychology but from Gertrude Stein's 1926 lecture "Composition as Explanation." In this lecture, written at the invitation of the Cambridge Literary Club and delivered at Cambridge and Oxford, Stein offered a meditation on the idea of composition as it defines the contemporary or what it means to be of one's time, followed by a chronological survey of twenty years of her writing and poetics. That is, "Composition as Explanation," Stein's first lecture as a mature writer, both explored composition as an explanatory idea for thinking about art or making in relation to time and history and was itself a composition that served to introduce and explain her exemplary writing to contemporary audiences.[2] This reflexive, at once implicative and explicative use of word and idea was characteristic of Stein and indexes her larger poetic project. As a very rough summary, this project could be said to include a constant effort to communicate meaning that refuses to abstract from the lived, present circumstances and conditions of meaning-making; consequently a remarkable attention to the varied material conditions for writing, whether to the sensory aspects (the sight, sound, and feel) of letters and words, or to the grammatical circumstances of writing, or to other situational aspects of writing and reading; and finally, an ability to fold such multiple awarenesses back into the writing itself. I think of these multiple forms of attention that Stein's writing required of her, and also invites from a reader, as *compositional* in that they place together elements that many of us are in the habit of keeping apart, often for what we think of as very good reasons, say, for the sake of clarity or intelligibility, propriety, or the appearance of sanity. But in returning again and again to the dynamic, compositional relations between words, whatever words name and the things that words are, the intricate grammatical structures they are embedded in, and the ideas and meanings that emerge from all of these together, Stein's writings offer some of the most sustained and precise explorations of the varieties of confusion integral to thinking, and to communicating thinking, that I know of.

These compositional aspects of Stein's writing may help us to understand both its so-called difficulty, or the tangle of confusion and frustration that readers may experience, and the excitement and enjoyment that her writing offers to the same readers. As Stein puts it in the lecture, confusion and composition tend to accompany one another in perception: "The only thing that is different from one time to another is what is seen and what is seen depends on how everybody is doing everything. This makes the thing we are looking at very different and this makes what those who describe it make of it, it makes a composition, it confuses, it shows, it is, it looks, it likes it as it is, and this makes what is seen as it is seen" (495). These sentences begin clearly enough: Stein analyzes difference over time as emerging from sensory, spatial experience ("what is seen"), itself dependent on activity—a broadly performative and constructivist understanding, it would seem. This grammatical clarity gets muddied when she foregrounds the specific activities of describing and making, and suddenly compositional agency becomes difficult to locate. Consider a close grammatical reading: "This," the first word of the second sentence, may refer to the preceding final phrase ("how everybody is doing everything"), or to the dependency relation just elaborated between perception and action, or to the analysis of difference that the entire sentence presents. The subsequent "this" can similarly refer to "the thing we are looking at," to its difference from itself, or to the same variety of things that the previous "this" referred to. When "it" is introduced and repeated there is an exponential explosion of grammatical parsings, a large (though finite) number that in the ordinary practice of reading creates a kind of overload (fig. 1). While an analytically minded reader may feel initially baffled, with the phrase "it makes a composition" this reader may begin to grasp the qualitative gist of these sentences: how, for Stein, composition is at once agent and patient, naming precisely the possibilities of dynamic self-differentiation conveyed in the grammatical activity of the sentence itself. With the insistent list and the mobile pronoun "it"—"it confuses, it shows, it is, it looks, it likes it as it is"—we may begin to get, in the rhythm of the sentence now, how the kinds of attention that composition invites lead toward both complexity and simplicity, a division and then recombination into some perceivable whole.

With the phrase *the compositional aspect of affect* I am aiming to name, follow, and explicate the necessary role that affects and feelings play in such divisions and recombinations or in the constitution of objects of perception. Tomkins and Klein offer vocabulary and conceptual tools for this project, as we will see, but so does Stein, who explores the role of feeling in composition most directly in the lecture "Poetry and Grammar" (1934). This lecture begins with a clear set of questions: "What is poetry and if you know what poetry is what is prose."[3] Stein pursues answers to these questions by describing her affective responses to a variety of parts of speech, for, as she puts it, "One of the things that is a very interesting thing to know is how you are feeling inside you to the words that are coming out to be outside of you" (209). She begins with her cowboy modernist preference for verbs and adverbs over nouns and adjectives: "Nouns are the name of anything and just naming names is alright when you want to call a roll but is it any good for anything else" (210). Nominal forms convert what Stein would understand to be essentially dynamic processes or forces into manageable, static, and habit-driven entities; she prefers verbal forms because "they are, so to

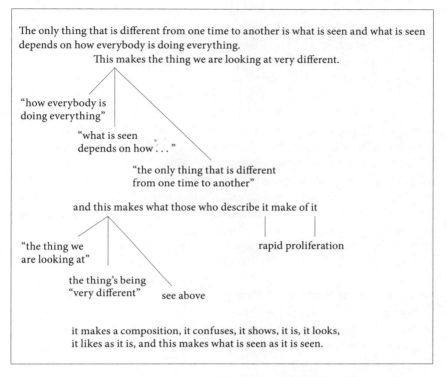

FIGURE 1. Gertrude Stein's "Composition as Explanation" (1926)

speak on the move" (212). While this emphasis on movement and process is a general characteristic of modernist thinking, less familiar is Stein's particular association of <u>movement with the productive possibilities of mistake, a</u>nd her further association of mistake with enjoyment. "It is wonderful the number of mistakes a verb can make" (211), asserts Stein, whose greatest enjoyment comes from those elements of language that can be most mistaken: "Prepositions can live one long life being really being nothing but absolutely nothing but mistaken and that makes them irritating if you feel that way about mistakes but certainly something that you can be continuously using and everlastingly enjoying" (212). What begins as an investigation into the nature of poetry and prose has become, at this point in the lecture, an articulation of Stein's poetics of mistake, a poetics for which use and enjoyment are crucial qualities.

Use, enjoyment, and also life or liveliness: "Verbs and adverbs and articles and conjunctions and prepositions are lively because they all do something and as long as anything does something it keeps alive" (214). Stein's enjoyment of those parts of speech that are active or promote activity is matched by her disdain for those that undermine activity or life itself. Consider her powerfully negative response to commas, which she describes as "servile": "they have no life of their own, and their use is not a use, it is a way of replacing one's own interest" (219). A comma, "by helping you along holding your coat for you and putting on your shoes keeps you from living your life as actively as you should lead it" (220). I hear in Stein's disdain rejections of dependence that are both masculinist and feminist: she casts the comma as at once chivalrous suitor and protective mother and rejects them both. But as she continues to explain her feeling for commas and the particular experiences that they interfere with, we may hear something else as well: "I have always liked dependent adverbial clauses because of their variety of dependence and independence. You can see how loving the intensity of complication of these things that commas would be degrading. Why if you want the pleasure of concentrating on the final simplicity of excessive complication would you want any artificial aid to bring about that simplicity" (220). Commas help a reader in parsing a sentence to reach the "final simplicity" or meaningful gist of a complicated sentence; Stein rejects this assistance, preferring to experience the varieties of dependence and independence, the mistakes and confusions that grammatical form makes possible.

While Stein appears to be naturalizing grammar by contrast with the "artificial" technology of the comma, the following passage makes clear that, for her, a sentence is also a tool, no less artificial or prosthetic. Her primary point is to enter into a lively circuit with this unusual tool:

> When it gets really difficult you want to disentangle rather than to cut the knot, at least so anybody feels who is working with any thread, so anybody feels who is working with any tool so anybody feels who is writing any sentence or reading it after it has been written. And what does a comma do, a comma does nothing but make easy a thing that if you like it enough is easy enough without the comma. A long complicated sentence should force itself upon you, make you know yourself knowing it and the comma, well at the most a comma is a poor period that lets you stop and take a breath but if you want to take a breath you ought to know yourself that you want to take a breath. (221)

Stein's point is not to distinguish the natural from the artificial (her approach, here as elsewhere, is post-Romantic) but to distinguish between different kinds of tools and experiences, those that promote life and its tangles and those that do not. If commas cut up or impose breaks on the rhythms of respiration, a long complicated sentence exerts a different kind of force. Both breathing and grammatical parsing are characterized by a movement back and forth between unconscious, automatic behavior and conscious, deliberate attention, and both nudge your attention toward reflexive awareness: as Stein puts it, just as a sentence should "make you know yourself knowing it," so "you ought to know yourself that you want to take a breath." Stein enjoys grammatical mistake, then, because it indexes a complexity she associates with life and requires her to pay attention to what is ordinarily automatic or unconscious, the subtle circuits of grammar and respiration. She aims to write sentences that induce a reflexive awareness of these circuits, that promote a lively determination of structure and meaning through readerly deliberation.

I use the word *deliberation* in order to echo Steven Meyer's description of Stein's approach to what he calls "deliberate error," "error that may nonetheless be correct, error, that is, with the means for correction built into it. If such error requires deliberation, it also rewards it."[4] Meyer discusses this aspect of Stein's poetics as part of his careful analysis of the relations between her early neuroanatomical training and later writing practices. As a student in the 1890s Stein had worked in the field of experimental physiological psychology, first as an undergraduate at Radcliffe and Harvard with William James and Hugo Münsterberg, and then at the Anatomical Laboratory at Johns Hopkins, where she pursued a medical degree. At Hopkins she made models of human brain tracts and encountered difficulties that led her ultimately to reject a career in medicine and take up writing as a medium for experiment. Meyer understands Stein's career change as in part a consequence of her resistance to anatomical perspective and to the exclusion, in her medical training, of what he calls a "neuraesthetic" perspective, which he defines as "a sensitivity to the physiological operations of one's own nervous system" (58). If an anatomical perspective on the brain gives an observer a clear visual sense of brain structure, it fails "to convey any sense of the actual conditions in which these structures exist—any sense, that is, of their physiological conditions" (96). In this way Stein was very much a student of William James, who emphasized the value for knowledge practices of paying attention to one's bodily, physiological experiences. But, as Meyer points out, Stein's insistence on writing and reading as the primary locus for a reflexive circuit of knowledge and feeling distinguishes her from James; for Stein, there appears to be some ultimate continuity between writing and physiology that permits writing to become not only a symbolic vehicle for communicating ideas but itself matter for experiment and experience.[5]

Stein's thinking on the liveliness of words and her attention to the role of feeling in composition engages critically with her nineteenth-century training in the life sciences. At the same time, her compositional poetics of deliberate error, with their implied notion of negative feedback as a means for correction, offered her access to aspects of what was not yet, in the first half of the twentieth century, called organized complexity (although ideas of circular causal relations and nested relations of dependence and interdependence between systems were percolating at the intersections of a number of disciplines). In this context consider how Stein's keen excitement for the combinations of grammar foregrounds the notions of emergence and self-organization, two important ideas from later biological systems theory: "when I was at school the really completely exciting thing was diagramming sentences and that has been to me ever since the one thing that has been completely exciting and completely completing. I like the feeling the everlasting feeling of sentences as they diagram themselves./In that way one is completely possessing something and incidentally one's self."[6] Here again Stein's activity and that of the sentence enter into feedback or circuit relations, permitting an eccentric self to emerge from the way that words can, under observation, self-organize into complex whole sentences. Both the words *complex* (in the sense of composite or compound) and *complete* (to make whole or entire, having all its parts or elements) inhabit the same semantic field as the word *composition*, so central to Stein's poetics.

I make these points about complexity and composition in order to bring Tomkins into my discussion, the American psychologist whose theory of what he called, from the mid-1950s on, "the affect system" was crucially informed by those midcentury sciences of organized complexity, cybernetics and systems theory. Stein and Tomkins are not as distant, either historically or conceptually, as I had initially assumed, connected as they are through William James and the laboratory tradition of physiological psychology. Strangely, their career trajectories, although a generation or two apart, are almost symmetrically reversed. In 1930, about thirty years after Stein dropped out of medical school, Tomkins completed his bachelor's degree at the University of Pennsylvania with a concentration in playwriting. He pursued graduate work in psychology and philosophy (also at Penn), taking two graduate seminars in the early 1930s with another student of James's, the philosopher Edgar A. Singer Jr., who was born a year earlier than Stein.[7] Tomkins finished his doctorate in 1934 and moved on to do postdoctoral work in philosophy at

Harvard (with the logician Quine, among others) before joining Henry Murray's group studying human personality at the Harvard Psychological Clinic (which had been founded by James's colleague Morton Prince). Whereas Stein left Harvard and the life sciences for writing, Tomkins moved from playwriting (and Pennsylvania, where Stein was born) to Harvard and the study of personality. These two very different writers and thinkers shared an explicit filiation with James, academic training in the psychologies of their moments, and a dissatisfaction with the forms of empiricism that guided this training. Tomkins, as much as Stein, became explicitly concerned with the role that affect plays in perception and cognition.

I introduced the basic elements of Tomkins's theory of affect in my introduction; here I would like briefly to explore those aspects of his work that offer theoretical traction on the idea of the compositional aspect of affect. Tomkins proposes specific roles for affective experience in the perception of objects, as, for example, in his theory of the role of positive affect in the development of infant perception. He suggests that the affect of interest-excitement sustains infant attention, acting as a motive for "perceptual sampling" (*AIC* 1: 347) or the many and various acts of perspective-taking that permit the infant to become acquainted with a new object: "In learning to perceive any new object the infant must attack the problem over time. Almost any object is too big a bite to be swallowed whole. If it is swallowed whole it will remain whole until its parts are decomposed, magnified, examined in great detail, and reconstructed into a new more differentiated object" (1: 347–48). Tomkins lists many kinds of perspective-taking, including looking at an object from different angles, watching its movement, switching between perceptual and conceptual orientations, remembering and comparing the object in time, touching, stretching, pushing, or squeezing it, putting it into one's mouth, making noises with it, and so on, and suggests that "without such an underlying continuity of motivational support there could indeed be no creation of a single object with complex perspectives and with some unity in variety" (1: 348). Enjoyment plays an equally important role in infant perceptual development: by providing "some containment" for the infant's distractibility, it lets the perception of an object remain in awareness longer (1: 487). The enjoyment of recognition then motivates the return to what is emerging, in perception, as a bounded object.

As in infancy, so in adult life: for Tomkins, both positive and negative affects continue to play essential roles in perception because of that most significant of the freedoms of the affect system, the freedom of object. Accompanying this basic freedom is what Tomkins calls "affect-object reciprocity," the ways that affects and objects come to be reciprocally interdependent. He puts it this way: "If an imputed characteristic of an object is capable of evoking a particular affect, the evocation of that affect is also capable of producing a subjective restructuring of the object so that it possesses the imputed characteristic which is capable of evoking that affect. Thus, if I think that someone acts like a cad I may become angry at him, but if I am irritable today then I may think him a cad though I usually think better of him" (1: 133–34). In this example anger may lead Tomkins to information about himself (his prior mood) or about others (their callousness), or both; just because Tomkins is irritable when he makes his observation does not mean that his friend is not a cad ("In a moment of anger, characteristics of the love object which have been suppressed can come clearly into view" [1: 134]). These dynamics, most often described in terms of (what psychoanalysis calls) the defenses of projection and introjection, are not easily avoided, nor should they be, according to Tomkins, since affect-object reciprocity plays a crucial role in experiences of coming to knowledge: "There is a real question whether anyone may fully grasp the nature of any object when that object has not been perceived, wished for, missed, and thought about in love and in hate, in excitement and in apathy, in distress and in joy. This is as true of our relationship with nature, as with the artifacts created by man, as with other human beings and with the collectivities which he both inherits and transforms" (1: 134–35).

Both Stein's compositional poetics and Tomkins's theory of the role of affects in perception offer access to a reflexive and dynamic middle ground, what Eve Kosofsky Sedgwick has termed "the middle ranges of agency."[8] I believe that these middle ranges are important to think about; the alternative, a continual oscillation between phantasies of omnipotence and abjection, is exhausting and unhelpful. But these middle ranges are difficult to conceptualize and inherently confusing because affective dynamics do not obey the logic of noncontradiction: "The logic of the heart," as Tomkins puts it, "would appear not to be strictly Boolean in form, but this is not to say that it has no structure" (*AIC* 1: 134). Where Tomkins addresses this difficulty by seeking a theory that can capture the complexity of affective experience, Stein explores confusion itself, seeking to make it palpable, available, and tolerable. For Stein, acquainting oneself with confusion is an important part of what it means to know and to experience understanding; as she puts it in her lecture "Portraits and Repetition," "There is another thing that one has to think about, that is about thinking clearly and about confusion. That is something about which I have almost as much to say as I have about anything."[9]

It turns out that the word *confusion* and its cognates do appear regularly in Stein's lectures. In "Paintings," for example, she writes toward the end, "I wonder if I have at all given you an idea of what an oil painting is. I hope I have even if it does seem confused. But the confusion is essential in the idea of an oil painting."[10] Etymologically *confusion* means "to pour together, to blend or melt in combination or union," a literal description of what happens with viscous oils when mixed and used for painting. But Stein insists on the necessary relation between confusion and "the *idea* of an oil painting" (emphasis added); at stake here is precisely the movement from the literal to the figurative or symbolic, from a perceptual experience of paint on canvas to a conceptual experience of picture or representation and back again. This confusing movement back and forth between medium and form has been the subject of Stein's lecture all along, and at this point she is wondering whether she has successfully communicated her poetics, for which such movement is crucial. These modernist poetics would become extremely influential in mid-twentieth-century visual art criticism, and it is usual to associate Stein's writing with a move toward abstraction in the arts, best captured, for example, in Clement Greenberg's arguments against figuration.[11] But Greenberg's program for postwar American abstraction is not Stein's, for whom abstraction poses the greater threat to experiences of understanding and communicating understanding than does confusion. For Stein (and, as we will see in chapter 4, the psychoanalyst Wilfred Bion as well), accommodating confusion and the frustration that accompanies it make thinking possible.

"The difference between thinking clearly and confusion," asserts Stein in "Portraits and Repetition," "is the same difference as there is between repetition and insistence."[12] What is this difference? Stein claims to have discovered the latter distinction, crucial for her poetics, at the age of sixteen or seventeen, when she spent a summer in Baltimore living with "a whole group of very lively little aunts who had to know anything" (168). Listening to her aunts talk and listen to each other taught Stein about the importance of emphasis: "expressing any thing there can be no repetition because the essence of that expression is insistence, and if you insist you must each time use emphasis and if you use emphasis it is not possible while anybody is alive that they should use exactly the same emphasis" (167). What appeared to be repetition of words and sentences in her aunts' conversation often involved variations in mood, modality, tense, or tension. When repetition did occur, it was due to a lapse of attention, to tiredness or boredom, to the failure of listening: Stein concludes that "Nothing makes any difference as long as some one is listening while they are talking" (170). She associates thinking clearly with a sustained attention to these differences in emphasis; in fact, for Stein, creativity or compositional difference itself emerges from a sustained attention to the affective circuits between listener and speaker, even or especially when these are the same person. Confusion, by contrast, takes place when this circuit of attention is interrupted, when insistence and difference subside into senseless repetition of the same, and when remembering takes the place of attention to the present.

Listening and talking at the same time, it turns out, is one of Stein's working definitions of genius: "it is necessary if you are to be really and truly alive it is necessary to be at once talking and listening, doing both things, not as if there were one thing, not as if they were two things, but doing them, well if you like, like the motor going inside and the car moving, they are part of the same thing" (170). Once again she offers a technological figure to describe what is most alive: here she figures the coordination of talking and listening by a coordination of a motor "going" and a car "moving," by the relation between motivation and behavior. Stein's interest in people's motors or what she calls "the rhythm of anybody's personality" (174), her whole portraiture project is a way to explore motivation at once continuous with and a radical break from her early training in physiological psychology. Her attention to "the motor going inside" can be heard in two ways at once, especially when she returns to this figure late in the lecture: "As I say a motor goes inside and the car goes on, but my business my ultimate business as an artist was not with where the car goes as it goes but with the movement inside that is the essence of its going" (194–95). Stein brings her awareness not to behavior (where the car goes) but to "the movement inside," that is, both to what is going on inside a person and what goes *to* the inside of a person, motivation within and without. Stein's language addresses the status of affects or motives as at once inside and on their way inside from elsewhere, and her method of doing portraits requires that she attend precisely to these movements of affect, especially between her portrait subjects and her self: "I must find out what is moving inside them that makes them them, and I must find out how I by the thing moving excitedly inside in me can make a portrait of them" (183). I will discuss Stein's affective, transferential portraiture method in chapter 4. For now I would simply point out that these movements are essentially confusing (in terms of location and belonging) at the same time that they make up the very liveliness she wants to capture in her portraits: "But I am inclined to believe that there is really no difference between clarity and confusion, just think of any life that is alive, is there really any difference between clarity and confusion" (174).

Certainly the lively mobility of affect, how affect moves between outside and inside, between selves or between self and object (what Tomkins describes in terms of affect-object reciprocity), makes affect a primary source of confusion. But this general characteristic is not the only source: "As I say a thing that is very clear may easily not be clear at all, a thing that may be confused may be very clear. But everybody knows that. Yes anybody knows that. It is like the necessity of knowing one's father and one's mother one's grandmothers and one's grandfathers, but is it necessary and if it is can it be no less easily forgotten" (173). Stein moves from a universal "everybody" to an individual "anybody," both as subjects of knowledge, then suddenly introduces a familial middle ground as an object of knowledge. Just as her gossiping aunts led her to the distinction between repetition and insistence, now she locates family as a primary source of confusion: the mixing up of environments, of genes, of persons that create family resemblances, strange throwbacks, and unpredictable mutations. The terrain of clear confusion summons up, one imagines rather surprisingly for Stein, the feelings of dependence and independence that accompany family life, the necessity both to know and to forget the difficult vicissitudes of infancy, childhood, and beyond.

The difficulties of infancy occupied Melanie Klein greatly; indeed for Klein, the intensity and volatility of especially negative emotional experience explains, in part, why the first year or two of life is generally unavailable to adult consciousness: it's too painful (and pleasurable) to remember. For Klein, these intensities continue to inform later mental experience and behavior, or, as Robert Hinshelwood puts it, "If Freud had discovered the child in the adult, then Klein believed she had discovered the infant in the child."[13] Born in 1882 (eight years after Stein), Klein was part of the early wave of central European psychoanalysis, undergoing analyses with Sandor Ferenczi and Karl Abraham before settling in London in the mid-1920s. The British-based school of object relations that she helped to initiate differed from what came to be called classical psychoanalysis, especially in emphasizing qualitative relations with the important early "objects" or people in the life of a patient. Where Freud's main clinical methods involved verbal techniques (free association and dream interpretation), Klein developed techniques of play and play interpretation in her work with children, for which the material of gesture, vocal intonation, spatial manipulation of toys, and other nonverbal communication became relevant for observation. Bringing her interpretive techniques to adult analysis, Klein developed the important understanding that infantile unconscious phantasies accompany all behavior and that these phantasies are enacted both verbally and nonverbally in the here and now of experience.

Such an emphasis on the here and now, or what Stein would call the "continuous present," is one common ground between Klein and Stein, between whom there was little overt historical connection. Unlike Tomkins and Stein, who can be intellectually and disciplinarily linked, Stein would appear not to share with Klein any such personal or professional filiations. In fact Stein staunchly and publicly rejected psychoanalysis, most famously in *The Autobiography of Alice B. Toklas*, where she claimed never to have had any "subconscious reactions."[14] By contrast with her brother, Leo, Gertrude shied away from Freud and the popular uptakes of psychoanalysis in the first decades of the twentieth century.[15] As a queer woman writer Stein had excellent reasons to reject heteronormative psychoanalytic and other psychological discourse and the threats it might pose to her. But Stein and Klein were participating in similar modernist projects in their efforts to become acquainted with and give verbal form to elements of experience that are difficult to access and entertain in consciousness. These efforts share a few basic methods or principles: in addition to an insistence on the present of awareness, they shared a form of attention to what in psychoanalysis is called the "total situation," a suspicion of abstraction as a way of coming to knowledge and a sense of the inevitable role for confusion in thinking.

To approach these shared concerns or methods, consider this long citation from an excellent essay by Lyn Hejinian on the role of compassion in Stein's early book *Three Lives*:

> Like Flaubert, Stein was interested in compassion *as an artist*, which is to say *formally*; this is at the root of Stein's desire (and ability) to "include everything." It is a clinical, not an encyclopedic, impulse; there is nothing that can be considered unworthy of attention, no subject that is too trivial, too grimy, too mundane, too abject, too foible-ridden, too ordinary. Inclusiveness in this context means a willingness to look at anything that life might entail; as such, it was a central tenet of the "realism" which claimed Flaubert for its "father." And the detachment which it requires is what permits the shift from manipulative to structural uses of compassion, a term whose connotations modernist realism transformed. What had previously served (antirealist) sentimentality now informed (merciless) compositionality.[16]

Detached and compassionate attention that includes everything: this closely resembles the total analytic situation in which nothing is too minor to be overlooked and everything may have value. For Klein, the importance of the total situation lies not in a fantasy of totalized description or knowledge but in the variety of ways that the patient expresses unconscious phantasy, including deeply negative wishes or thoughts aimed toward the analyst. Klein tried to give what she called "deep interpretations" or verbalizations of unconscious phantasies and discovered that these often had the surprising and therapeutic effect of freeing the patient to engage in more varied creative activity. Interpreting especially negative phantasy tended to open up a generous space in which the most destructive impulses can be voiced and entertained rather than inhibited or repressed for fear that they might trigger immediate, dangerous reprisal (by an other or by a different part of the self). In this context the analyst's merciless attention becomes a version of what Hejinian calls the structural use of compassion, characteristic of Stein's (and other modernists') compositional practices.

What might be structural about this use of compassion? Stein's emphasis on compositional differences, that is, on differential relations as themselves constituting objects or identities, shares a basic insight with Ferdinand de Saussure's linguistic theory, including an emphasis on nonmimetic understandings of language. Stein puts it this way in "Poetry and Grammar": "Language as a real thing is not imitation either of sounds or colors or emotions it is an intellectual recreation."[17] But where Saussure's structuralism and its uptakes in later anthropology and literary criticism focused on groups of static binary oppositions as productive of value and meaning, Stein's structuralism is much more Kleinian, involving acts of what Susan Howe calls "linguistic decreation" as well as intellectual re-creation.[18] The poetic project of *Tender Buttons* (written in 1912–13, around the same time Saussure gave his course in general linguistics) offers the most striking examples of Stein's Kleinian structuralism, beginning with its title, which invites a reader to think of everyday household objects as well as exceptionally sensitive body parts (nipples, clitorises, fingertips). In three sections this writing traces a broad itinerary from "objects" to "food" to "rooms," that is, from poems that attempt to decreate/re-create things that one can see outside of one's body, to decreations/re-creations of those kinds of things that can be taken into the body as food and digested, to interior spaces that are formed from such processes of incorporation. The first poem in this collection, titled "A carafe, that is a blind glass," offers a sense of the structuralist aspect of Stein's project:

> A kind in glass and a cousin, a spectacle and nothing
> strange a single hurt color and an arrangement in a system
> to pointing. All this and not ordinary, not unordered in not
> resembling. The difference is spreading.[19]

A carafe is, among other things, a container used for pouring, while a "blind glass" is, again among other things, a nonreflecting mirror: the linguistic "system to pointing" that *Tender Buttons* begins with offers a moving viscosity and opacity rather than a still clarity and mirroring of meaning. The poem's "kind" and "cousin" evoke the familial as a model for differences, an "arrangement" that is neither "ordinary" (ordinal, numbered) nor "unordered": the representational system here is structured but not static. Its mobility is in part a consequence of its destructive energies, the sense of shattered crystal and spilled "spreading" of bruised difference or "hurt color" in a continuing present of the writing.

Many of the poems in the first section communicate the sense of taking a perceived object to pieces and putting it together in a new way so as to see it, and say it, as if for the first time. In "Poetry and Grammar" Stein describes the poetic project of *Tender Buttons* this way: "I began to discover the names of things, that is not discover the names but discover the things the things to see the things to look at and in so doing I had of course to name them not to give them new names but to see that I could find out how to know that they were there by their names or by replacing their names."[20] As an infant discovers "the things to see" through bodily manipulations of the thing it is perceiving, including a discovery of a thing's solidity, persistence, and usability through efforts at destroying it, so Stein enacts this process of perception in language, a process that involves discovering how names and things are intimately, intricately related: "After all one had known its name anything's name for so long, and so the name was not new but the thing being alive was always new."[21] The modernist goal of generating new poetic form to accord with the newness of things in nonhabituated perception brings her attention to the dynamics of writing itself as a space of recreation or childlike play. Consider another poem, "Objects," from the first section it shares a title with:

> Within, within the cut and slender joint alone, with sudden equals and no more than three, two in the centre make two one side.
> If the elbow is long and it is filled so then the best example is all together.
> The kind of show is made by squeezing.[22]

Stein begins this poem by counting feet: one iamb ("Within"), two iambs ("within the cut"), three ("and slender joint alone"), as if generating these feet from the idea of "within" and the word that names this idea. Counting serves to modify the anxiety of "the cut" (between word and thing), a technique that turns into a balancing act or an effort to fill in the gap or even out the sentence ("with sudden equals and no more than three"). The following phrase continues reflexively to count the center feet, but what counts as the center keeps changing as this long, jointed sentence goes on. A new sentence or joint appears next, an "elbow" that may disappear from sight or become filled in when the arm stretches out; the poem now encourages us to look at the sentence or arm "all together" rather than anxiously to count feet or body parts separately. In the final sentence Stein announces something about her compositional method, how it feels to make a poem or "show" of the kind we are reading: slow and gradual, as if squeezing something out of the body (excretion).

This poem reads like a set of instructions or a recipe for how to produce a middle or third space in and of writing, an exemplary recipe for Stein's project insofar as any of her poems are exemplary. Not that it's particularly easy to follow Stein's recipes; rather she offers readers specific examples of de-habituated linguistic and perceptual experience and opportunities to step away from habit ourselves. Of course, *objects* is also a verb, and in these poems Stein gives us her objections to reifications of nominal forms. In order to read Stein at all it would appear that one needs to give up any sense of dialectical mastery that language use ordinarily comes with and begin, as it were, all over again. For example, here's a poem called "Oranges in" from the end of the second section "Food."

> Go lack go lack use to her.
> Cocoa and clear soup and oranges and oat-meal.
> Whist bottom whist close, whist clothes, woodling.
> Cocoa and clear soup and oranges and oat-meal.
> Pain soup, suppose it is question, suppose it is butter, real is,
> real is only, only excreate, only excreate a no since.
> A no, a no since, a no since when, a no since when since, a
> no since when since a no since when since, a no since, a no
> since when since, a no since, a no, a no since a no since, a no
> since, a no since.[23]

I hear the word *nuisance* repeated in what strikes me as a stubborn, irritated or despondent nursery rhyme that takes constipation ("Whist bottom whist close") or some other excretory difficulties as subject. These difficulties are accompanied by the memory of childhood foods ("Cocoa and clear soup and oranges and oat-meal") used to treat a painful condition ("Pain soup"), memories that deliver a depressing sense that "real is only, only excreate." This feeling that the world and one's writing have gone to shit ("cocoa" to caca) may be one natural and fitting conclusion to a section on food, but one that triggers a tantrum of sobs: the poem appears to struggle against returning ("since when") to some early, fraught moment. The title "Oranges in" evokes *origins*: the poem recognizes how origins and the felt imperatives of origin stories (both to tell these stories and to feel determined by them) are a nuisance, distracting from the presence of new perception; the poem also recognizes how such distractions are nearly inevitable, natural, difficult to counter—you can't say it too often, a real nuisance.

For object-relations theory, the near inevitability of being distracted from the here and now of perception is a consequence of the constant activity of the basic defenses of projection and introjection in unconscious phantasy. Klein differed from Freud in her theory of phantasy. For Freud, fantasy is a form of (sometimes conscious) hallucinatory wish-fulfillment resorted to by the infant when an instinctual desire is not gratified. But for Klein, as Hinshelwood defines it, "unconscious phantasies underlie every mental process, and accompany all mental activity. They are the mental representation of those somatic events in the body which comprise the instincts, and are physical sensations interpreted as relationships with objects that cause those sensations."[24] Unconscious phantasies are ubiquitous and accompany any experience of thinking or perception; rather than substituting for external reality, in object-relations theory "the investigation has been into the way in which internal unconscious phantasy penetrates and gives meaning to 'actual events' in the external world; and at the same time, the way the external world brings meaning in the form of unconscious phantasies."[25] If the term *compositional* involves the bringing together of elements that we are often in the habit of keeping apart, this notion of unconscious phantasy offers the most sophisticated and thoroughgoing interpretation of the mixed-up nature of composition that I am aware of. Like Tomkins's understanding of affect-object reciprocity, Klein's notion of phantasy complicates any simple subject-object and interior-exterior oppositions, requiring reciprocal understandings of the role of mental experience in the constitution of objects in perception and the role that external objects play in the constitution of subjective experience.

The epistemological stakes of Klein's notion of phantasy emerged during the 1930s as her differences from Freud grew. These differences were sharpened and exacerbated when a number of Viennese psychoanalysts, including Freud and his daughter, Anna (who also specialized in child analysis), moved to London in 1938 to escape the war, eventually prompting the so-called Controversial Discussions of the first half of the 1940s, in which Klein and her supporters tried to consolidate their theories and defend themselves against rejection by the British Psychoanalytic Society. Klein asked Susan Isaacs to write and deliver the first paper, "The Nature and Function of Phantasy," a lucid and provocative treatment of the idea.[26] As Meira Likierman puts it in her description of this paper, "Isaacs' account intimates that phantasy creates the earliest system of meaning in the psyche. It is the element that gives blind human urges a direction, and so is an instinctual mode of thinking based on the response to worldly impingements."[27] If for Freud instincts "were the fundamental motivational forces in mental life . . . neither purely physiological nor purely mental," then, as Isaacs put it in her essay, "Phantasy is the mental corollary, the psychic representative of instinct. And there is no impulse, no instinctual urge, which is not experienced as (unconscious) phantasy."[28] Phantasy gives psychic shape, texture, volume, or sense to the instinctual urges and forces that we constantly undergo; it is, as Hinshelwood puts it, "the nearest psychological phenomenon to the biological nature of the human being."[29]

One significant value of Tomkins's affect theory is its redescription of what Freud called "instinct" or "drive"; for Tomkins, qualitatively different affects (which, like instincts, are at the border between the psychic and the physiological) provide more varied kinds of motivation than the Freudian dualisms (either of libidinal and hunger instincts or, later in his theory, life and death instincts). In the interest of working out a compatibility between Klein's and Tomkins's theories, I suggest that affects may be thought of as specific qualities of relation that become worked over in or as phantasy. Where affect gives quality to phantasy, phantasy lets affect take shape and move as part of the process of composing objects. For example, for Tomkins, the infant's hunger is amplified by its distress: the cry of distress communicates both to the infant and to its mother that something is wrong. In Klein's theory the hungry infant has a phantasy of something biting its stomach from the inside. Bringing these descriptions together we have the negative affect of distress (along with fear and anger) motivating and qualifying a phantasy that gives these affects specific psychic content; the phantasy itself can then reactivate this particular affective bundle for the infant even when it is not literally hungry. Likierman puts it this way: "the particular scenario out of which a phantasy is composed is always and specifically based on object relations, in which an object is either treated in a particular way, or else itself meting out a particular kind of treatment to the subject. . . . [Isaacs's and Klein's understanding of unconscious phantasy] portrays the basis of our mental operations as relational in nature, and suggests that we cannot make sense of our experiences, nor indeed our identity, without referring continually to an internal scenario in which meaning is actualized in an exchange between a subject and an object."[30]

This notion of phantasy as "an internal scenario in which meaning is actualized" goes even further than Tomkins does in insisting on the composite nature of thinking and feeling, of perception and conception, and of sensation and imagination. While it is not the case that these binaries are collapsed in Kleinian thinking, nonetheless there is an awareness of the impossibility of ultimately separating these out *in experience* and a refusal to subordinate experiential awareness to more abstract theoretical descriptions and goals. In this way Kleinian thought shares an attitude with William James's radical empiricism, and it is no accident that Isaacs cites James early in her essay in answer to the criticism that Klein confuses the perceptual and conceptual "mode of thought." Isaacs responds by insisting that, while we necessarily use words and concepts in discussing thinking, perceiving, and other mental processes, nonetheless "the mind and mental process, thinking itself, *are not in themselves abstract*," that is, we experience thinking as well as perceiving, feeling, and sensing. She goes on: "The concepts we use in talking about perceiving or thinking are alike the result of focusing in attention certain elements in the total content of experience. Even a sensation or a perception is from one point of view partly abstract, since each is attended to by abstracting certain aspects of experience from the total." For Kleinians, the partly abstract nature of concepts and the words we use to represent them (in this case, the words *conception, sensation,* and *perception*) should not replace an awareness of the psychic reality that underlies the experience and gives them meaning. Isaacs writes that "phantasies are, in their simple beginnings, *implicit meaning*, meaning latent in impulse, affect, and sensation" and goes on a few sentences later: "But words are by no means an essential scaffolding for phantasy. We know from our own dreams, from drawing, painting and sculpture, what a world of implicit meaning can reside in a shape, a colour, a line, a movement, a mass. We know from our own ready and intuitive response to other people's facial expression, tone of voice, gesture, etc., how much implicit meaning is expressed in these things, with never a word uttered, or in spite of words uttered."[31] For Kleinian thought, there's always more going on than we are able to say; it shares with James's radical empiricism a commitment to the possibility of becoming aware of such meaning-giving experience. Unlike James's, however, Klein's thinking and techniques share with Stein's poetic project a commitment to the possibility of communicating this experience in partly symbolic form in the here and now of perception.

The controversial aspects of Klein's work share something with those of Stein's: both women were accused of being too confusing, whereas what is confusing and difficult is the object of their investigations and the nature of their projects. During the discussion following Isaacs's paper Edward Glover, one of Klein's staunchest opponents (and Klein's daughter's analyst), accused Klein and Isaacs of misunderstanding Freud's theory and inventing a new metapsychology that could accommodate the notion of phantasy. The word *confusion* appears repeatedly in his angry response as he accuses Isaacs and Klein "of confusing concepts of the psychic apparatus with psychic mechanisms in active operation in the child's mind, or, again, of confusing both psychic concepts and functioning mechanisms with one of the psychic derivatives of instinctual stress, namely phantasy." He concludes his angry accusations this way: "I maintain that the compatibility of her ideas with accepted Freudian theory cannot be maintained. It is not possible to have it both ways."[32] This classic paternal expression of the law of the excluded middle accompanied a criticism of what these practitioners considered to be unscientific epistemology: a confusion between the analyst's descriptions of the mechanisms or psychic processes in actual operation and the analyst's attempts to understand the patient's own phantasies of these processes. Hinshelwood points out how "extensive problems of validity, generalizability and communicability in a 'science of the subjective'" unsettle claims for scientific authority, an uncomfortable situation that often provokes attempts to distinguish a language of metapsychology from a phenomenological language of the patient's phantasies.[33] Here we encounter what Wittgenstein calls the impossible dream of a metalanguage, a separation that can never ultimately secure the desired distance because, as Hinshelwood goes on to point out, psychic experiences are themselves productive of the objects of perception under discussion, or, to put it another way, phantasy underlies and itself becomes theory.

I do not mean to imply that confusion itself is to be valued positively, but I am interested in when it is dismissed in anger and when it is possible to have some other affective and cognitive relations to it. Klein herself theorized confusion in a discussion of envy in the late paper "Envy and Gratitude" (1957). Taking up Freud's controversial notion of the death instinct, she defined envy as an innate or constitutional destructiveness directed against what is good or the sources of life itself, in the first instance the feeding breast. Freud had claimed that these powerfully destructive tendencies were "clinically silent," but Klein observed or inferred them from her analytic experiences, for example, when she describes "a patient's need to devalue the analytic work which he has experienced as helpful [as] the expression of envy."³⁴ She goes on to suggest that some patients use confusion as a defense against their own tendency to criticize or devalue: "This confusion is not only a defence but also expresses the uncertainty as to whether the analyst is still a good figure, or whether he and the help he is giving have become bad because of the patient's hostile criticism" (184). This uncertainty over good and bad in the "negative therapeutic reaction" is both an expression of envy as well as a defense against it, and throughout her essay Klein consistently presents confusion in this double role.

To elaborate further: according to Klein, the infant lives the first few months of its life in what she called the paranoid-schizoid position, which is characterized by the perception of part-objects that are either entirely good (prototypically the breast that comforts and feeds the infant) or entirely bad (the absent breast, the one that withholds or denies milk). Such "normal splitting" permits the infant to begin to internalize the good object at the core of the ego, and eventually this leads, around the middle of the first year, to the integration of what is good and bad into a mixed, contaminated, more realistic whole object, the achievement of what Klein called the depressive position. Confusion enters the developmental picture if "excessive envy, an expression of destructive impulses, interferes with the primal split between the good and bad breast, and the building up of a good object cannot sufficiently be achieved" (192). "I believe this to be the basis of any confusion—whether in severe confusional states or in milder forms such as indecision—namely a difficulty in coming to conclusions and a disturbed capacity for clear thinking. But confusion is also used defensively: this can be seen on all levels of development. By becoming confused as to whether a substitute for the original figure is good or bad, persecution as well as the guilt about spoiling and attacking the primary object by envy is to some extent counteracted" (216). While the confusion that expresses envy is somewhat different from the confusion that acts as a defense against it, both these confusions are fundamental to life insofar as envy is constitutional or innate. If life is accompanied by the instinct toward death or a return to the inorganic state, then some varieties of confusion of the kinds that Klein describes are inevitable.

The concept of envy introduced yet another division among Klein's colleagues, this time within the group of object-relations analysts, many of whom rejected what they perceived to be a deeply pessimistic idea about innate human self-destructiveness; indeed Freud's own thinking on the death instinct has been stringently modified by later psychoanalytic theorists. As Laplanche and Pontalis put it, "The difficulty encountered by Freud's heirs in integrating the notion of the death instinct leads to the question of what exactly Freud meant by the term '*Trieb*' in his final theory."[35] My interest in these pages has been, in part, to bring together Klein's and Tomkins's approaches by foregrounding their approaches to affect. I suggest that Tomkins's differentiated vocabulary of affect offers more descriptive traction than does the psychoanalytic vocabulary of instinct or drive, and I propose recasting at least some of the phenomena that Klein associates with envy and the death instinct in terms of a variety of innate, negative affects that threaten any sense the very young infant (and at times the older adult) may have of a more coherent or integrated self. In their more intense forms the negative affects offer experiences of extreme bodily destabilization: the rending cries of grief, the burning explosions of rage, the shrinking or vanishing compressions of terror, the transgression of the boundary between inside and outside the body in retching or disgust, all these wreak havoc with any more integrated bodily sense the infant is also in the process of developing.[36]

For Klein, envy and the defenses against it give rise developmentally to the need to modify envy in the depressive position. Some time in the middle of the first year of life the infant comes to recognize its mother as a whole object who integrates in herself good and bad. This integration is both a subjective experience and an objective change in the infant's mental structure, a gathering of fragmented ego parts into a more coordinated psychic identity that depends on the infant's perceptual and affective capacity to recognize the mother's face. Importantly for Klein, this integration triggers aggression, ambivalence, and a fluctuation between depressive states and the defenses against them, until a more stable understanding of the flawed object permits a more secure relationship or experience of it, along with a commitment to reparative processes. In this context consider how Stein offers up a Kleinian understanding of Cubist method in her short book *Picasso* (1938). She describes that artist's vision in terms of the way a small child sees the face of its mother: "the child sees it from very near, it is a large face for the eyes of a small one, it is certain the child for a little while knows one feature and not another, one side and not the other, and in his way Picasso knows faces as a child knows them and the head and the body." Whereas in ordinary vision "everybody is accustomed to complete the whole entirely from their knowledge"—ordinary vision involves habitual gestalts that permit us to experience whole figures—in Picasso's vision, "when he saw an eye, the other one did not exist for him and only the one he saw did exist for him and as a painter, and particularly as a Spanish painter, he was right, one sees what one sees, the rest is a reconstruction from memory."³⁷ Picasso tries to communicate a vision that does not make use of the generalizations or abstractions of memory but rather insists on the present of experience as much as possible, no matter how fragmented.

To put this another way, Picasso's compositional techniques—as well as Stein's, whose descriptions of Picasso are almost always also of herself—try not to assume any integrated forms that preexist the act of composition itself. If this notion of composition has the sense of bringing together parts into a whole, such an integration is necessarily accompanied by confusion because of the great variety of defensive strategies working to mitigate the pain of the depressive position. Recall, Stein puts it this way: "But I am inclined to believe that there is really no difference between clarity and confusion, just think of any life that is alive, is there really any difference between clarity and confusion."³⁸ Perhaps it ought to be possible to distinguish, at times, between kinds of confusion—those that express envy and those that defend against it—as well as between these confusions and the rather different experience of integration of whole objects in the depressive position. But it does not feel like any of this should be particularly easy. This is due to the vitality of affects and the ways they act as compositional agents in the perception of objects: they necessarily both clarify and confuse, motivating the constitution, maintenance, and dissociation of objects. This, I believe, is the basic premise and promise of the idea of composition. Unlike those of her colleagues who took up the modernist slogan "Make it new," Stein does not renovate anything but rather attends to the contemporariness of awareness and unawareness. The relevant slogan might be "Make it now," a *now* that we cannot know whether it is now or not except through forms of attention to affects and their confusing consequences for composition.

2 / Expression and Theatricality, or Medium Poe

In a Jack Cole comic from November 1949 Plastic Man nearly meets his match.¹ The villain, hangdog-faced escaped criminal Phil Sanders, has gone straight and avoided the law for the past two years. Everything changes when he tries out for a theatrical role, rather minimally specified: the part of a sad character whose "facial expression must break hearts of audience." The director finds that Sanders suits the part and coaches his expression slightly, until they both realize that his face can bring everyone around him to tears (fig. 2). Plastic Man's sidekick, who happens to be at the same audition, starts the train rolling: "Here are my last two bucks . . . er . . . Sadly-Sadly! It's the only name I can think of for you!" And so the newly renamed Sadly-Sadly returns to his life of crime with his new unbeatable weapon, a face that causes people to want to make him feel better by handing over their cash and jewels. Bounding away from the audition with an armful of money, he thinks, "All I have to do is remember what Camden [the director] taught me about the tone of my voice and the expression on my face! I'll be able to pull anything and maybe even win Plastic Man's sympathy!" (fig. 3). For the duration of the comic this face renders its diegetic viewers helplessly sad while giving many of us outside the frame of the comic great pleasure, a pleasure taken not only in Sadly-Sadly's face and its exorbitant effects on his viewers or victims but more generally in the great assortment of exaggerated faces and warped and twisted bodies. In Cole's extraordinarily vital, manic style, Plastic Man's slapstick abilities to stretch, bend, expand, and compress are exaggerations of the distortions of every body

FIGURE 2. "A little sadder . . . more pathetic." Plastic Man™, DC Comics. Used with permission.

in every frame; as the subtitle of Art Spiegelman's Plastic Man edition puts it, "Forms Stretched to Their Limits!"

In one sense Cole's version of the sad man who provokes sympathy in his onlookers takes to the ridiculous limit that manipulative role played by distressed straight masculinity, especially in U.S. political performance.[2] Not that there's explicit satire here, but the queer energy of Cole's drawing and the refreshing absence of any self-pity in this comic contrast with, say, a contemporary Frank Sinatra singing "Willow Weep for Me." Sadly-Sadly is much more up front about his new power: "What an angle! I should work when I've got this new gift for getting easy dough?" Less satire than burlesque, this comic offers an over-the-top treatment of the idea of sympathy itself, both the pity that one feels for another's pain and distress and the more general sense of sympathy, in Adam Smith's understanding, as the mechanism by which anyone can feel what another person is feeling. Famously, for Smith, "As we have no immediate experience of what other men feel, we can form no idea of the manner in which they are affected, but by conceiving what we ourselves should feel in the like situation."[3] In Smith's model, emotional contagion takes place only through an act of wholesale imaginative identification with another person, a sympathetic identification that operates in the mode of the hypothetical. Cole's story glosses sympathy very differently: when viewers see Sadly-Sadly's extreme expression, they experience an analogously extreme distress with nothing hypothetical about it; no need for a viewer to imagine himself or herself in Sadly-Sadly's shoes, as distress is somehow communicated more directly, and to overwhelming effect.

Figure 3. Sympathy in Cole's burlesque. Plastic Man™, DC Comics. Used with permission.

Cole's gloss on sympathy as a kind of instant contagion of affect closely resembles a theory that Smith briefly entertains only to reject: "Upon some occasions sympathy may seem to arise merely from the view of a certain emotion in another person. The passions, upon some occasions, may seem to be transfused from one man to another, instantaneously, and antecedent to any knowledge of what excited them in the person principally concerned. Grief and joy, for example, strongly expressed in the look and gestures of any one, at once affect the spectator with some degree of a like painful or agreeable emotion" (11). For Smith's interest in developing theories of social order, equilibrium, and propriety, this is a dangerous theory. For one thing it leaves open the possibility of a quick spread of passion through a crowd; for another, and relatedly, it bypasses the discriminating abilities that eighteenth-century psychology located in the faculties of imagination and judgment (as indexes of class) in favor of a sensationalist account of emotional communication that depends on the sense of sight. Smith offers a counterexample to dismiss this account—"the furious behaviour of an angry man is more likely to exasperate us against himself than against his enemies" (11)—but this example offers yet another instance of the transfusion model he wishes to reject. While we may not be angry with the same thing as the angry man, we are, as Smith points out, "exasperate[d]" or, like him, ourselves angry. Smith would like sympathy to depend on judgments or evaluations of the propriety of emotion (the propriety, that is, of the relation between emotion and object) but cannot avoid those more physiological aspects of emotional experience that take place before or to one side of propriety and judgment. Cole's comic foregrounds these less evaluative aspects. Sadly-Sadly's viewers have no idea what the object of his sadness might be; indeed they are prevented from making any judgments at all about the propriety of his feeling. What counts here is expressive intensity rather than emotional authenticity.

Cole's burlesque fits well with Silvan Tomkins's theorization of the affect system as I have been making use of it in this book: its primary location on the face (and in the voice), its freedom with respect to object, the lability, volatility, and mobility of affect across physiologies, and its status as generally autonomic, involuntary, or, in the terms of information theory, redundant to a large degree. For example, in a discussion of the redundancy of affects Tomkins explores what he calls their "*syndrome* characteristic" (*AIC* 1: 146), the innervation of all parts at once in affective response (as when we break into a full-body sweat in sudden fear or literally leap for joy), and goes on to suggest that as a consequence of this redundancy, affect tends to rearouse itself, resulting in the phenomenon of contagion.[4] In this context consider a quick thought experiment: could some facial expression other than sadness fit Cole's story? Joy might work for this criminal plot as an expression that can inspire money-giving acts of gratitude, though a certain animated Stimpy's "Happy-happy Joy-joy" tends to have an opposite effect on his cranky partner, Ren. Fear or anger might not so easily fit the bill here— or could they? My sense is that it is the coached, pitch-perfect intensity of Sadly-Sadly's facial expression that creates the redundancy and syndrome effects in Cole's depictions, a swamping and rearousal of affect that renders viewers incapable of thought. If the villain in this comic were a woman, something called sex appeal would likely replace sadness as the physiologically overdetermining, hypnotic quality in an artifact of mid-twentieth-century U.S. popular media, as in film noir's femme fatale. "GRAWK! What have we done? What came over us?" "How could we do it? We weren't ourselves . . . couldn't even think rationally!" In

Cole's comic, the communication of exorbitant affect as it overwhelms reason and makes one's self unrecognizable takes effect as a kind of mesmeric power, a power often thought to have its source in sexuality and which here appears on the face of things.

I use the term *mesmeric* to evoke the historical coincidence of Adam Smith's writing and Franz Anton Mesmer's life and work. Sympathy theory and mesmerism are flip sides of the same coin, both mid- to late eighteenth-century attempts to understand what we now associate with the phenomena of affective communication that set the terms for later investigations into both individual psychology and group behavior. Mesmerism (a model for the labile movement of emotion across physiological boundaries) and sympathy (a model for feelings that, although they may be for others, are only ever authentically our own) come in deconstructive tandem, something that can be seen clearly in Freud's work. As several historians have pointed out, only after his early attempts to use hypnosis failed did Freud develop techniques of free association and dream analysis to treat his patients. Mikkel Borch-Jacobsen has convincingly argued that the disciplinary identity of psychoanalysis has depended on the repression or disavowal of hypnosis as a technique, even while related phenomena of suggestion and emotional contagion continue to surface in the realm of the transference.[5] If I begin with Cole's comic and the mesmeric, material underside of the coin of affective communication, it is in order to develop a theory of expression that can describe exorbitant affect dynamics without resorting to depth models of psychic causality. Cole's comic, along with Tomkins's affect theory, model affective communication in terms of intensity and quality rather than interiority and authenticity as these are supposed mutually to guarantee one another within depth models; the mesmeric model offered by Cole's comic offers overt and excessive expression that, in a sense, obviates (for the moment) epistemological questions of authenticity or true feeling.

Much twentieth-century criticism, informed by modernist antisentimentalism, had difficulty treating such highly expressive aesthetic forms as comics. I approach this aesthetic terrain by turning to a similar maximization of affect in Edgar Allan Poe's prose romances and poetics. Poe's writing both forcefully communicates specific feelings and claims to know something about what it does. In theorizing his practice Poe elaborated over the course of his career a well-known poetics of effect that makes explicit an intention to produce "Passions" in his readers. According to these poetics, all writing (whether poetry or prose, science or romance) aims for pleasures or satisfactions of varying kinds: "A poem, in my opinion, is opposed to a work of science by having, for its *immediate* object, pleasure, not truth; to romance, by having for its object an *indefinite* instead of a *definite* pleasure."⁶ This three-way generic distinction from "Letter to B—" (between poetry, scientific prose, and prose romance) reappears in "The Philosophy of Composition" (published ten years later): "Now the object, Truth, or the satisfaction of the intellect, and the object Passion, or the excitement of the heart, are, although attainable, to a certain extent, in poetry, far more readily attainable in prose. Truth, in fact, demands a precision, and Passion, a *homeliness* (the truly passionate will comprehend me) which are absolutely antagonistic to that Beauty which, I maintain, is the excitement, or pleasurable elevation, of the soul."⁷

This reference to "homeliness" would tend to invite critics to route Poe's poetics of passion through Freud's thematics of the uncanny and the depth dynamics of repression and the unconscious. I turn instead to Tomkins's reinterpretation of these thematics by way of a set of conflicts between what he calls the General Images, or goals of the affect system. I argue that Poe's most effective stories are roughly equivalent to Cole's comic book depictions in that both serve as overtly expressive masks that stage relations between the four Images of the affect system: maximize positive affect, minimize negative affect, minimize affect inhibition, and maximize power. These Images or goals generate a set of conflicts with one another and, in conjunction with what Tomkins terms the taboos on looking, work to regulate or control the expression and communication of affect. This chapter maps the prominent facial dynamics of Poe's tales in terms of Tomkins's affect theory and reads Poe's narrators' fascinations with their loved objects as enactments of his poetics or proposals to his desired readers. I have two main goals here: first, to offer a revised notion of expression that criticism appears to be seeking, one that can describe affect dynamics without falling back into an idealized, self-authenticating interiority; and second, to read out of Poe's peculiarly shameless narration (in "The Tell-Tale Heart") a specific affect strategy, what Tomkins describes as a masochistic strategy of "reduction through magnification" of negative affect. This strategy helps to explain the considerable appeal of Poe's writing more generally, especially in the terms that I began to discuss in the introduction of the theatricalization of writing. At the same time, this strategy offers an alternative description of the phenomena we have come to associate with the return of the repressed.

Consider, first, the frequent descriptions of faces in Poe's tales, less in the service of elucidating character than in a series of attempts to frame relationships with readers. A Poe narrator will often offer a minutely detailed depiction of the face of some beloved or compelling person within the tale's first few paragraphs, directly after confessing to the difficulties he has remembering origins. "I cannot, for my soul, remember how, when, or even precisely where, I first became acquainted with the lady Ligeia"; "I cannot just now remember when or where I first made the acquaintance of that truly fine-looking fellow, Brevet Brigadier General John A. B. C. Smith."[8] These self-consciously nervous, melancholy narrators tend to follow such gestures with extensive, obsessive, idealized physical descriptions, as if to correct the impressions they have just given of their memory loss and to sketch a picture of, say, Ligeia's ivory skin, raven hair, Hebrew nose, sweet mouth, brilliant teeth, Greek chin, and extraordinarily large eyes, or of the general's jet-black hair and whiskers, brilliant teeth (again), clear voice, and (yet again) "exceedingly large" eyes. But these long, mostly visual descriptions are bizarre, somehow never quite adding up, for what Poe's narrators seem to want to make perfectly clear is less a picture of a person than a problem with expression.

This problem, or set of problems, clusters around the various meanings of *expression* that the narrator of "The Man That Was Used Up" makes explicit. The first is a problem with verbal capacity, an inadequacy of linguistic expression or a failure of words fully to capture the narrator's meaning: "There was something, as it were, remarkable—yes, *remarkable*, although this is but a feeble term to express my full meaning—about the entire individuality of the personage in question" (378). The second, related problem is with the location of the identity expressed by the beloved or fascinating individual, a problem that the narrator has in locating essence or substance: "I could not bring myself to believe that *the remarkable* something to which I alluded just now ... lay altogether, or indeed at all, in the supreme excellence of his bodily endowments" (380). These two problems of locating and communicating meaning, his difficulties grasping an idealized identity and speaking about it intelligibly, are brought together when the narrator stares into his beloved's eyes and attempts to describe the facial expression that he sees: "there was perceptible about them [his eyes], ever and anon, just that amount of interesting obliquity which gives pregnancy to expression" (379). The narrator of "Ligeia" moves through a similar set of problems with even more emphasis on the eyes of his beloved: "The 'strangeness,' however, which I found in the eyes, was of a nature distinct from the formation, or the color, or the brilliancy of the features, and must, after all, be referred to the *expression*. Ah, word of no meaning! behind whose vast latitude of mere sound we intrench our ignorance of so much of the spiritual" (313).

Expression, for Poe's narrators, names a host of basic problems: how can they possibly tell "spiritual" feeling given the "mere" material features of sounds, words, and faces? That is, how can they tell how their beloved feels, or how they feel about their beloved—and how can they possibly tell these feelings in turn to a reader, who is often directly, desperately addressed? The narrators of these tales all seem to believe that their problems of expression are specific to their beloved, and it is true that, in these tales, their objects are unusual: something about Ligeia's volition or force of will is so immense that it permits her to return from the grave to possess her husband's second wife, and the title character of "The Man That Was Used Up" turns out to be entirely made up of artificial parts and prostheses. In another story, "A Tale of the Ragged Mountains," the narrator begins by offering us a detailed, blazon-like description of Augustus Bedloe's face, a man of whom he can get no information concerning his family or history. By the end of the tale it seems Bedloe is the reincarnation of a man named Oldeb, who died in a colonial rebellion more than thirty years before. These depictions of faces and the accompanying problems of expression tend to take place at the start of tales about bodies that threaten to belong to no one or to someone else, or to take over someone else; these are tales about persons who are never properly singular or individual in their bodies.

Insofar as we are born from bodies not our own, of course, none of us is properly singular. These Poe tales investigate the connection between the nonsingular nature of bodies or persons and a variety of problems of expression. Perhaps these narrators are struggling to remember some lost image of a parent, engaged in the process that Poe calls "mournful and never-ending remembrance" (the title of Kenneth Silverman's psychobiography and a citation from "The Philosophy of Composition").[9] This would help to make sense of several aspects of these scenes: the narrator's difficulty remembering origins (just when, again, do we meet our parents for the first time?), his infant-like proximity to facial features or other body parts that do not quite cohere as an identity, the fact that these beloved persons have a tendency to return unexpectedly from the past. My intention in bringing forward this psychoanalytic observation is not at all to begin a psychological investigation into the narrators themselves, their particular characters or psyches; indeed the persons in Poe's prose romances tend to have nothing readers skilled by realist writing would recognize as three-dimensional or well-rounded characters, as Poe's writing is not interested in delineating idiosyncratic surface features to index buried or ingrained character traits.[10] Part of the peculiar power of Poe's writing is its ability to step away from privileging the depth side of the opposition between surface and depth, especially in its prescient understanding of analysis: "The Purloined Letter" and the other detective stories define analysis in terms of an attention to what is right under our nose yet remains hidden or unreadable. Both Poe's detective stories and his tales of terror are centrally concerned with the legibility of expression and pose fundamental questions about the communication of affect between individuals as well as within individuals who, precisely in experiencing multiple and contradictory feelings, may not experience themselves as singular or individual.

At the same time, Poe's tales are centrally concerned with affective communication between text and reader. In this way the problems of expression, like the dynamics of analysis, occupy the terrain that psychoanalytic theory describes by way of the notion of transference. Poe's tales have been uniquely available to psychoanalytically informed and especially deconstructive theory because they continually and hyperreflexively stage the basic enabling condition and problem for analysis, that of the transference. Transferential relations have been explored at length in largely linguistic terms in the Lacan-Derrida-Johnson debate, those theoretical approaches canonized in the 1980s that avoided the epistemological oppositions surface/depth and interior/exterior by pursuing the more complex topographies that come to be associated with writing (signifier, signified, the circuit of the letter).[11] One major motive for bringing affect theory such as Tomkins's to literary study has been to think the interimplications of writing and affect without beginning from or ending with theories of exclusively linguistic signification. If I focus on the set of problems associated in Poe's writing with expression rather than analysis, it is because the basic critical thematic of the purloined letter applies equally to facial affect as to linguistic signification. A survey of the detective stories shows that Poe defines analysis precisely in terms of a transferential identification that takes place through facial affect. For example, the prefatory remarks in "The Murders in the Rue Morgue" adduce examples from games such as draughts (checkers) and whist in order to describe the successful analyst's proper object of observation, "the countenance": "he notes every variation of face as the play progresses, gathering up a fund of thought from the difference in expression of certainty, of surprise, of triumph, or of chagrin" (530), keeps track of the "manner" and "air" of the players so that he can play his cards "as if the rest of the party had turned outward the faces of their own" (530). Similarly "The Purloined Letter" insists on the play of facial identification in the schoolboy's game of even and odd.[12]

I have already discussed Melanie Klein's understanding of transference and unconscious phantasy. Here I want to suggest that object-relations theory offers an approach to expression (whether by way of words, gestures, or other means) as enactments of phantasy in the here and now of the analytic situation. Recast in these terms, expression becomes a play of enacted relations or reenactments of conscious and unconscious relations to objects of phantasy. In those of Poe's tales that begin from attempts to depict a beloved's face, expression names both the possibility and the problem of successfully enacting phantasy relations, not to Poe's narrators' parents but to the texts' primary objects, its readers. Consider how we readers are positioned in these tales both with the narrator, by way of the first-person perspective, and with the beloveds who are described as specifically "remarkable": they bear a graphic nature that pertains both to writing and to a vivid, unusually violent or literalizing death or death-in-life scene. For Poe, these meanings of graphic are densely intertwined. For example, Bedloe's name is almost exactly the inverse of the name of the man whom he reincarnates (Oldeb), and both die similar deaths when an arrow or leech penetrates their skull; Ligeia's force of will is exemplified both by her passionate text-based learning and by her zombie revival; and the General John A. B. C. Smith, as his name attests, is both a bodily and "textual precipitate."[13] Poe's beloveds tend to allegorize the readers he seeks to please, manipulate, and control, especially in their iterated, serial, or mass aspect, and the relations between narrators and beloveds can be read as mapping the phantasy relations his writing attempts to enact with readers.[14] In this context the detailed depiction of faces that do not quite come together or cohere can be thought of as ways to reach out and touch a reader, or at least try to touch us.

It follows that Poe's strategies for depicting faces differ from many of his contemporaries' more typical uses of physiognomy to idealize expression as transparent, legible, or indicative of inner moral qualities.[15] "The Man of the Crowd" thematizes this difference most explicitly. The tale begins with physiognomy's highly conventional association between reading print and reading faces: the male narrator, a sensitive convalescent, sits at a large window in a London coffeehouse alternately "poring over advertisements ... observing the promiscuous company in the room ... [and] peering through the smoky panes into the street" (507). Emphasizing the hazy graphic continuity between the newspaper and the populated city spaces, the tale repeats the word *press*, which, along with *throng* and *crowd*, name the primary object of study. After pages of the narrator's detailed descriptions of the "dress, air, gait, visage, and expression of countenance" (507) of the myriad types and classes he sees through the window, his taxonomic approach is suddenly interrupted by a man whom he is entirely unable to classify: "Any thing even remotely resembling that expression I had never seen before" (511). The narrator can only list the set of ideas that "arose confusedly and paradoxically within my mind, the ideas of vast mental power, of caution, of penuriousness, of avarice, of coolness, of malice, of blood-thirstiness, of triumph, of merriment, of excessive terror, of intense—of supreme despair" (511). He is unable to make this overwhelming list of feelings cohere or attach to an existing social type and leaves the coffee shop to stalk the man through the streets of London. A full twenty-four hours later he finally stops the man and looks him full in the face but receives no acknowledgment; the narrator returns to the taxonomizing impulse and concludes that he is "the type and genius of deep crime. He refuses to be alone. *He is the man of the crowd*" (515).

But who is it, after all, who cannot be alone? Certainly both men in the story answer to this description of "the man of the crowd." Once again Poe offers us the failure of a first-person narrator to read or tell the physiognomy of a fascinating figure, although here the illegibility is specifically a crime as well as a problem for the narrator. Critics have observed how this tale gives us the flaneur as a prototype for the detective who reads the urban space and its inhabitants in the service of a new form of social control that requires exhaustive typologizing; unreadability becomes a crime in this specific sociocultural context.[16] Another, perhaps related reading returns to the point that Poe's beloveds tend to allegorize the readers that Poe wants, and their unreadable faces give us these phantasy relations: the man of the crowd who cannot be alone becomes a reader stalked by Poe's compulsive writing style, who, after all, must stay with the text's narration at least for the duration of the reading experience. In a strange (at once estranging and too intimate) manner, Poe's writing acknowledges our unreadability: the tale ends by echoing its physiognomic beginning and comparing the man to a book that "does not permit itself to be read" (506). We are quite literally unknown to Poe or future to his act of writing, criminal in the sense of being beyond his control or that of the proto-detective. In this context the tale's epigraph from La Bruyère, "Ce grand malheur, de ne pouvoir être seul" (This great unhappiness, not to be able to be alone), hints that the story be read as a sly, slightly sadistic punishment, both for being beyond the writer's control and for the unhappy crime of reading, which in this story names the inability or unwillingness to be alone with whatever crowd of thoughts or feelings we might want some distraction from.

Like other Poe tales, in "The Man of the Crowd" man *is* a crowd, never only singular or individual, nor even only double, but multiple, dynamic, self-contradictory, and perverse. This man's face, like the other Poe faces I have described, is unreadable not in being blank but rather in being overly legible or too intensely expressive of too many things at the same time, an intensity that overwhelms the narrator, who can only create an impressive list of disparate feelings. (The "pregnancy" of expression in "The Man That Was Used Up" also implies this kind of multiple or nonsingular aspect of feeling-states.) In order to unfold those aspects of Poe's poetics that turn on intensity, multiplicity, and especially the excessive expression of negative affect, I turn now to Tomkins's affect theory, both to his understanding of the faciality of affect and to his theory of what he calls the General Images.

In the introduction I described how, for Tomkins, "affect is primarily facial behavior" (*AIC* 1: 205–6) and how facial expressions are not consequent to inner, prior feeling-states but lead the rest of the body in the enactment of affect. Tomkins's approach to affect's faciality permits physiognomic reading to look rather different from usual: rather than revealing inner, ideal, or essential feeling-states or moral traits, faces index layered histories of complex affective experience, or, to use Tomkins's terms, faces index the scripts or theories that serve to organize and navigate our motivational realities, scripts that are both stable and open to revision. One name for the history of such scripts as they appear on the face might be "character."

I would like to approach Tomkins's understanding of such scripts and theories by way of his important distinction between affect and image: affects as the primary motives in humans (and some other animals), images as specific purposes or goals. This distinction hinges on Tomkins's way of taking up first-order cybernetic theory, in which an intention, aim, or purpose should itself be understood as an emergent property of some complex system.[17] Tomkins called such emergent aims that direct the human feedback system "images," a term that may strike a reader as idiosyncratic but serves to illustrate a basic aspect of cybernetic approaches to purposive behavior: cybernetics understands such behavior not by reference to the notion of an originating will or consciousness but by reference to the observation of a sensorimotor apparatus of sufficient complexity capable of mistake or trial and error. For example, the image of room temperature (say, 68 degrees Fahrenheit) becomes the target and guide for a thermostat and heating and cooling system; an image of social justice or a more equitable economic system becomes the target and guide for activist politics (such as the Occupy movement). An image, as Tomkins puts it, is "a blueprint for the feedback mechanism: as such it is purposive and directive" (1: 120); by contrast, affects are motives, "by which we mean immediately rewarding or punishing experience mediated by receptors activated by the individual's own responses" (1: 120). The excitement that I may experience reading Poe and the shame that I experience thinking about why I am interested in his work (more on this shortly) are affective motives that have something to do with my choice to make it a subject of my writing. But these affective experiences are distinct from my stated purpose of demonstrating the usefulness of affect theory for criticism. This latter purpose is what Tomkins would call an image, in this case a conscious one, and there will always be less conscious images or purposes at work as well.

Because of the inherently self-rewarding and self-punishing aspects of the affects, Tomkins suggests, there is an extremely high probability that any human will generate four "General Images" that guide or give purpose to the (somewhat independent or autonomous) affect system: maximize positive affect, minimize negative affect, minimize affect inhibition, and maximize power to the other three images. These General Images can and do interfere with one another, and the varieties of interference and the different ways of weighting their importance, as well as distinct strategies for their attainment—our scripts—offer satisfyingly complex descriptions of behavior and motivation. Whether conscious or not, these Images guide an affect system that is primarily located on the face. I suggest, then, that we think about the overtly expressive faces in Poe's tales as they offer a staging ground both for the multiple affects and the conflicting images and scripts that guide them; indeed Poe's depictions of these faces should tell us something about the affect strategies of his writing, or, to put this another way, the terms of his poetics as phantasy, wish, image, or purpose.

At first glance it would seem that Poe's poetics of "Passion" or pleasure are guided by the first General Image of maximizing positive affect, and this may be true in the broad sense in which all verbal behaviors, including writing, count as "modes of communion."[18] For Tomkins, the enjoyment of communion with others is the major motive for speech and other verbal behavior; his discussions of oral gratification, claustral pleasures, mutual staring and visual intimacy, and other preverbal modes of communion, all set up a powerfully simple analysis: "The major motive to speech is, paradoxically, the intensely rewarding claustral and preverbal social affect. Speech is in the first instance a continuation of that kind of communion in which the distinction between subject and object is attenuated. It is only because the infant feels so close to the other, we think, that he wishes to mimic the sounds he hears from the other" (1: 428). Affective and verbal communication need not be in competition with one another (although they may also be) because for Tomkins speech is in the first instance a medium for affective communication. Poe's poetics certainly participate in this way of thinking about verbal behavior. Whatever else is going on, Poe's writing aims to please.

It may strike readers of Poe as perverse to foreground something as pleasant or nice as the enjoyment of communion as central to his poetics. Yet this first General Image of the affect system turns out to be a capacious category that happily includes a number of perverse possibilities, among which Tomkins lists "controlling others as a mode of communion," "the enjoyment of the expression of negative affects as a mode of communion," and even "the attenuation of communion as a mode of communion" (1: 454–63). Particularly the second of these helps us to understand Poe's writing as it characteristically communicates a host of mostly negative and intense feelings of confused terror, humiliated disgust, self-abasement and contempt, or any combination of these and others with a high-wire pitch of excitement or thrill and a push to the edge of sanity or figuration. This first Image gives purpose to a host of contradictory feelings, and matters become even more complex when considering the conflicts between Tomkins's second General Image, minimizing negative affect, and the third one, minimizing affect inhibition. When the fourth Image powers both of these at the same time, the stage is set for some of Poe's most sublime scenarios, those involving the binding of fear-terror by shame-humiliation, and vice versa.

Before turning to "The Tell-Tale Heart," as it offers this kind of conflict between these two General Images (along with a strategy of affect magnification for dealing with this conflict), I want briefly to explore an important aspect of Tomkins's discussion of the third general goal of the affect system. Unusually in his treatment of this goal Tomkins makes use of what appears to be a psychoanalytic mechanism of repression, something he usually does without; for example, he writes, "The inhibition of the overt expression of any affect will ordinarily produce a residual form of the affect which is at once heightened, distorted and chronic and which is severely punitive" (1: 330). He goes on to describe the possibility of any affect being suppressed and the resulting pain of this chronic suppression. But what becomes clear over the course of this discussion, as well as other discussions throughout the volumes of *Affect Imagery Consciousness*, is that he proposes no single mechanism of suppression. Rather affects themselves occupy the pivotal role of controllers or inhibitors. For example, "an individual may be distressed much of his life, but never overly complain or exhibit his suffering because of shame" (1: 330–31), or "he may be incapable of expressing his excitement, sexual or otherwise, because he is afraid or ashamed to express these positive feelings" (1: 331). Especially fear-terror and shame-humiliation can act to control or inhibit the expression of other affects, positive and negative, and participate in what he calls affect theories and scripts. Suppression becomes less a single mechanism or multiple instances of one thing than a set of constraints on behaviors and feelings that may be described in terms of the contradictory motives and goals emerging from a dynamic and complex affect system interacting with its various environments.[19]

The notion that inhibition itself may be an emergent phenomenon of the affect system brings us closer to the de-idealized notion of expression that I am trying to elaborate by way of Poe's tales. As illustration, consider one of Cole's throwaway frames from early in the comic, which depicts Plastic Man's sidekick hurtling into a line of auditioning men, one of whom is squeezed up and partly out of the crowd (fig. 4).

This image offers a way of linking the first two dictionary definitions of the verb *express*, "to press or squeeze out" and "to portray, represent." Expression becomes quite literally a matter of physical emergence, with its representational qualities following upon changes in force and configuration such that the composition of the line changes as these other variables change. The meaning of *express* here does not rely on a movement from interior to exterior; in fact the initial force is directed from the outside. The six or seven individuals in Cole's ragtag line can, in this context, be considered metaphorically as a configuration of affects in dynamic interaction. For if, in Tomkins's theory, affects can bind each other for the purposes of inhibition, they can also bond in order to amplify one another: shame may serve to suppress fear, or it can amplify excitement, or both; fear may serve to suppress enjoyment or to amplify contempt, or both. The effects of expression will depend on the scripts or strategies that guide the dynamics of the specific affects in question. Curiously, in both Cole's comic and Poe's writing, overt expressiveness accompanies an intense crowdedness or multiplicity: Cole's comic depicts a long scene in which Sadly-Sadly induces a sympathetic mob to beat Plastic Man to death. Expression, for these artists, involves the forceful squeezing or crowding out of persons, states, or feelings, a crowding out that need not imply some container that can hold only so much. Crucially, of course, *crowding out* can mean in at least two ways, as expression and as something more like suppression. In this latter sense we are finally approaching a way of describing the graphically destructive aspect of expression in Poe's tales, one that does not require a depth model of psychic causality and that may begin to compass the puzzle around exorbitant expression that Poe's tales offer.

Figure 4. Expression as crowding out. Plastic Man™, DC Comics. Used with permission.

To unfold these dynamics of the affect system a little further, I turn now to "The Tell-Tale Heart." I find it a little embarrassing to be writing about this story, which is strange given how much I have already written about Poe's tales without encountering the particular feeling that I am betraying my preadolescent tastes or a distinctly uncritical attraction to this most out-there of Poe's tales. Then again it is precisely this tale's exemplariness—exemplary of Poe's poetics generally and of what I will argue is a very particular affect strategy—that makes any attention to it a matter of some shame. This tale practices what Tomkins calls a masochistic strategy of amplifying negative affect for the purposes of making it disappear; in this story fear-terror is especially amplified, and shame-humiliation is made to vanish from the tale (perhaps to be communicated to a reader). The shamelessness of Poe's writing gives us an affect strategy that comprises a particularly theatricalizing aesthetic form. Poe's usefulness to a number of twentieth-century traditions (especially to American underground or B-movie aesthetic practices such as Roger Corman's) that have adapted his work into film, audio, and comics lies precisely in the skill with which his writing makes this masochistic affect strategy available or communicable to its readers. At the same time, this affect strategy covers terrain very similar to what critics have tended to understand in terms of repression: the attraction that Poe's writing has held for psychoanalytically informed criticism is, I would suggest, not distinct in kind from the attraction that it holds for dramatic adaptors. It is something about the writing's shameless theatricality that has drawn so many different readers, and this something is what I will try to specify or describe.

As we can gather from its title, "The Tell-Tale Heart" takes affective communication as its subject, and more specifically the inevitability or uncontrollability of affective communication. It also offers the most efficient or condensed version of the problem of expression with which I began: we are given, once again and very quickly, a nervous narrator ("True!—nervous—very, very dreadfully nervous" [792]), his beloved object ("I loved the old man" [792]), and a difficulty remembering origins ("It is impossible to say how first the idea entered my brain" [792]). Once again we have the beloved's face, or simply the old man's eye; the entire problem of expression in writing appears to get boiled down to the narrator's conviction, "I think it was his eye! yes, it was this!" (792). And finally, we have a marked incoherence of facial features as well as a fragmentation of body parts (the eye, the heart, the old man's eventually dismembered body). All of the indications of the problem of expression appear in this tale, here enlisted in a particularly overt, destructive goal: the narrator's desire "to take the life of the old man, and thus rid myself of the eye forever" (792). And just as "The Man of the Crowd" invites us to pose the question, Why is the man's illegible face a crime?, this tale invites the question, What's so bad about the old man's eye?[20]

More generally, what's so evil about the evil eye? Tomkins approaches the evil eye in its enormous variety of transcultural and transhistorical manifestations as instancing what he calls the taboos on looking.[21] These taboos—on looking, on being looked at, and on mutual looking or interocular interaction—follow from his theory of facial affect, arguing as it does for "the unique capacity of the look-look with respect to the expression, communication, contagion, escalation, and control of affects" (*AIC* 2: 158). The affect of shame-humiliation plays a privileged role in Tomkins's discussion of the taboos on looking because of its innate activator, "the incomplete reduction of interest or joy" (2: 123): when curious or interested staring (or communion) is partially inhibited by these taboos, shame can become implicated in "the whole spectrum of affect expression" (2: 182). Think, for example, of a shy child looking through her fingers at a stranger as the child's attempt to negotiate the shame of transgressing these taboos. Or think of the basic situation of

64 / EXPRESSION AND THEATRICALITY, OR MEDIUM POE

attending live theater, one situation in which we are permitted the experience of uninhibited staring at the face of a stranger. But think too of the potential for acute embarrassment if your stare, as an audience member, is suddenly returned by the performer on stage and you are picked out for some interaction. This may be one reason why live theater or performance is considered risky in a way that film never is. The risk is specifically one of humiliation, and not only for the performer who may make a mistake and the audience member who may experience the vicarious shame of this mistake. More basic, I think, is the shame that can at any time take place upon the reinstallation of the taboos on looking: the risk of the humiliating acknowledgment of the structural, affective conditions of live theater.²²

Remarkably Poe's tale manages to communicate something like this theatrical risk in writing. It does this in part by taking the evil eye or the taboos on looking as subject: the tale offers a meditation on the murderous aim of getting rid of the evil eye, getting rid, therefore, of the shame-humiliation that accompanies the taboos on looking. The possibility of shame in this tale is located in the interrupted relations between the narrator and the old man's "pale blue eye, with a film over it" (792), an eye that is apparently covered and that may or may not be able to meet the narrator's look. Every night for a week the narrator attempts to stare at the eye without the old man's knowledge and casts a ray of lantern light while he sleeps, "so that a single thin ray fell upon the vulture eye" (793). While the eye remains closed he cannot "do the work; for it was not the old man who vexed me, but his Evil Eye" (793). To put this another way, until the taboos on looking are activated, the shame-humiliation of the look-look does not occur and there is no motive to get rid of it. Once the eye opens—that is, once the eye takes center stage, lit by the narrator's spotlight in this tale's bizarrely condensed, literalized version of theatricality—all hell breaks loose: "It was open—wide, wide open—and I grew furious as I gazed upon it. I saw it with perfect distinctness—all a dull blue, with a hideous veil over it that chilled the very marrow in my bones; but I could see nothing else of the old man's face or person: for I had directed the ray as if by instinct, precisely upon the damned spot" (795).

All the strained staring or gazing in this tale still fails to make any facial expression cohere; quite the opposite. This lack of coherence of facial figures, emphasized here but present also in other of Poe's tales, manifests a particular defense against the humiliation of the taboos on looking. As Tomkins explains, at the same time that the taboos on looking constrain intimacy and expression of affect generally, they keep shame in intolerable focus by way of a double bind: "One may not defend oneself against looking into another's eyes by looking away or by hiding one's face. The expression of shame or shyness is quite as shameful as shameless looking" (*AIC* 2: 170). The narrator's fury stems from an encounter with this double defense against both looking and not looking, a double defense that magnifies not only the basic shame of the taboo but other negative affects as well. The narrator's shiver is one of terror, rage, *and* humiliation, all triggered by his inability to determine whether or not the old man's veiled eye can return his look. Generally in Poe's tales humiliation may be readable not through any explicit depictions of the facial expressions of shame (a blush or the head or eyes turned down or away) but precisely in the failure of visual coherence or of figuration, the failure of facial features to come together and offer any single, legible expression. What Poe offers instead is a shameless self-exposure (rhetorically a confession) that yet fails to offer what we would recognize as a coherence of self, a self that we would expect to be, as Tomkins suggests, "located phenomenologically on the face and in the eyes" (2: 180).

This lack of coherence of self is accompanied in this tale by a very distinctive coherence of sound and a peculiar maximization of terror communicated through sound. Consider this list: the lantern's creaky hinges, the old man's groan, the beating heart, a yell and a shriek that alert the police, a bell that tells the hour (4 a.m.), a knock on the door, a ringing in the ears, and again, most dramatically, the beating heart and final yelled confession: "it is the beating of his hideous heart!" (797). Sound tells this tale to offer not a spatialized facial coherence but a temporalized coherence of narrative movement, and the specific sound that repeats, metrically, thematically, analogically—from the "death watches in the wall" (794), to "the low, dull, quick sound, such as a watch makes when enveloped in cotton" (795), to "the hellish tattoo . . . which grew quicker and quicker, and louder and louder every instant" (795)—is the beating heart-watch. The heart, of course, has been traditionally cast as a seat of feeling. Like the eye, it is an organ that serves as a medium for the expression and communication of affect, but it is a kinesthetic and aural medium that usually communicates within a single physiology or organism. It is the narrator's excessive aural sensitivity that constitutes his "madness": "The disease had sharpened my senses—not destroyed—not dulled them. Above all was the sense of hearing acute. I heard all things in the heaven and in the earth. I heard many things in hell" (792). We are invited to experience this madness when Poe gives us the sound of a beating heart throughout the entire tale, by way of poetic meter and other technical devices: the repeating trochees and anapests at the high-pitched start, the adverbial repetitions throughout the tale ("slowly—very, very slowly"; "steadily, steadily" [793]), the several moments of emphatic direct address. The tale's signal rhythm, stillness or extremes of slow motion followed by sudden violent movements, echoes the sound of the beating heart, and (like the signature soundtrack music from Steven Spielberg's *Jaws*) aims to create overwhelming suspense and terror, its particular version of madness.

But while madness may be one name for what Poe is giving us to experience, sympathy may be another. To return to Adam Smith, consider that one intertext for the particular analogy between the ticking of a watch and the beating of a heart is Smith's writing on "keeping time" with another's emotions, and especially the difficulty of doing so. Smith suggests that the major obstacle to shared feeling between spectators and a person expressing suffering is "the thought of [the spectators'] own safety, the thought that they themselves are not really the sufferers," and that this creates a wish in the sufferer: "He longs for that relief which nothing can afford him but the entire concord of the affections of the spectators with his own. To see the emotions of their hearts, in every respect, beat time to his own, in the violent and disagreeable passions, constitutes his sole consolation."[23] This wish, redescribed, is Tomkins's goal of minimizing affect inhibition, here negative affect. But Smith does not condone this wish (not outside of the theater, anyway);[24] instead he advises the sufferer to minimize negative affect, to "flatten . . . the sharpness of its natural tone, in order to reduce it to harmony and concord with the emotions of those who are about him" (22). He tracks the importance for this harmony of the spectatorial relation to oneself. Sympathy, in permitting the self's imaginary identification with an other that produces the "somewhat analogous" feeling that is less intense, also permits the self to imagine the other's imaginative identification. This "reflected passion," weaker than the original one, "abates the violence of what he felt before he came into their presence" (22). This will eventually unfold in Smith's writing as the "impartial spectator" within our breast that regulates our feelings to keep time with others, the impartial spectator that keeps a watch on our hearts.[25]

Not only does Poe literalize and exceed this pun (it's a death-watch), but he also gives us a dangerously partial spectator who longs for sympathetic concord with the beloved, that is to say, with the old man and also with the reader. The narrator's explicitly spectatorial relation to the old man becomes one of identification when, on the night of the murder, the man wakes up and groans in "mortal terror" (794): "I knew the sound well. Many a night, just at midnight, when all the world slept, it has welled up from my own bosom" (794). This identification of an experience of self and other returns at the conclusion of the tale, when the narrator once again hears the beating of what he presumes to be the old man's heart but that we may presume to be his own, misrecognized or projected outward. To wonder whose heart you're hearing is to wonder whose feelings you're having. We could say that the narrator has some boundary issues, or we could say that the tale is determined to communicate feeling in writing. If by the end it remains undecideable whether the beating heart is the old man's beneath the floorboard or the narrator's own, whether the tale is supernatural or explained supernatural, this is because Poe is aiming to make the narrator's boundary issues ours. If the tale succeeds in communicating "Passion," then the old man's or the narrator's beating heart may well have become the reader's.[26]

Unlike Smith's writing, Poe's does not prefer to minimize negative affect (to put it mildly). In this tale we encounter a maximization of especially fear-terror and a version of what Tomkins would call a masochistic affect strategy of "reduction through magnification" of negative affect. This strategy can play out whenever the general goal of minimizing negative affect comes into conflict with that of minimizing affect inhibition. Tomkins lists several instances of this strategy, including drunken avowals of humiliation or self-contempt, but think of any sought-out experience of distress, rage, or fear, such as going to movies to "have a good cry" or to be safely horrified or to experience righteous anger, triumph, and revenge.[27] He describes it this way:

> The human being will strive to minimize the experience of negative affect at the same time that he longs to express overtly the affect which grows stronger just because of his effort to suppress and minimize it. There will be much suppression and avoidance of affect which will be successful, and under these conditions the second general strategy will provide a clear directive. There will also be failures of suppression which will grow to intolerability until they are released and reduced by overt expression. The self which is so overwhelmed is necessarily a divided self, siding both with and against the affect within, which was his own but which has become alien.
> It is the discovery of this basic ambivalence which constitutes Freud's most significant contribution to our understanding of human nature. He mistakenly identified this conflict as one between the drives and the threat of castration which produces anxiety, rather than between the affects themselves. (*AIC* 2: 269)

Note that, for Tomkins, suppression of negative affect can be successful, so that the strategy of magnifying negative affect takes place only when suppression does not work, in other words, when the second General

Image of minimizing negative affect does not succeed in directing the show. What appears to be a magnified return of the repressed takes place only when the third General Image or goal directs the human feedback system. In such cases, when negative affect can neither be simply suppressed nor expressed, this affect may become intolerable and the masochistic strategy of negative affect magnification comes into play.

In Poe's story shame is double-bound by the peculiarities of the taboos on looking and can neither be suppressed nor simply expressed. These conflicting goals of minimizing shame and, at the same time, of minimizing the inhibition of shame create the conditions for the binding of shame by terror and "a quest for maximizing rather than minimizing negative affect" (*AIC* 2: 268). That is, Poe's tale seeks to "express" (to squeeze or crowd out) the shame-humiliation associated with the evil eye and the taboos on looking; it must, somehow, be gotten rid of or expressed by way of being projected outward, as it were, on the back of terror, an intensive magnification of terror that swamps or presses all other feelings to the vanishing point. The sublime exhilaration that may be experienced in reading this story comes from the binding of shame by fear in this particular affect strategy, as it is used both for and against a reader. The evil eye, as it connotes the shame associated with the taboos on looking, also connotes the shame of any encounter with an other. The narrator's desire to destroy the evil eye, then, is also a desire to destroy any other, that is, to destroy any reader. Poe's power as a writer is largely composed of this remarkable ability to please us by showing how much his writing wants to, or needs to, destroy us.

I will conclude by returning to comic books and a specific image by a contemporary American visual artist, Charles Burns. Burns has adapted the outsized eyes and breasts of Japanese anime style (specifically, hentai, or perverse drawing) to offer what I think of as an emblematic depiction of the strategy of reduction through magnification of negative affect (fig. 5).[28]

Try the experiment of isolating the girl's various facial features by blocking off parts of the image. Doing this, you can see an iconic depiction of each of the negative affects: her eyebrows depict anger; she is wide-eyed with fear and surprise (the startle lines); she cries with distress; her nose is crinkled with contempt; her skin entirely blushes with shame. If you see the snake as a tongue, then she expresses disgust as well. Here are all of Tomkins's negative affects iconically depicted, and in this context her prominent breasts and nipples connote total expressiveness. These affects practically cancel each other out. It is the other face in this picture, the snake's bucktoothed, sweaty, nervous excitement,

FIGURE 5. Reduction through magnification of negative affect. Copyright 1996 by Charles Burns. Published by Fantagraphic Books. Used with permission.

that registers the perverse success of this strategy of amplifying all the negative affects at once, a strategy that aims at splitting and annulment, suspension, or making something disappear.

"It must be nice to disappear / To have a vanishing act": Lou Reed's strange Poe tribute album *The Raven* includes at least four songs that treat "The Tell-Tale Heart." Of these, "Vanishing Act" best understands this affect strategy and its murderous, paradoxically self-conscious shamelessness. This shamelessness, so characteristic of Poe's writing as it responds to the excruciating double binds of the taboos on looking, forms part of the basis for his appeal, especially to twentieth- and twenty-first-century readers powerfully drawn both to the play of language as such and to composition in mediums that make use of audiovisual materials. The sheer number of Poe adaptations into film and audio indicates that something about this writing works well as a medium, specifically as a medium for communicating and disinhibiting negative affect.[29] Poe's writing shares with mask work, minstrelsy, many comic books, and other excessively iconic, highly stylized facial representations opportunities to power the goal of minimizing affect inhibition. In other words, Poe's writing knows how to touch a reader, and in this chapter I have been unfolding what this affective knowledge consists of.

When we think of Charles Burns's and Jack Cole's comics, Poe's tales, exploitation and psychotronic films, or other gonzo-manipulative aesthetic forms, we are likely thinking of work that offers a kind of gamble to readers, an opportunity to maximize expressions of negative affect that is shameless in the sense that shame does not work to inhibit this expression. Literary and cultural criticism has often devalued aesthetic compositions that work this way, offering the generic terms *sentimentalist* or *sensationalist* to describe them, though especially within feminist and queer critical uptakes of the past twenty-five years these valuations have been reversed, complicated, or theorized. Poe is especially interesting as a test case because his work belongs to complementary genealogies, at once central to a modernist trajectory (Baudelaire, French Symbolism, high modernism) and to several mass-cultural genres.[30] In bringing Tomkins's work on the Images to Poe, I have been aiming in part to find approaches to this terrain of modernism and mass culture or entertainment using fresh terms for phenomenological description; by locating and theorizing a variety of shamelessness in Poe's writing I want to avoid opposing these various trajectories. The method of transferential poetics offers a way to begin mapping a field of aesthetic compositional strategies using the vocabulary of affect, without, I hope, getting bogged down by distinctions between literary cultures and their others.

Not only does the vocabulary of affect hold promise for a nonhierarchized approach to poetics that is to one side of the evaluations of modernist antisentimentality. It also departs from too great a modernist investment in analyses of the specificities of medium, analyzing instead a variety of expressive goals or affect strategies. I do not reject approaches to medium; generally I find it valuable to attend to the differences between experiences of print, film, and television, for example. Nonetheless I want (and I think that contemporary criticism is seeking) a vocabulary that permits me to move in and out of a greater variety of aesthetic experience. The notion of theatricality that I offer in this book foregrounds the vocabulary of affect for this purpose. Poe's writing in particular has led me to identify what is at once a writerly technique for the communication of affect and the basis for theatrical expression. Its shattering shamelessness offers one (if not the) affective engine for theater. In this way experiences of writing and theater share something significant: both let us suspend or transgress the taboos on looking. If it is possible for *expression* to mean in a manner that is not entirely bound by notions of idealized interiority and self-presence, I expect these meanings will have to address the continuities and discontinuities between writing and theater, both of which involve the affect dynamics that Poe, Cole, and others permit us to read.

3 / Maisie's Spasms: Transferential Poetics in Henry James and Wilfred Bion

How useful might it be to think of Henry James's *What Maisie Knew* (1897) as a study in group psychology? The particular group I have in mind consists of all the characters in the novel who take on or are given the task of bringing its main character, Maisie, successfully to the end of her childhood. Ordinarily or normatively this would be the work of the family group, but the motivating interest of James's plot is exactly the degree to which the members of Maisie's immediate family, and later of her unusual extended one, are just not up to the task. The novel tells the story of a young English girl of divorced, hateful parents (Ida and Beale Farange) who use Maisie in their warfare against one another— "the little feathered shuttlecock they could fiercely keep flying between them."[1] When both parents remarry (Ida to Sir Claude, Beale to Maisie's governess Miss Overmore), the child's movement between households eventually brings together her new stepparents, who care for Maisie more attentively than her biological parents but whose guardianship serves, at the same time, as a pretext for the emerging adulterous relationship between them. Add to this middle-class late Victorian mix another governess, Mrs. Wix, the maid Susan Ash, and brief but crucial appearances by Ida's and Beale's various lovers, and one gets a quick sense of just how large, varied, and otherwise preoccupied a group of guardians and near-guardians James's plot forms around its central figure.

Perhaps it would be more accurate to describe Maisie as slightly off-center, given to us by way of the narrator's intimate distance. Not exactly a character, James's narrator is (as much of the criticism has noted) a definite presence in this novel, which has as its guiding conceit, according to the preface in the New York edition, the telling of the tale through the child's perceptions: "To that then I settled—to the question of giving it *all*, the whole situation surrounding her, but of giving it only through the occasions and connexions of her proximity and her attention; only as it might pass before her and appeal to her, as it might touch her and affect her, for better or worse, for perceptive gain or perceptive loss" (7). The narrator is formally positioned, as it were, very close to and just behind Maisie's head, an analyst's position, which permits him (although never specified, it does seem to be a masculine narrator)[2] to make informed guesses as to what Maisie is feeling at any moment and whose job is to offer translation: "Small children have many more perceptions than they have terms to translate them," and so "our own commentary constantly attends and amplifies" (8). I cast James's narrator as a kind of analyst not to assign him a position of analytic mastery but rather to take account of his motivated attentiveness to stressful situations, what the novel repeatedly calls "muddle." The preface puts it this way: "The effort really to see and really to represent is no idle business in face of the *constant* force that makes for muddlement. The great thing is indeed that the muddled state too is one of the very sharpest of the realities, that it also has colour and form and character, has often in fact a broad and rich comicality, many of the signs and values of the appreciable" (11). The distressed comedy of James's novel follows upon the narrator's patient, ironic, gently sadistic willingness to let Maisie stumble through any number of painful situations in order that we may profit from her perceptions and confusions, revisions to her understanding, and a gradually gained ability to give verbal form to the "appreciable."

The position of James's narrator is surprisingly similar to that of Wilfred Bion's in his book *Experiences in Groups* (1961), whose approach to group psychology I take up in this chapter. Bion, an early practitioner and theorist of group therapy, means something quite different by this than the therapy of individuals assembled in a group; as he dryly explains in the first paper in his book, he means rather the therapy of a group as such, or the attempt "to make the study of their tensions a group task.... It was disconcerting to find that the Committee seemed to believe that patients could be cured in such groups as these."[3] The first seven papers recount Bion's often pained, awkward experiences with various groups, his estranging attempts to interpret a group's dynamics to itself, and his constantly revised inductive theorizing of these dynamics. He describes his theories as "educed in the situations of emotional stress that they are intended to describe" (142), and like both Maisie and her narrator, Bion is very much in the thick of things: "These occasions [of stress] provide the raw material on which interpretations are based, but the interpretation itself is an attempt to translate into precise speech what I suppose to be the attitude of the group to me or to some other individual, or of the individual to the group" (143). Both James's narrator and Bion act as amplifiers and translators of perception, especially perception of "the muddled state" that each associates with emotional stress and experiences of earliest childhood. Moddle is the name of Maisie's first nurse, or the first she can remember, and Bion puts the particular, sometimes unbearable difficulties of being in a group this way: "The adult must establish contact with the emotional life of the group in which he lives; this task would appear to be as formidable to the adult as the relationship with the breast appears to be to the infant, and the failure to meet the demands of this task is revealed in his regression" (141–42).

Bion's concluding overview essay makes explicit his book's theoretical concern to bring Melanie Klein's work on object relations to the study of groups to supplement Freud's accounts in *Group Psychology and the Analysis of the Ego* (1921) and *Civilization and Its Discontents* (1929). For Freud, the family offers the basic pattern for group dynamics: individuals become members of a group by introjecting a father or leader figure, creating a shared ego ideal, conscience, or sense of guilt. Bion, on the other hand, brings Klein's less paternalist thinking about infant experience to approach the varied, often discomfiting weirdness of groups: "the group approximates too closely, in the minds of the individuals composing it, to very primitive phantasies about the contents of the mother's body" (162). For Bion, groups form because of the inevitable regressive defenses against these phantasies; indeed his working definition of a group is "an aggregation of individuals all in the same state of regression" (142). However, unlike most crowd psychologists before him who pathologize group behavior in masculinist and primitivist terms, Bion asserts that "the apparent difference between group psychology and individual psychology is an illusion" (169). He places great value on what he calls the mental activity of the work group, or the skilled participation of a number of individuals in the cooperative performance of a task (143). Such productive, task-oriented activity is always diverted or undermined by unconscious "basic assumptions" that give rise to various images of the leader, who, in Bion's understanding, is more a consequence than a cause of group cohesion, someone (or something) that fulfills phantasy (projectively) rather than primarily threatening punishment (introjectively).

In the pages that follow I will unfold Bion's understanding of groups in a reading of James's novel; for example, I hope to show that one of Maisie's talents lies in her abilities to evade the leadership roles projected onto her and to stay focused on the task at hand: her own upbringing. But I am equally interested in how Bion's writing itself exhibits Jamesian characteristics or complexities, as if something about both writers' approaches to group dynamics leads to shared poetics. Bion's style is especially reminiscent of James's in its ironic depictions of the awkwardness of group experience. He conveys the discomfort of these situations while seeming to permit the reader a privileged distance from them, a distance that quickly vanishes as we become implicated in the group dynamics that are being described. For example, the book's first paper begins with a narrative account of a typical encounter in group therapy. Bion points out the group's inflated expectations of him and, "while waiting for the group to settle on its new course" (31), digresses to explain to the reader what he thinks he is doing:

> We are constantly affected by what we feel to be the attitude of a group to ourselves, and are consciously or unconsciously swayed by our idea of it. It will be seen at once that it does not follow that one should blurt it out in the way I have so far described myself doing in the group. This, I confess, must be regarded as peculiar, although if precedent were required, we are all familiar with certain types of people, particularly those who tend to feel persecuted, who behave in this manner. Not a happy precedent, the reader will think, and it will not be long before it is evident that the group thinks so too. But it is necessary now to return to the group, whom we left in the process of changing course. (32)

I find this passage strangely comic, with its abrupt, slapstick movements through multiple perspectives, mirrorings, and forms of address. The "we" that includes both Bion and his reader is rapidly followed by a shift in perspective ("It will be seen at once") that distinguishes Bion from those of us who do not "blurt out" our perceptions of group attitudes toward ourselves—a "peculiar" form of confession that Bion reflexively emphasizes ("This, I confess"). The perspective then moves back to a "we" who are "all familiar with certain types of people," presumably not us, immediately followed by Bion's identification with precisely these people: his claim to know what "the reader will think" exemplifies the paranoia or persecution that he ascribes to others. By the time we are returned to the narrative, we may be left chuckling uncomfortably, wondering at the implications of these lurching movements or, more likely, wondering whether we are in the presence of a writer who might not be a little crazy.

Robert Hinshelwood, in a brief discussion of this style, suggests that Bion "perfected a trick of describing certain psychic processes, while at the same time engaging in just that process during the act of describing it."[4] In the example above, one effect of this style is to communicate something like the discomfort experienced by members of the group: a reader is invited to participate in a set of oscillating dynamics of identification and differentiation that takes place both in Bion's narrative and in the nondiegetic, reflexive relation between the book and its readers. I understand these abrupt movements, both within the narrative and between narrative and reader, as one aspect of a transferential poetics shared by both Bion and James. Bion hesitates to use the term *transference* because he is not certain whether his interpretive method with groups is identical with psychoanalytic method (31). But I find the term useful to summarize what is shared by both writers (as well as the other writers of my study): a close attention to emotional states and movements of affect, both within and between individuals; an amused, patient, and nonmoralizing attitude to the messes or muddles that accompany these states and movements; a willingness to risk humiliation or contamination in describing these aloud; and an allowance for sudden, unpredictable changes of course that might follow these descriptions. As discussed in my introduction, the term *transferential poetics* generalizes a Kleinian notion of transference, which Hinshelwood describes this way: "In the transference something is *constantly* going on, the analyst is constantly being used. This is not the analysis of resistance and defence, it is the playing out, in the relationship with the analyst, of subtle and often extremely obscure object-relations" (214). To subscribe to a transferential poetics, then, would be to propose that all interactions (including those between reader and text) play out obscure object relations. As a consequence it pays to be attentive to the fundamentally transferential and group-ish nature of knowing or learning: how the activity of knowing takes place between or among persons or between a person and other objects; how knowledge changes depending on context or situation, becoming possible or emergent in some relationships or configurations and impossible, forgotten, or recessive in others.[5]

James's commitment to a transferential poetics underlies his novel's turbulence, the sense it conveys of a rollicking, rambunctious romp, enjoyable, exciting, and also somewhat nauseating, especially for graduate students reading it in seminar.[6] One of the novel's running jokes is Maisie's lack of proper education, her shuttling between households and caregivers making any progressive, formal schooling, or the fantasy of such schooling, impossible to sustain. Her frequent changes of location and shifts of allegiance involve sharp movements through steep learning curves that the narrator depicts in terms of sudden drops and losses of balance—these are the spasms of my title. When, for example, without warning, Sir Claude moves Maisie from her mother's home back to her father and Mrs. Beale's, "it was like being perched on a prancing horse, and she made a movement to hold onto something" (108). The narrator associates these rollicking movements almost definitionally with Maisie's changing knowledge. In this same scene Sir Claude and Mrs. Beale bond over what they describe as Maisie's "fatal gift of beauty," by which they claim to mean her "charm of character." "'Oh I know all about that sort of thing!'—she fairly bridled with the knowledge" (107): the narrator's description of Maisie's response likens her to the "prancing horse" of the next page, as if her knowledge threatens to knock her off balance and trample her underfoot or needs to be reined in. At the same time Maisie's "bridling" knowledge is associated with the possibilities of her child-bride appeal and the accompanying dangers that she seems to become aware of in the very next sentence: "It gave Maisie somehow a sudden sense of responsibility from which she sought refuge" (107).

Such sudden movements and drops around Maisie's knowledge, or our being made acutely aware of them through the narrator's attention, signal James's attempt to drop to "some deeper depth of irony than the mere obvious" (4), as the preface puts it. Presumably the obvious irony is the juxtaposition of innocence and guilt, the irony of a young girl being thrown into a milieu in which she is exposed to promiscuous sexuality and becomes a pretext for adultery. But James's explanation of the "full ironic truth" (4) of his tale involves a complicated reversal between the adults who are supposedly in the know and the child who is not nearly so innocent. Maisie's name connotes mazes of bewilderment and confusion, as well as the *may*s of plural permissions and possibilities, and it is her ability to induce vicarious wonder, shame, and fearful self-awareness in her guardians that, according to James, makes for the deeper irony. My larger goal in placing Bion and James alongside one another, then, is to approach from a less familiar angle what might otherwise be cast as a child's acculturation, socialization, and loss of innocence. With Bion's work on groups in mind we might redescribe Maisie's trajectory not so much in Freudian (or even Kleinian)[7] developmental terms but this way: over the course of James's novel Maisie is continually acquainted with the particular necessity and extraordinary difficulty of making contact with the emotional life of the group in which she lives.

The novel's great contribution is to cast this frustrating necessity and its consequences in theatrical terms. From the start Maisie is figured as a passive spectator to events beyond her understanding and control, "a mite of a half-scared infant in a great dim theatre" (18). As I will show in more detail, Maisie's spectatorship structures the novel until, in its final chapters, she takes the stage and begins to speak so that her words have significant consequences for the actions, feelings, and decisions of those around her. In my reading the novel's transmutation of spectatorship into acting offers a narrative of vindication rather than development, a reading that contrasts with those critics who attempt to determine what Maisie knows in reductively sexual terms. James does not permit his readers this kind of determination; his transferential poetics motivates the interrogative mood and tense of the novel's title. What Maisie knows at any given moment is only ever anybody's best guess, including her own, routed through fundamentally vicarious relations and assessed only retrospectively. The novel's ending—"'Oh I know!' the child replied. Mrs. Wix gave a sidelong look. She still had room for wonder at what Maisie knew" (275)—comes full circle to offer readers a sense of continuing, lively possibility for this uncanny young person with the capacity for getting what she needs from those around her.

Before diving into the novel's group dynamics I would like to explore how vindication, for James, partly comprises theatricality in a number of interesting ways. Consider how James puts theatrical form and vindication into relation in one of his notebook entries on *Maisie*, part of a set of notes in which he develops his famous remarks on the "scenic method." He first describes his pursuit of "a really detailed scenario" for the novel, how he seeks an "intensely structural, intensely hinged and jointed preliminary frame," and goes on to assert that "each little chapter *is*, thereby, a moment, a stage."[8] The critical literature has long pointed out that *Maisie* was one of a handful of novels written just after James's five-year effort to gain financial support by writing for London's commercial stage, which ended with the opening night of his play *Guy Domville* in the winter of 1895. While his two main biographers differ in their interpretation of his theatrical career and the consequences of the partly negative audience reaction at this opening night, both agree that James did not succeed in reaching the larger theater audience he was hoping for.[9] As the story goes, James recouped his emotional losses by developing a compositional method that used act and scene structure as well as drawing-room dialogue in the novels he wrote during the second half of the 1890s, including *The Other House* (1896), *The Spoils of Poynton* (1897), *What Maisie Knew* (1897), and *The Awkward Age* (1899), a scenic method that crucially informs his late style. In the notebook entry on *Maisie* that I have been quoting from, James's theatrical self-talk culminates in a sort of ecstasy: "Ah, this *divine* conception of one's little masses and periods in the scenic light—as rounded ACTS; this patient, pious, nobly 'vindictive' application of the scenic philosophy and method—I feel as if it still (above *all*, YET) had a great deal to give me, and might carry me as far as I dream!" (162). The editors' footnote at the word *vindictive* reads, "HJ corrects this to 'vindicating' in a note at the top of the manuscript page" (162). Certainly this notebook entry can be read as expressing James's vindictiveness toward the audience that rejected him, as well as his sense of vindication of his chosen métier, the novel form. But the note also raises two questions that I want to pursue here: how, specifically, are vindictiveness and vindication related? And how might they both accompany or motivate the scenic method and, perhaps by extension, theatricality itself?[10]

The novel helps to answer these questions by immersing us in the dynamics of vindication from its first sentence: "The litigation had seemed interminable and had in fact been complicated; but by the decision on the appeal the judgment of the divorce-court was confirmed as to the assignment of the child" (13). James's mock officious style sets the stage for characters who struggle to clear themselves from censure, to assert their interests, to claim ownership or possession, in other words, to vindicate themselves. Each "bespattered" parent fights to keep Maisie from the other, but they both fail when the court decides to share her equally between them. Their own motivations are absolutely vindictive: "They had wanted her not for any good they could do her, but for the harm they could, with her unconscious aid, do each other. She should serve their anger and seal their revenge, for husband and wife had been alike crippled by the heavy hand of justice" (15). In presenting his novel's concern with the consequences of divorce, James's first few pages draw a powerful link between vindication and vindictiveness: how the affective force of a righteous, punitive anger and resentment underlies the legal and performative dimensions of vindication. *Vindicare*, etymologically "to claim, set free, punish, or avenge," conjures up an archaic scene of slavery undone by violence, or conversely, mastery enforced. Vindication invokes the general question of rightful claim to ownership and, with regard to persons, the legal relations between guardian and dependent. The novel's modern theme of divorce taps the ancient political problem of relations between full citizens or subjects and their dependents, political ties that are affectively structured.

If James's prologue immediately establishes its concern with the performative dynamics of vindication and the feelings of anger, resentment, and humiliation that underlie them, it also locates these dynamics in an intensely public, theatrical social space. The judgment to divide Maisie's time between her parents is considered "odd justice in the eyes of those who still blinked in the fierce light projected from the tribunal" (13), and it is this stage lamp of justice that shows both parents to be entirely artificial or superficial, their good looks, showy clothes, and outrageous behavior making them unsuitable parents and perfect objects of gossip in a chattering world. Despite the "reverberation, amid a vociferous public" (14) that the child be left with "some proper third person, some respectable or at least some presentable friend" (13–14), the novel's prologue leaves the child alone and unprotected—except for the narrator, whose first-person pronoun a reader encounters for the first time in the sentence that introduces Maisie's proper name. The narrative style quickly moves from the officiously impersonal to the subtly perspectival, bringing the child under the narrator's, and therefore the reader's, protection, both improper (because neither biologically nor legally assigned) first-person protections of the child. While Maisie is financially secure "thanks to a crafty godmother" (17), this only serves to make her an ideal nineteenth-century heroine: emotionally vulnerable and economically a going concern.

By placing a young girl with dubious protection in a spectacular public realm, the novel offers an updated version of the plot of innocence or virtue in distress, a plot informed as much by nineteenth-century French melodrama as by earlier English novels of sentiment. As Peter Brooks has suggested in an influential argument, melodrama should be considered an important aspect of James's poetics insofar as it allows him to explore fundamental psychic sources of meaning and value, or what Brooks terms "the moral occult."[11] Brooks characterizes melodrama as "the desire to express all," in which "the characters stand on stage and utter the unspeakable, give voice to their deepest feelings, dramatize through their heightened and polarized words and gestures the whole lesson of their relationship" (4). If this style of utterance would initially appear as distant as possible from James's own, Brooks offers convincing arguments for the specific place of melodramatic forms, plots, and goals in what he terms James's "melodramas of consciousness." The significance of expression or saying all lies in melodrama's "rhetorical breaking-through of repression" (42), the effort to name and make legible those emotional or psychological states and relationships that constitute ethical choice in a postrevolutionary, "post-sacred era" (15): "melodrama as a form exists to permit the isolation and dramatization of integral ethical forces, to impose their evidence and a recognition of the force of the right" (157).

I would like to redescribe Brooks's valuable insights in the rather different theoretical terms of this book so that I can specify the relations between vindication and theatricality. Brooks operates within a classical Freudian framework that opposes repression to expression, but as my previous chapter argues, these should be understood in deconstructive tandem, not as distinct mechanisms so much as emergent properties of a motivational system in which the affects themselves serve both to amplify and inhibit one another. Where Brooks recasts the unconscious as "the moral occult," thereby assimilating affective to ethical considerations, I would turn to what Silvan Tomkins calls the General Images, those guiding goals for the affect system, conflicts between which generate a great deal of complexity, as it were, before moral considerations come into play. The conflicts inherent in our fractured and multiplied affective lives underlie and help to constitute what we tend to describe in the more cognitive terms of ethics or beliefs. If melodrama is viewed primarily as a form of expression that is, like Poe's writing, strongly guided by Tomkins's Image of "minimizing affect inhibition," then its pleasures come more from experiences of an intensity, range, and combination of positive and negative affects and their amplified expression than from ideological or ethical resolutions of plot and character per se. These resolutions, which Brooks analyzes by way of what he calls "the aesthetics of astonishment," are fundamental to melodrama: virtue must be made to suffer by going unrecognized, then must be acknowledged and vindicated in a "drama of recognition" (27); and villainy, which "constitutes the active force and the motor of the plot" (34), must astonish as much as or more than virtue. The ethical resolution to the drama should primarily be understood in terms of an affective balance between these forces, in which the vindication of virtue depends upon an equivalently intense vindictiveness that can be assigned, or conveniently handed off, to the villain, whose anger and resentment are necessary to motivate the vindication of virtue. It is the affects themselves that are vindicated by melodrama, or to put this another way, melodrama is the literary form that vindicates their expression.

In this context melodrama may be taken to highlight a fundamental aspect of theatricality itself, that aspect which aims to minimize the inhibition of affect.[12] James's scenic method takes up the melodramatic mode for his own compositional purposes: to put it to work as an instrument of lucidity when faced with the muddle of confused or contradictory affective states. Consider Brooks on the notion of character: "if one conceives character as that theatre for the interplay of manichaeistic forces, the meeting place of opposites, and his [sic] self-expressions as nominations of forces at play within himself—himself their point of clash—the role of character as a purely dramaturgic center and vehicle becomes evident" (101). Redescribing these "manichaeistic forces" as positive and negative affects (or good and bad part-objects) permits me to offer a somewhat different reading of James's novel than Brooks does. Brooks proposes that "What is never seen—and is queried in the last line of the novel as in its title—is the extent to which Maisie knows what lies *behind* the behavior of different adults, and combinations of adults, in her regard," which is the "essentially sexual" nature of human motivation of which Maisie remains "largely ignorant" (166). But to take up this particular psychoanalytic privilege and assert, as a reader, that we know what Maisie doesn't is to miss something fundamental: that Maisie permits the relations that form around her to become richer, deeper, and more complex precisely by not becoming predictable or determined in the manner that the "essentially sexual" risks. In Tomkins's terms, the sex drive becomes an interesting source of motivation only in the context of an affect system that amplifies and transforms it; the sex drive becomes sexuality, in all of its complexity and relations to knowledge, only in proximity to the freedoms of the affect system.

James's novel invites an attention precisely to the relations between affect and sexuality. I would like to return now to Bion's understanding of group psychology in a more sustained reading of the novel's theatricality. From the start Maisie is figured, in Brooks's terms, as a "purely dramaturgic center and vehicle," a spectator at a violent, confusing performance whose ability to understand is a function of her vision:

> It was to be the fate of this patient little girl to see much more than she at first understood, but also even at first to understand much more than any little girl, however patient, had perhaps ever understood before. Only a drummer-boy in a ballad or a story could have been so in the thick of the fight. She was taken into the confidence of passions on which she fixed just the stare she might have had for images bounding across the wall in the slide of a magic-lantern. Her little world was phantasmagoric—strange shadows dancing on a sheet. It was as if the whole performance had been given for her—a mite of a half-scared infant in a great dim theatre. (18)

James casts Maisie as the hyperbolic heroine of an epistemic romance whose "patience" or passivity is a consequence of the way her parents enlist her in their battles. Not only does each freely abuse the other in the child's presence, but each also requires her to repeat their insulting messages to the other, and these insults and adult talk more generally constitute her phantasmagoria. The second chapter introduces Maisie's first important lesson: how not to parrot or repeat her parents' words. She arrives at "the idea of an inner self or, in other words, of concealment" (23) from an exchange with her first governess at her mother's house, the pretty and upwardly mobile Miss Overmore. In response to a question from the child as to whether she should convey yet another insulting message from her mother to her father, Miss Overmore blushes and laughs, then communicates her negative answer nonverbally: "her companion addressed her in the unmistakeable language of a pair of eyes of deep dark grey" (24). This look brings to Maisie's mind a memory of an accidental meeting at the park between the flirtatious governess and the child's father, which Miss Overmore had asked Maisie not to mention to her mother. At the same time that we receive a glimpse of what will become a sexual relationship between Maisie's father and her first governess (they eventually marry), we are also given the progress of Maisie's spectatorial skills: she begins to read facial expressions, to understand what is not said but expressed by way of the eyes. While adult talk may be confusingly phantasmagoric, Maisie learns quickly about nonverbal expression and the motives for speaking and keeping silent.

Immediately, then, Maisie is given to us as someone for whom the skills of spectatorship are crucial for her survival. James's narrative technique manages to convey Maisie's expanding perceptions at the same time that it communicates, at least partially, the increasingly complicated sexual and financial transactions among the adults. But the novel is careful neither to oppose our knowledge and Maisie's nor to identify them; rather it tracks and ironizes the ways that the adults use their relationships with Maisie to work out their own situations. For example, in a conversation between Maisie and her stepfather, Sir Claude, she proudly asserts that, just as she has brought together her father and her former governess, now Mrs. Beale, she has also brought Mrs. Beale together with Sir Claude (72). He laughs at the implications of this, and when Maisie goes on to assert that she has brought him together with her current governess as well, the ugly and elderly Mrs. Wix, he laughs again and half-jokingly asks the child to bring him together with Ida, his wife and her mother. This exchange conveys both the growing antagonism between Sir Claude and Ida and the emerging relationship between Sir Claude and Mrs. Beale—which Mrs. Wix terms the "extraordinary muddle" (67) of their situation. It also places Maisie at the projected center of what Bion would call a "pairing" group. This is one of the three kinds of "basic assumption" groups that, Bion suggests, exist alongside any work group, the other two being the dependent and fight-or-flight groups. Bion describes the pairing group after observing in his meetings the emergence of specific pairs who monopolize group discussion; these pairs are accompanied by "a peculiar air of hopefulness and expectation" (150) in the group, which finds verbal expression in ideas about the future. Bion characterizes this feeling of hope or expectation as "both a precursor of sexuality and a part of it":

> The optimistic ideas that are verbally expressed are rationalizations intended to effect a displacement in time and a compromise with feelings of guilt—the enjoyment of the feeling is justified by an appeal to an outcome supposedly morally unexceptionable. . . . For the feelings of hope to be sustained it is essential that the "leader" of the group, unlike the leader of the dependent group and of the fight-or-flight group, should be unborn. It is a person or idea that will save the group—in fact, from feelings of hatred, destructiveness, and despair, of its own or of another group—but in order to do this, obviously, the Messianic hope must never be fulfilled. (151)

In James's novel it is Maisie herself, or more precisely the idea of her education, pursued but never fulfilled, that acts as the leader of the pairing group. The adults brought together around Maisie argue over which possible configuration of caregivers will best serve the child; meanwhile the actual task of teaching her is jeopardized precisely by feelings of hope for her salvation and their own. The more she is cast in the role of either savior or saved, the more the adults pair off.

The work of raising Maisie is made more difficult by the other basic assumption groups as well, especially the dependent group, which, Bion writes, assumes that it has met "to be sustained by a leader on whom it depends for nourishment, material and spiritual, and protection" (147). Rather than a strong individual with a magnetic personality, the leader is "an individual whose personality renders him peculiarly susceptible to the obliteration of individuality by the basic assumption group's leadership requirements" (177). Sir Claude gets cast in the leadership role for the dependent group most often. Attractive and charming (all the women in the novel love him), weak and susceptible, he fits Bion's description as a "leader by virtue of his capacity for instantaneous, involuntary (maybe voluntary too) combination with every other member of his group" (177). The dependent group is instanced whenever Mrs. Wix and Maisie imagine Sir Claude leaving Ida and taking a house for the three of them. The fight-or-flight group makes its appearance, with Mrs. Wix as its leader, when Sir Claude finally acts at the governess's instigation and steals Maisie away from her stepmother's place to bring her across the English Channel. Rather than offer detailed readings of the appearances of these various basic assumption groups in the novel, the point I would like to take from

Bion's writing concerns the relation between individual experience and the basic assumptions: "I think the struggle of the individual to preserve his distinctness assumes different characteristics according to the state of mind of the group at any given moment.... Individual distinctness is no part of life in a group that is acting on the basic assumptions" (170). While the work group demands cooperation from individuals and therefore requires that individuals recognize themselves and their own distinctive skills or contributions, the basic assumption groups, which exist alongside the work group, encourage phantasies of dependence, pairing, or fight-or-flight; in these basic assumption groups individuated experience becomes indistinct in the various phantasies of projected leadership. Bion agrees with Aristotle's assertion that the human is a political animal but asserts that "the power of the group to fulfill the needs of the individual is ... challenged by the group mentality" (55). Group dynamics, both necessary and frustrating, always involve a movement between the assertion of individual needs or aims and the forgetting, overwriting, or indistinction of these needs or aims in group phantasy.

Maisie must use the group that has formed around her to fulfill her needs, but her success—her ability to make individuated emotional contact with the group—will require its dissolution. As she grows older and learns to recognize and accommodate her fear of the increasingly precarious instability in her situation, her sphere of perception gradually widens. The first two-thirds of the book can be read, chapter by chapter, in terms of Maisie's increasing perceptual abilities to understand what is going on around her; recall James's explanation in one of his notebook entries on the novel that "each little chapter *is*, thereby, a moment, a stage." The novel continues to figure "the sharpened sense of her spectatorship" as "the child's main support," which "gave her often an odd air of being present at her own history in as separate a manner as if she could only get at experience by flattening her nose against a pane of glass" (90–91). But two-thirds of the way through the novel the narrator gives up on the chapter-stage structure that had carried him, and us, so far: "Maisie had known all along a great deal, but never so much as she was to know from this moment on.... It was granted her at this time to have divinations so ample that I shall have no room for the goal if I attempt to trace the stages" (159). The last hundred pages describe a compressed roller-coaster ride of several days (by contrast with the preceding decade or so, covered by the first part of the novel), during which Maisie's knowledge grows exponentially as she confronts each of her potential guardians, imagines herself in several different configurations, and finally forces a choice between them.

Maisie's exponential growth is a consequence of her genuinely difficult situation: she has finally been cut off from her biological parents, who have each taken still other lovers and given Maisie up to her stepparents. The scenes in which Maisie is given up are remarkable, as the narrator manages to communicate the parents' extraordinary selfishness and narcissism to the reader and, at the same time, to convey their "goodness," in Maisie's eyes, giving her a crucial emotional stability. At Mrs. Wix's instigation, Sir Claude steals Maisie away from her father's house and takes her across the English Channel; Mrs. Wix wants to "save" Sir Claude, as she puts it, from the predatory women he is surrounded by, a desire prompted in part by her own love for him. Mrs. Beale has other ideas: she wants to adopt Maisie with Sir Claude to legitimate their adulterous relation. The conflict between Mrs. Wix and Mrs. Beale over Maisie's allegiance leads Maisie to ask her governess, "Why shouldn't we be four?" (209), which prompts Mrs. Wix to try to explain to the child the precise "crime" (210) she is being asked to abet. Maisie's struggle to understand the differences and similarities between the various emotional, financial, and sexual transactions among her parents, stepparents, and guardians (who pays whom, in what currency, with which binding consequences) eventually brings Mrs. Wix to her own sharp question: "Haven't you really and truly *any* moral sense?" (214).

It is one of the ironies of James's novel that he locates the moralizing and sexualizing reading of Maisie's knowledge together, rather precisely, in the character of Mrs. Wix. Introduced as poor, uneducated, and bespectacled, Mrs. Wix is saved from complete caricature by offering Maisie something no other character does: a "sense of a support, like a breast-high banister in a place of 'drops,' that would never give way" (31). Mrs. Wix is *the* maternal figure in the novel, a consequence of the intensity of their vicarious relation: Maisie serves as a replacement for her dead daughter. This vicarious relation emerges in an early scene, when Maisie leaves Mrs. Wix to return to her father's house, a separation the narrator compares with a recent visit to the dentist to have a tooth pulled: "Maisie, at the dentist's, had been heroically still, but just when she felt most anguish had become aware of an audible shriek on the part of her companion, a spasm of stifled sympathy" (33). Mrs. Wix's spasm is a vicarious lurch that enacts Maisie's anguish; her shriek, reproduced when they part, now gives voice to the pain of both. James's irony is not aimed at their vicarious relationship as such but rather at Mrs. Wix's role as storyteller. Instead of offering Maisie lessons in specific subjects, she "took refuge on the firm ground of fiction. . . . Her conversation was practically an endless narrative, a great garden of romance" (32). Of course, this puts her in direct competition with the narrator, who seeks to protect Maisie from Mrs. Wix's sense of what fiction should offer, the kind of instruction that results in "a moral sense."

For Mrs. Wix, a moral sense—which includes, most relevantly, a condemnation of sex outside of marriage—is the one thing remaining for Maisie to learn, and she sets about teaching it, despite the narrator's misgivings, on a carriage trip the two of them take through the French port town: "She began, the poor child, with scarcely knowing what it was; but it proved something that, with scarce an outward sign save her surrender to the swing of the carriage, she could, before they came back from their drive, strike up a sort of acquaintance with" (215). James here invokes the literary historical connection between carriages and sex (scenes of "if this van's a rockin', don't come a knockin'" in, for example, Sterne's *A Sentimental Journey* and Flaubert's *Madame Bovary*).[13] Maisie does begin to acquire some new knowledge, as indexed by the rocking movement of the carriage, but what she learns is not the condemnation that Mrs. Wix teaches. From this scene on, the theatrical figure of spectatorship changes and permeates the novel differently. It changes, first, by way of another expansion of the child's perceptions: her capacity to enjoy her surroundings, "the splendour of the afternoon sea, and the haze of the far headlands, and the taste of the sweet air" (215). No longer behind glass, Maisie begins to feel a new, sensuous relation to her knowledge as she strolls down the beach with her governess at sunset: "She looked at the pink sky with a placid foreboding that she soon would have learned All. They lingered in the flushed air till at last it turned to grey and she seemed fairly to receive new information from every brush of the breeze" (216). Maisie, it appears, has lost her virginity (one kind of virginity) to Mrs. Wix, and later that same evening in their hotel room Mrs. Wix is "bewail[ing]" the fact that, in order to introduce to Maisie a moral sense, she has had to explain so much, to "throw up at you the badness you haven't taken in" (218). Maisie, somewhat oppressed by this conversation, lingers on the balcony:

> The night, this time, was warm and one of the windows stood open to the small balcony over the rail of which, on coming up from dinner, Maisie had hung a long time in the enjoyment of the chatter, the lights, the life of the quay made brilliant by the season and the hour. Mrs. Wix's requirements had drawn her in from this posture and Mrs. Wix's embrace had detained her even though midway in the outpouring her confusion and sympathy had permitted, or rather had positively helped, her to disengage herself. But the

casement was still wide, the spectacle, the pleasure were still there, and from her place in the room, which, with its polished floor and its panels of elegance, was lighted from without more than from within, the child could still take account of them. (218)

The balcony with its rail, the space of the spectator, continues to support Maisie as she watches the spectacle; but suddenly, by a trick of the light, the space changes—the hotel room, "with its polished floor and its panels of elegance," reflects the lights coming from outside to become continuous with the spectacle itself. When Maisie turns inside to respond to Mrs. Wix, she takes the transformed domestic stage and begins to act: "She appeared to watch and listen; after which she answered Mrs. Wix with a question" (218). Maisie moves back and forth from balcony to hotel room—"She hung again over the rail: she felt the summer night; she dropped down into the manners of France" (218)—and listens to a musical performance, "a song about 'amour.' Maisie knew what 'amour' meant too, and wondered if Mrs. Wix did: Mrs. Wix remained within, as still as a mouse and perhaps not reached by the performance" (218–19). Maisie's knowledge of love, with all its undecideable sexuality, is here equated with a knowledge of performance. The reader soon sees Maisie dissemble and observe herself (220), choosing words with the intention to convey specific meanings, for example, words that "she hoped as she looked away, would guarantee her moral sense" (221). Instead of a moral sense, Maisie has developed the art of acting.

Maisie has been developing this art during her many years as a spectator, and her skills are not confined to self-observation and dissembling. They are transmutations of spectatorship by way of an increasingly sensuous perception and an expanded attention to nonverbal communication. In the definition that I think James is implicitly offering in this novel, acting is equated with "amour": the capacity to enter into complex affective circuits or relations with one's self (or selves) and others, to speak and act, with regard to one's self, in ways that have meaningful consequences for the feelings and behavior of others. Rather than simply watching while others make decisions that alter her life, Maisie begins to impede and transform their actions and meanings. These new capacities are exhibited in all the remaining scenes of the novel, but they are most forcefully expressed when she goes out for breakfast with Sir Claude and he asks her if she is willing to give up Mrs. Wix and join him and Mrs. Beale in an unconventional household arrangement in the south of France. This conversation takes place at a café "with wide, clear windows and a floor sprinkled with bran in a manner that gave Maisie something of the added charm of a circus," a space of performance where she senses "a sort of ordered mirrored licence, the haunt of those—the irregular, like herself—who went to bed or who rose too late" (247). As she "watched the white-aproned waiter perform as nimbly with plates and saucers as a certain conjurer her friend had in London taken her to a music-hall to see" (247), Maisie begins to experience herself as one of these bohemians or performers, that is, someone who does not need to subscribe to her governess's norms of sexuality or morality. But, as becomes clear from the conversation with her stepfather, neither will she subscribe to Sir Claude's.

At the beginning of their conversation Maisie notices his fear, which she reads as fear of himself, and this permits her to recognize and understand her own fear of herself, one of the many instances in which her learning is vicarious. Maisie is afraid of her newfound agency, her capacity and willingness to act on her desires, to love or hurt one person and not another. At the train station she suddenly proposes to her stepfather that he take her to Paris. They are both terrified at the prospect—is it a proposal or a proposition?—and he hesitates until it's too late. Maisie's fear then dissipates: "She had had a real fright but had fallen back to earth. The odd thing was that in her fall her fear too had been dashed and broken" (262). This sudden movement indexes a new awareness, and she is finally able to answer Sir Claude: she will give up Mrs. Wix if he gives up Mrs. Beale. He is startled, and Maisie sees how afraid he is of what she thinks of as his "weakness," that is, his inability to be consistent with his own strongest intentions, in this case, his love for Maisie. In the extraordinary, climactic scene at the end of the novel, which takes place in the hotel room, Maisie finds herself at the excruciating center of contention between the adults. Mrs. Beale insists that the child belongs with the stepparents; Mrs. Wix refuses to leave her with them; and Sir Claude finally makes it clear that he cannot take Maisie up on her offer and that he is willing to let her go. In the middle of all this extreme melodrama Mrs. Wix reminds Maisie of her moral sense and demands, "*Haven't* I, after all, brought it out?" But all Maisie can summon is a dim memory: "Then it left her, and, as if she were sinking with a slip from a foothold, her arms made a short jerk. What this jerk represented was the spasm within her of something still deeper than a moral sense. She looked at her examiner; she looked at the visitors; she felt the rising of the tears she had kept down at the station. They had nothing—no, distinctly nothing—to do with her moral sense. The only thing was the old flat shameful schoolroom plea. 'I don't know—I don't know'" (268). Maisie is crying for the train that left the station, that is, the dashed fantasy or wish of the pairing group, that she and Sir Claude would finally be together. Her spasm indexes her acknowledgment of despair and destruction, the end specifically of the relationship with the stepfather she wants. But she is also crying because of a different conclusion, the success of the work group that, against all odds, has brought her to the end of her childhood. Maisie has learned to assert her needs, to make individuated and forceful contact with the group, even while this contact also destroys the very group that has both failed to fulfill and succeeded in fulfilling these needs.

This reading of James's novel itself participates in the basic assumption of the pairing group. "It is as if there could be no possible reason for two people's coming together except sex" (62), writes Bion in describing this group mentality, and my suggestion that Maisie's proposal to Sir Claude may amount to a proposition certainly partakes in it. But I hope that I have also achieved my primary task, which has been to show that James's novel offers specifically theatrical terms for understanding the difficult relations between individuated experience and group phantasy. As much as these theatrical terms apply to Maisie's own narrative experience, or her uneven development from spectator to actor, they also apply to James himself, whose powerful identification with Maisie may account for some aspects of the uncanniness of this child. The concluding sentences of James's preface bring out the nature of this identification: "The active, contributive close-circling wonder, as I have called it, in which the child's identity is guarded and preserved, which makes her case remarkable exactly by the weight of the tax on it, provides distinction for her, provides vitality and variety, through the operation of the tax—which would have done comparatively little for us hadn't it been monstrous. A pity for us surely to have been deprived of this just reflexion" (11–12). James distinguishes Maisie along the lines of her affective-perceptual capacity for "wonder," claiming that this wonder both protects her identity and justifies the "tax" he puts on it, in other words, his narrative's sadism. According to James, then, Maisie's wonder distinguishes and protects her while distinguishing and vindicating James himself, his narrative choices and clinical, case-study perspective, all in the service of offering readers a seemingly detached experience of "reflexion."

This set of gestures firmly locates readers in what Joseph Litvak has called the Jamesian "theater of embarrassment," which, rather than offering any reliable position of detachment, "shows both author and readers moving back and forth across the footlights."[14] Tuning in to James's (and Bion's) transferential poetics has permitted me to pay attention to the relations between theatricality and not only embarrassment or shame but also vindication and the anger or resentment that underlies it. In my reading of James's novel, vindication appears to operate with respect to theatricality on at least three levels. Within the narrative Maisie vindicates herself: she takes the stage and asserts her individual distinctness from the group on which she depends by refusing the various projected leadership roles. At the level of method James's melodrama of consciousness works as a compositional technique that vindicates the expression of positive and negative affects themselves and their complex, muddled relations. Finally, vindication takes place metanarratively, as James distinguishes and justifies his own choices for an audience that he presumes to be hostile to some aspects of his project. His presumption of hostility is not wrong; the defensive tone of the concluding sentences of his preface should not be read simply in terms of misguided projection. As Litvak has shown, critics of James have often expressed anger toward his writing, whether in terms of its supposed vagueness, abstraction, moral confusion, or its queerness. I suggest that the hostility that James addresses and tries to ward off points, once again, to the strained relations between individual and group, or what Bion, in a later emendation of his thinking, describes as the relation between the genius and the Establishment.

These terms resonate with 1960s-era romanticism, but Bion's use both taps and expands these meanings: "I propose to borrow this term [the Establishment] to denote everything from the penumbra of associations generally evoked, to the predominating and ruling characteristics of an individual, and the characteristics of a ruling caste in a group (such as a psycho-analytical institute, or a nation or group of nations)."[15] His use of the word *genius* or *mystic* is similarly inclusive, meaning both "exceptional individual" and a mode of exceptional thinking that Bion seeks for the purposes of improving psychoanalysis. Indeed what makes these essays (especially "The Mystic and the Group" and "Container and Contained") so strange is that Bion is sketching a theory of the relation between individual and group and, at the same time, a theory of thinking which he casts in the most general terms of the relation between container and contained. I will take up Bion's theory of thinking in some detail in my next chapter, on Gertrude Stein's poetics of landscape theater. For now, it is enough to point out that Bion understands the mystic, both person and idea, as a creative and destructive force whose existence the group requires but seeks to control or manage. At the same time, the mystic person or idea needs the group in order to exist at all but exerts an uncontrolled explosive force: "The function of the group is to produce a genius; the function of the Establishment is to take up and absorb the consequences so that the group is not destroyed" (82). In what sounds like a borrowing from Gregory Bateson's anthropology, Bion proposes that the relationship between group and mystic may be "commensal, symbiotic, or parasitic" (78): they may simply coexist, they may produce mutual growth, or they may be mutually destructive. But even the symbiotic or growth-producing relationship may be troublingly hostile, as the "mystic contribution is subject to close scrutiny" (78) precisely because it holds the possibility of dangerous change for the group. By bringing this later understanding of Bion's into the discussion, I do not mean to assert James's genius in the face of the critical establishment. Rather I read James's defensiveness and self-vindication at the end of the preface as an index to the often hostile relationship between individual and group. James identifies with Maisie's "distinction," her "vitality and variety" as they emerge in necessary relation to the "tax" that his narrative exacts, a tax that serves, precisely, as an image of the group and its demands.

By way of conclusion, I would like to draw out some implications of my reading of *What Maisie Knew* for understanding James's late style, of which the preface is an example, as well as the perhaps surprising relations between this style and the twentieth-century theatrical medium of television. My approach to this subject shares something with David Kurnick's understanding of Jamesian theatricality. Kurnick reads a number of James's middle and late texts (written just before and after *Maisie*) to unfold a productive generic uncertainty in this mature writing, an equivocation between the spaces of the page and those of the stage. He argues that James "was unwilling to abandon the theatre as an imaginary referent. Instead, James created a bizarre fictional medium to convey the sense that these texts are sketches for a more robust but deferred theatrical enactment." Kurnick goes on to read the uniformity of James's late style—the odd way that many of the characters in his late novels sound, more or less, alike—against the grain of the critical tradition that insists on James's mastery of the novel form and its investments in individual psychology.[16] He proposes instead that "one thing Jamesian style wants is to replace the differentiating energies of the drama of consciousness with an equally compelling vision of collectivity and universalism" (146), one that depends on rhetorical techniques that are indebted to a "phenomenology of theater" (147); for example, Kurnick observes that James's characters share an "actorly purposiveness" (147) and "extra-diegetic consciousness" (149) that are fundamentally theatrical and move toward a utopian, democratic group consciousness.

Jamesian theatricality is "a technology of collectivization, a mechanism for the production of the plural" (109), an attempt to envision an idealized, unattainable experience of collectivity.

As will be clear, I entirely agree that James's writing offers us access to collectives or groups in specifically theatrical terms. However, I do not agree with Kurnick's argument that James describes group or collective experience in a primarily utopian mood or register, nor (relatedly) do I think there is any need to oppose individual to collective psychology in the way that interior is opposed to exterior. A great strength of Bion's understanding of groups is that he theorizes the collective elements and energies of group experience as both positive and negative. By insisting on the productivity of the work group and the constant challenges posed by the basic assumption groups, Bion offers a sense of the constant and complex impact of group psychology on individual experience and thinking, and indeed the occasional continuity between them. This conceptual continuity is a consequence of his Kleinian emphasis on unconscious phantasy and is closely related to what I described in my introduction as the hinge nature of affect. I would recast some of Kurnick's astute observations about late style in terms of James's commitment to a transferential poetics and close acquaintance with the theatricalization of writing. I would also suggest that the "bizarre fictional medium" that James seeks to create may usefully be compared with television, a medium whose emergence coincides with the beginning of his late style. (Television was first named in a paper given in French at the 1900 World's Fair in Paris, at the International Congress of Electricity.)

My point here is less causal-historical than aesthetic-formal: I want to draw out a set of analogies between writerly and televisual techniques, something I will do again at the end of my next chapter. For as it turns out, James's late work makes unexpectedly good television. I'm thinking in particular of the 1972 production of *The Golden Bowl*, perhaps the most successful of the James adaptations produced by the BBC.[17] This novel would seem to be as unlikely a choice for television as almost any I can think of. But Jack Pulman's script, which uses the novel's language to a remarkable degree, understands how James's intricate sentences, which sometimes need to be read aloud to be read at all, lend themselves to the near intimacies of the small screen. By turning a minor character, Colonel Assingham, into the narrator, Pulman offers television viewers a perplexed, calm, at once wryly detached and intensely interested guide to the narrative's complex emotional transactions. Each episode begins with the colonel sitting in an armchair in his study or club, speaking directly to the camera for minutes on end, smoking a pipe and, as one commentator puts it, "imparting to the viewer faintly conspiratorial confidences after his wife has retired to bed."[18] Played with understated charm by the very talented Cyril Cusack and shot from medium-close to close range, the colonel's narration engages viewers as if it were an unusually insightful and sustained series of after-dinner gossip sessions. Suddenly James's late style makes all the sense in the world.

But what exactly makes televisual sense here? How can the particular intimacies or proximities of James's late style be described? As a way to answer this question, consider examples of narrative style from works that have not been much explored, James's plays, and more specifically his parenthetical stage directions. Whereas in James's earlier plays the directions are spare and usually confined to descriptions of physical actions or clear, simple emotional states (e.g., *looking at his watch*; *with rising impatience*), the later plays offer greater numbers of directions of ever-increasing subtlety.[19] By the time he wrote *The Saloon* (1908), parenthetical directions precede almost every line of dialogue and often pose as much a challenge as a help to an actor: "*as with something between a shrug and a shudder of apprehension*" (662); "*with a certain arrest, a certain dryness*" (662); "*with his hands in his pockets and his eyes on her; as if thinking of more things than he can say or than she'll understand*" (664). These later directions, while they still describe precise physical actions and emotional expressions, are not easily captured by simple verbal description. James seems to want actors to convey affective states that are in between, both in between more ordinarily named and perceived feelings or movements (between a shrug and a shudder) and often defined in between two (or more) characters. It is difficult to imagine how any actor, no matter how talented, could convey such in-between feelings to an audience seated at any great distance from the performance. I think that the implied audience of James's late stage directions, then, is only as distant as the other actors on the stage, and as attentive.[20]

In characterizing his later style as televisual I am proposing that James's writing realizes a parlor scale of intimacy: he draws out circuits of affective communication between and among a handful of individuals who are physically proximate in the sense that they can hear each other speak at a conversational volume and can notice subtle inflections of voice, face, and body, and his writing places readers at a comparable imaginary distance. It may be useful to contrast James's narrative voice and its forms of intimacy with Poe's. Both writers implicate a reader by mixing insinuation with analysis, presuming intimacies without making clear the source of the presumption, which may therefore always be the reader himself or herself. But where Poe's intimacies take place as extreme close-ups (in-your-face, as my previous chapter suggests) and concern individuals and their destruction, James's interest is less in individual coherence and decoherence than in the relations between individuals and groups. What I am calling James's televisual style accompanies his commitment to representing the movements of feeling among a handful of persons, including the reader or viewer, at a certain scale of intimacy. On television this intimate and inclusive spatial scale is accompanied by the expanded temporal scale of the serial, itself rooted in nineteenth-century novel form. Television's seriality offers another reason why James's writing works well on television.[21]

Interestingly these spatial and temporal scales resemble the ones that Bion requires in his weekly group sessions, arranged with approximately eight or nine people. Bion chooses this size not because he believes that group psychology comes into existence only when a certain number of people are present; "in fact," he insists, "no individual, however isolated in time and space, should be regarded as outside a group or lacking in active manifestations of group psychology" (169). Rather this scale is convenient for the purposes of demonstrating the transferential or affective relations among the individuals of the group, for sharing evidence of these relations, and for giving "an interpretation without shouting it" (168). If, as Bion suggests, the difference between individual and group psychology is an illusion, then James's late style, as it represents his increasing use of theatrical devices to stage affective relations among a number of persons, should be understood as part of a technique for investigating and making appreciable the phenomena of group psychology.

4 /   Loose Coordinations: Theater and Thinking in
      Gertrude Stein

This chapter begins with a scene of mixed audience response, not entirely unlike the response that greeted Henry James at the opening night of his play *Guy Domville*. The performance was Gertrude Stein's delivery of the lecture "Plays" to a specially invited New York audience of fifty at an apartment on the Upper East Side on October 30, 1934. Having just stepped off the boat from Paris the week before, Stein had not yet adjusted to her new celebrity following the best-selling success of *The Autobiography of Alice B. Toklas*, published the year before. Seeking practice before her first official lecture (to be given two days later to a much larger audience of five hundred), she found help in a young artist named Prentiss Taylor, who arranged a dress rehearsal. According to Taylor, Stein's performance was well received but not a spectacular success. He wrote in a letter to his mother, "She read the lecture & it was not always easy to follow. Some of it was in her nearly vague style & always she uses simple words with fresh emphases that are difficult to catch as they go quickly by."[1] Interestingly the difficulty that Taylor described echoes fairly precisely the main concern of "Plays" as Stein gave it to her audience early in the lecture: "The thing that is fundamental about plays is that the scene as depicted on the stage is more often than not one might say that it is almost always in syncopated time in relation to the emotion of anybody in the audience."[2] Taylor's lagged responses to Stein's words going "quickly by" and his difficulty comprehending her were very much a part of the theatrical experience that she was investigating; it "is what makes one endlessly troubled about a play, because not only is there a thing to know as to why this is so but also there is a thing to know why perhaps it does not need to be so" (94). Stein's lecture offers a close analysis of this experience, followed by her own solution to the problem: to write a play as a landscape with which anyone can keep time.

While "Plays" was the first, it was also the least often delivered of the six lectures Stein had prepared that summer in France before going on her American tour, likely because its questions were her most pressing, present, and confusing ones. As she emerged (along with Toklas) onto the stage of modern, mass American culture, Stein wondered what it would be like, at the age of sixty, to come into contact with very large audiences for the first time.[3] She represented these worries to herself very clearly in a short piece written in September just before leaving France, "Meditations on Being about to Visit My Native Land," in which she anticipated the behavior of her lecture audiences: "Will they ask me questions and will I ask them questions and which will ask the questions most and first, and will they listen to me and will I listen to them."[4] Taylor's description of the audience reaction to her lecture shows that Stein's worries were entirely realistic: "There was considerable complicated and subtle development I couldn't begin to give you here, but most of us came away with a sympathetic approach, much more understanding. Not Mrs. Colby, she groaned I'm told & afterward was quietly scathing, but she always gauges her reactions to claim an audience for herself."[5] Once again Taylor's response echoes Stein's lecture: in its central concern with the different emotional tempos of audience members and the action on the stage, "Plays" takes up what an older tradition of writing on the theater calls sympathy, a mechanism by which spectators may imaginatively identify with an actor's situation. I would include even unsympathetic Mrs. Colby under this broader rubric of what Adam Smith called sympathy insofar as she precisely identified with Stein's situation and her efforts to "claim an audience for herself."

In the pages that follow I offer a reading of Stein's lecture that considers her treatment of questions of audience identification alongside some of the twentieth-century theories of affect and emotion I have been exploring in this book, those of William James, Silvan Tomkins, and Wilfred Bion. I juxtapose Stein's lecture with these works for conceptual reasons: I hope that her close, technical investigation into the problem of theatrical identification will make more sense when read in relation to this explicitly theoretical writing. The eighteenth-century model of sympathy remains useful, however, since it sets up the terms for the problem of emotional syncopation and provides a historical context for linking theories of emotion with theatricality. As I pointed out in my chapter on Poe, Adam Smith uses the figure of keeping time with another's emotions to imagine the moderation of affective response; more generally Smith invokes the theatrical situation to ensure that emotions are properly situated, anchored to shared objects and narratives, and thereby transformed from passions to moral sentiments. While Stein is not convinced that sympathetic identification at the theater offers the best model for explaining emotional phenomena, her lecture can nevertheless be read as it reinhabits and transforms a problematic most fully laid out not in Smith's writing but in Jean-Jacques Rousseau's *Lettre à d'Alembert sur les spectacles* (1758): "The Stage is, in general, a painting of the human passions, the original of which is in every heart. But if the Painter neglected to flatter these passions, the Spectators would soon be repelled and would not want to see themselves in a light which made them despise themselves."[6] As David Marshall has shown, Rousseau's text, which argues at length against establishing a theater in Geneva, demonstrates the unavoidable theatricality of social relations and state power; it touches on the basic question of how one can know others in the context of such a theatricalized social and political space.[7] Stein's lecture can be seen similarly to move from a narrower understanding of the theater as a specific institution and literary form to broader treatments of the theatricality of social relations and accompanying epistemological problems.

Given her twentieth-century modernist, scientific sensibilities, Stein sought a less normative understanding of emotion than that implied by the theory of sympathy, as well as a less narrative approach to theater. Her plays and poetics, in avoiding earlier identificatory models, share something with Bertolt Brecht's epic theater and its techniques of alienation, distantiation, and defamiliarization. "The art of the epic theater," as Walter Benjamin put it in 1939, "consists in producing not empathy but astonishment."[8] Brecht's rejection of empathy does not reject emotion per se but seeks instead to develop roles for specific emotions, such as surprise, in a project of awakening critical attitudes in a relaxed, alert audience. Stein's poetics focus on the dynamics of excitement with a related but distinct goal: her plays aim to create loose affective coordinations between audience and stage, as well as among audience members themselves, to permit experiences of reverie, which, according to Bion, names a crucial emotional component of thinking itself. Stein's poetics, less programmatic than Brecht's, are centrally concerned with the question of whether and how plays can permit audiences, or indeed actors, to experience new knowledge.

My use of Bion's work builds on the preceding chapter's argument that theatrical terms offered Henry James a way to address the phenomena of group psychology. As I remarked toward the end of that chapter, Bion's efforts to understand the continuities between group and individual psychology led him to develop a general theory of thinking that I take up here in more detail. Because my avenue of approach to Bion's theory is not direct, however, it may help to have something of a roadmap for the discussion that follows. My reading begins with Stein's use of William James's well-known theory of emotion in an analysis of what she calls audience "nervousness." I then turn to Tomkins, whose theorizing, in the Jamesian tradition, gives more precision to what Stein sees as the basic emotional problem of the theater; in particular I use Tomkins's writing on interest-excitement to gloss the prominent place given to this affect in Stein's lecture. I then introduce object-relations theory, offering an explication of Bion's theory of thinking. My discussion concludes by returning to the context of Stein's performance in America and suggests a way to understand why her poetics of landscape theater have been so influential for contemporary performance practices. I keep Stein's writing in the foreground throughout this chapter because my overriding concern is to read her lecture as it poses a fundamental question: Can theater offer the emotional conditions that permit experiences of new knowledge?

Stein's lecture "Plays" begins by assessing the theatrical problem, the emotional syncopation between audience and stage, in psychophysiological terms: "Your sensation as one in the audience in relation to the play played before you your sensation I say your emotion concerning the play is always either behind or ahead of the play at which you are looking and to which you are listening. So your emotion as a member of the audience is never going on at the same time as the action of the play" (93). She returns many times over the course of the lecture to the felt discrepancy between sensation (looking and listening) and emotion (feeling): "The thing seen and the emotion did not go on together" (94). Her use of these terms is indebted to her studies in the field of experimental physiological psychology during the 1890s. Steven Meyer's work offers the most sustained and cogent analysis of the continuities and discontinuities between Stein's early studies and her later writing practices; he suggests that Stein's writing be understood as a "poetic science" that responds to the limitations of empiricist method.[9] A crucial aspect of this poetic science, according to Meyer, involves the forms of reflexive attention that William James invites, for example in his chapter "The Emotions" in *Principles of Psychology* (1890): "If the reader has never paid attention to this matter, he will be both interested and astonished to learn how many different local bodily feelings he can detect in himself as characteristic of his various emotional moods.... Our whole cubic capacity is sensibly alive; and each morsel of it contributes its pulsations of feeling, dim or sharp, pleasant, painful, or dubious, to that sense of personality that every one of us unfailingly carries with him."[10] Stein's use of physiological terms depends on and can be understood in the context of James's definition of emotion, what has come to be called the James-Lange theory, "that the bodily changes follow directly the perception of the exciting fact, and that our feeling of the same changes as they occur IS the emotion" (449).

In James's theory emotion is identified with what Meyer calls "autosensation," a kind of second-order sensational experience.[11] The problem with theater, at least in Stein's initial formulation, is that it interferes with this autosensation, the feeling of bodily changes that "follow directly" upon perception. For Stein, attending to the action on the stage, to the development of plot and character, makes it difficult to experience one's emotions, that is, to feel one's own feelings in time with the action. "This that the thing seen and the thing felt about the thing seen not going on at the same tempo is what makes the being at the theater something that makes anybody nervous" (94–95); nervousness, which Stein defines as "needing to go faster or to go slower so as to get together" (95), becomes explicable in the context of James's theory in that the second-order autosensations need to catch up with the first-order perceptions for an audience successfully to feel the emotions in time with the action on the stage. According to Stein, the nervous-making elements of theater interfere even before the play begins since the curtain "already makes one feel that one is not going to have the same tempo as the thing that is there behind the curtain," and so does the audience, "the fact that they are or will be or will not be in the way when the curtain goes up" (95). These images of Stein waiting impatiently or anxiously in her seat, craning to see past someone's head, let me characterize her theatrical experiences, both before and during the play, in terms of anticipation. Not only does she anticipate the performance before it begins, but she also anticipates the story as the action unfolds and links the current action on the stage with what may have preceded it. Nervous excitement accompanies and motivates these back-and-forth movements, a familiar cognitive and emotional experience, I suspect, for many of us who attend narrative theater.

"And is it a mistake that that is what the theater is or is it not" (95), Stein goes on to ask in her lecture, and we may wonder with her why anticipation should be a problem rather than a cognitive challenge and a pleasure. Tomkins's affect theory may help to answer this question by offering a more qualitative analysis of this experience of anticipation. In particular I turn to Tomkins's unusual understanding that excitement, the more intense form of interest, is one of a handful of innate affects in humans. Tomkins argues that this affect, overlooked by Darwin and other theorists, plays a fundamental role in human experience as a support for organizing perception, learning, and creativity. In his discussion of interest-excitement he proposes that "any affect may have any 'object'" (*AIC* 1: 347). Not only is it possible to be excited by anything, but different objects will partly transform the quality of the excitement itself as well as the person feeling the excitement. "I am, above all, what excites me," suggests Tomkins, one of whose primary interests was to make available to thought "the extraordinary differentiations of personality" (1:347), a project he shared with the early Stein, as we shall see. One way that Tomkins's theory accommodates such differentiation is through its distinction between affect and emotion, between a relatively few innate affects and an infinite number of emotions. For Tomkins, emotions are made up of affects "co-assembled" with specific objects, with drives, with cognitions, or with other affects. For example, the same affect, shame-humiliation, is at the biological core of a variety of emotional experiences, such as shyness, embarrassment, and guilt; different situations "flavor" the affect of shame to create a variety of social and moral emotions (2: 119). For Tomkins, intellectual curiosity and sexual lust share the affect of interest-excitement at their core, while their co-assembly with different objects, aims, and situations leads to very distinct emotional experiences.

Stein's nervous anticipation at the theater can be analyzed, in Tomkins's terms, as a complex emotion: at its core the affect of interest-excitement taking the performance of the play as an object, further co-assembled with an orientation toward the future of the performance. For Stein, this orientation toward the future can become, inevitably does become an obstacle to her excitement in and enjoyment of the present moment of performance itself. Anticipation of the action or plot of the play competes with her attention to theatrical mise-en-scène, or the dynamic relations among the actors on stage with one another and with the elements of their setting. Because of this competition (or channel overload), anticipation can lead to irritation or the activation of negative emotions such as impatience or worry, which, for Tomkins, are based on the affects of anger and fear. For Stein, then, the "mistake" of live theater is a consequence of the particular emotional dynamics of an anticipatory excitement that interferes with and reflavors the present experience of the play's performance and whatever affects or emotions she may be experiencing toward that present moment.

But this anticipatory excitement becomes a problem only in the context of the defining role that excitement otherwise plays in Stein's poetics as at once motive and method for her portraiture project and fundamental to her ways of coming to knowledge of persons. Stein began doing literary portraits toward the end of the process of writing her long novel *The Making of Americans* (composed between 1905 and 1912); as several critics have noted, the early portraits move away from that novel's exhaustive typologizing ("a history of every one who ever was or is or will be living") and toward an attempt to convey the specificity and intensity of her subjects in the mode of what William James called "knowledge of acquaintance."[12] James used this term, along with the phrase "knowledge-about," to help map what other languages have two words for (*kennen* and *wissen*, for example, or *connaître* and *savoir*). While James roughly associated knowledge of acquaintance with feeling and knowledge-about with thought and verbal articulation, these kinds of knowledge remain complexly interimplicated, both in his writing and, even more so, in Stein's. In "Portraits and Repetition" (1934), one of the lectures she gave most often during her tour, Stein represents the goal of her portraiture this way: "I wondered is there any way of making what I know come out as I know it, come out not as remembering. I found this very exciting. And I began to make portraits."[13] The excitement in making portraits contrasts with what she calls the "soothing" quality of novels, which she associates with memory, habitual associations, familiarity of story, and resemblances of character. Whereas her earlier novel writing was partly based on extensive notes, charts, and graphs that permitted her to distinguish character traits and arrive at kinds and categories of persons in the mode of knowledge-about, her portraits required a different kind of attention: "I had to find out inside every one what was in them that was intrinsically exciting and I had to find out not by what they said not by what they did not by how much or how little they resembled any other one but I had to find it out by the intensity of movement that there was inside in any one of them" (183). Stein's method of acquaintance, not primarily comparative or behaviorist, is essentially (and for my book, exemplarily) affective and transferential: "I must find out what is moving inside them that makes them them, and I must find out how I by the thing moving excitedly inside in me can make a portrait of them" (183). Stein attends to the movement of her excitement as it indexes that of her subject. If, as Tomkins puts it, "I am, above all, what excites me," then the affective coordination of excitement can become Stein's way of acquainting herself with someone for the purposes of composing their portrait, in other words, of knowing them.

The nervous or anticipatory excitement of theater interferes with Stein's compositional method and knowledge practices: it overlays or compounds excitements, threatening her efforts to coordinate her own and her subject's movements in a present moment. And because theater poses this problem, her lecture goes on to pursue a careful phenomenological analysis of a variety of excitements: "Let us think of three kinds of things that are exciting and that make or do not make one nervous. First any scene which is a real scene something real that is happening in which one takes part as an actor in that scene. Second any book that is exciting, third the theater at which one sees an exciting action in which one does not take part" (96). Stein treats the second situation, that of reading an exciting book, briefly but revealingly for my argument here: "In the first place one can always look at the end of the book and so quiet down one's excitement. The excitement having been quieted down one can enjoy the excitement" (100). Note the compatibility between Tomkins's understanding that affects may take any object, including other affects, and Stein's sense that one can, for instance, enjoy excitement. Her implicit contrast is with a form of excitement that she does not enjoy, an excitement that accompanies suspense or the anticipation of story. Her reading strategy exchanges the denser excitements of anticipation for quieter, more spacious experiences of positive affect. (Stein enjoyed Trollope's novels, which often simply tell readers how they will end midway through.)

Stein's lecture is specifically concerned with the different ways that an exciting scene can end or "culminate": "In the real thing it is a completion of the excitement, in the theater it is a relief from the excitement" (96). By using the word *relief* to label the conclusion and goal of theatrical performance, Stein implicitly invokes the definition of tragedy in Aristotle's *Poetics*, in particular the difficult notion of catharsis as the purification of and pleasurable relief from pity and fear that tragedy is supposed to effect.[14] The literature on catharsis is vast (as vast as mentions to it are brief in Aristotle's own remaining works) and would take me too far afield to offer even a cursory survey. However, I would like to point out that the problem of catharsis as it has been cast by modern critics addresses the value of tragedy (and, often by extension, all theater) as educative, social, or political. As Andrew Ford puts it in a useful essay, "*katharsis* belongs to a complex organization of musical and artistic activities in the state," and its philosophical and aesthetic questions directly feed the political perspectives on theater that Rousseau and Brecht, among others, take up.[15] I will touch on the political implications of Stein's poetics later. For now I would simply suggest that emotional questions of theater are always linked to specific political perspectives, and vice versa.

To return to "the fundamental difference between excitement in real life and on the stage" (97–98): what does Stein mean by contrasting relief with what she calls "completion"? She is not simply authenticating "real-life" excitement by invidious contrast with some artificial, theatricalized kind. Her first attempt to clarify the difference seems to complicate matters by introducing the operation of memory: "As you go over the detail that leads to culmination of any scene in real life, you find that each time you cannot get completion, but you can get relief and so already your memory of any exciting scene in which you have taken part turns it into the thing seen or heard not the thing felt" (98). Stein aligns memory with theater in that it too delinks sensation from feeling (or autosensation). (Here we return to the inhibitions necessary to the scene of writing, as Derrida calls it, those relations between perception and memory discussed in the introduction.) In both cases a form of self-splitting observation (although perhaps not the same one) interferes with emotional participation. Stein contrasts the observational mode with the dynamics of emotional participation in a long paragraph that describes "anything exciting in which one takes part":

> There one progresses forward and back emotionally and at the supreme crisis of the scene the scene in which one takes part, in which one's hopes and loves and fears take part at the extreme crisis of this thing one is almost one with one's emotions, the action and the emotion go together, there is but just a moment of this coordination but it does exist otherwise there is no completion as one has no result, no result of a scene in which one has taken part, and so instinctively when any people are living an exciting moment one with another they go on and on and on until the thing has come together the emotion the action the excitement and that is the way it is when there is any violence either of loving or hating or quarreling or losing or succeeding. But there is, there has to be the moment of it all being abreast the emotion, the excitement and the action otherwise there would be no succeeding and no failing and so no one would go on living, why yes of course not.
> That is life the way it is lived. (99–100)

Stein understands that taking part in lived, exciting scenes is violent and consequential. Such taking part involves being taken apart, that is, experiencing different, often conflicting motives ("hopes and loves and fears"). When this emotional turbulence reaches a crisis or moment of decision, the scene must have a result that, in Stein's analysis, provides a sense of completion. But this result is possible only if the scene's participants realize "a moment of coordination," in the first instance a self-coordination: "one is almost one with one's emotions, the action and the emotion go together." Note Stein's "almost," which puts off any reading of this as a moment of transcendence or unification of self or emotion. Rather she is describing the dynamics of coming into a set of coordinated affective relations: first, a coordination of one's own motives, a difficult task precisely because of the nonsingular, often contradictory nature of affect; and second, a coordination between one's motives and actions, that must itself be coordinated with the motives and actions of others or the situation itself. Completion, then, names the feeling that accompanies a set of brief momentary intra- and intersubjective coordinations that have some result or consequence.

Perhaps the clearest examples of such exciting scenes are quarrels or arguments between lovers or family members that resolve, if they do, with some new understanding or situation. Completion here would name the feeling that some new state of affairs has been achieved. (Rarely committee meetings can offer something similarly productive, although more often they end with relief that the conflictive meeting is over.) Completion can take place only when participants are persistent enough to "go on and on and on" until a moment of crisis can be reached, and Stein's paragraph conveys this persistence, itself going on until "the moment of it all being abreast." With this phrase I would like to introduce another theoretical context into my reading of Stein's lecture: the object-relations theory of Melanie Klein and her followers. In a Kleinian understanding these turbulent dynamics of emotional coordination resemble the movements of an infant struggling to make contact with the mother's breast. This basic, frustrating experience involves violent movements back and forth as the infant struggles with perceptual and physical limits as well as conflicting motives; if "one would go on living," as Stein puts it, then these movements must result in some moment of connection or coordination that she identifies with life itself. The feeling of completion in the exciting scenes that Stein describes would, in this Kleinian reading, be based on early infantile experiences of physical as well as emotional fullness: the satisfactions of a successful feeding.

As I suggested in chapter 1, object-relations theory shares something with the Jamesian tradition: both emphasize qualitative, phenomenological aspects of emotional or affective experience, and both attempt to theorize such experience in ways that neither oppose nor reduce affect to cognition. Stein and Klein, I suggested, participated in similar modernist projects—to become acquainted with and to give verbal form to elements of experience that are difficult to access and entertain in consciousness—and they shared in particular a commitment to investigating the emotional conditions for the emergence of new knowledge. Bion, arguably Klein's most important follower, investigated these conditions intensively in his innovative theory of thinking published in the early 1960s. This work came out of Bion's efforts, like those of other Kleinians, to understand and treat disorders of thought in schizophrenic patients. In his clinical experience Bion repeatedly observed what he called "the destructive attack on a link," an attack on the bond between analyst and patient that is, at the same time, an attack on the patient's own mind, specifically his or her capacity to create emotional and cognitive connections.[16] Bion described the effectiveness of such attacks in terms of the defense that Klein called projective identification, an unconscious phantasy in which unwanted parts of the self are aggressively projected outward and located elsewhere.[17] Bion attributed the particular violence and frequency with which some patients rid themselves of bad or unwanted elements either to inborn disposition (what Klein called envy) or to inborn disposition combined with a failure in the patient's early environment (the mother's inability or unwillingness to accept or contain the painful projected elements). Bion's understanding of such disorders in schizophrenic patients led him to think more generally about the emergence, or the failure of emergence, of an apparatus for dealing with such projected elements, in other words, an apparatus for thinking.

Bion developed this work in a book called *Learning from Experience* (1962), written in his interestingly idiosyncratic, opaque style. His writing, like Stein's, is distinctly hard to summarize without extensive quotation; this is because, to recall Hinshelwood's description, Bion "perfected a trick of describing certain psychic processes, while at the same time engaging in just that process during the act of describing it."[18] To put this in William James's terms, Bion (like Stein) attempts to communicate the interimplication of knowledge of acquaintance and knowledge-about, for which an attention to the here and now of experience, including the experiences of writing and reading, is crucial. A reader of Bion's book expecting to walk away with an easily articulated grasp of a full-blown theory of thinking may be frustrated. At the same time, such a reader, in undergoing the experience of reading Bion's book, may have a new and more precise understanding of the role of frustration itself in thinking. "The link between intolerance of frustration and the development of thought is central to an understanding of thought and its disturbances," suggests Bion, or as he puts it a little later, "The choice that matters to the psycho-analyst is one that lies between *procedures designed to evade frustration and those designed to modify it. That is the critical decision.*"[19]

According to Bion, an apparatus for thinking develops (or may develop) in the mother-infant dyad, that is, in the scene of the infant at the breast. To summarize briefly, the infant experiences a need for nurture, which may be physical (a need for milk) and/or psychical (a need for love). The absence of a nurturing breast is itself experienced by the infant as an intolerable presence, a bad breast. "Is a 'thought' the same as an absence of a thing?" (35), asks Bion, and it seems that his answer is a qualified yes. Under certain circumstances the infant can exchange the bad breast for a good one: the maternal object offers the infant not only milk but love, expressed in the form of "reverie" (36). In the specific sense in which Bion uses it, "reverie is that state of mind which is open to the reception of any 'objects' from the loved object and is therefore capable of reception of the infant's projective identifications whether they are felt by the infant to be good or bad" (36.). The mother contains and transforms the bad breast, thereby permitting the infant to reintroject a good breast, accompanied by a feeling of satisfaction. For this transformation to take place, the infant's frustration must be tolerated. A modification of frustration, on the part of both infant and mother, is the condition of possibility for an apparatus to emerge for thinking the thoughts of absence. The infant may eventually take in this containing apparatus, that is, internalize the conditions for thinking itself. Bion puts it this way toward the end of the book: "To summarize. The relationship between mother and infant described by Melanie Klein as projective identification is internalized to form an apparatus for regulation of a preconception with the sense data of the appropriate realization" (91).[20]

Bion introduces the more general terms of *container* and *contained* into his theory of thinking and casts the relation between these as necessarily reciprocal. For example, while the apparatus for thinking may be contained by the infant, it may also be projected out at a later date, say, into the analyst, who then (re)plays the role of container for a patient, with the goal of permitting him or her to regain, or to develop for the first time, the capacity for thinking. Because of the constant to-and-fro movements of projective and introjective identification (as Kleinian theory understands these), the analyst and analysand may and often do reverse roles. In several later essays Bion applies these terms in other contexts: not only mother-infant and analyst-patient, but also group-individual, thinker-thought, and word-idea, each of which becomes imagined as a reversible container-contained relation. One interesting consequence of Bion's theory: the activity of thinking is definitively transindividual, originating in the mother-infant dyad and characterized by the to-and-fro dynamics of identification. Reverie helps to create an analytic space for thinking that may span across the boundaries of individual bodies and is suffused with emotional dynamics.

I would like to return to Stein's lecture with some of these ideas in mind. Consider, first, how often Stein brings up the question of knowing and how to go about it, often accompanied by a transaction between grammatical first and second persons, as well as a variety of third persons (such as *anybody, nobody, one*). Here is a quick selection of such moments:

> This is a thing to know and knowledge as anybody can know is a thing to get by getting.
> And so I will try to tell you what I had to get and what perhaps I have gotten in plays and to do so I will tell you all that I have ever felt about plays or about any play. (94)

> I ask you.
> What is knowledge. Of course knowledge is what you know and what you know is what you do know.
> What do I know about plays.
> In order to know one must always go back. (94)

> [A]s I have said knowledge is what you know and I naturally tell you what I know, as I do so very essentially believe in knowledge. (101)

> And in asking a question one is not answering but one is as one may say deciding about knowing. (102)

> I have of course always been struggling with this thing, to say what you nor I nor nobody knows, but what is really what you and I and everybody knows. (121)

These sentences express Stein's powerful commitment to forms of knowing that suit the dynamic, reciprocal, and transindividual relations that Bion's theory of thinking describes. She takes up the position of the analyst or knower and at the same time assumes the patient's more vulnerable position of someone who seeks to discover her own mind. The audience or reader, then, is placed in the position of a (more or less patient, often frustrated) listener who may be able to piece together some interpretation, or not. Bion writes, in a discussion of knowing (what he terms "the K link," xKy) in *Learning from Experience*, "As I propose to use it it does not convey a sense of finality, that is to say, a meaning that x is in possession of a piece of knowledge called y but rather that x is in the state of getting to know y and y is in a state of getting to be known by x."[21] Bion is particularly concerned with developing this kind of knowledge when y is animate, a person or a mind. He wants a theory of knowing that does not need to render its objects lifeless, still, or static in order to know them: "The procedure I am proposing, as part of K for the purposes of knowing 'xKy' and what it represents therefore involves identification with a person that comes for analysis" (49). Because the patients Bion has in mind are schizophrenic the otherwise bland-sounding procedure of "identification" should be heard in terms of the infantile, powerfully strange experiences of projective and introjective identification that characterize Kleinian theory and clinical practice, the volatile and reciprocal relations of container and contained.

For Stein, the problem with plays is that they do not bring about these fundamental, both vitalizing and destructive emotional conditions. Theater does not easily offer the possibilities for reverie, for reciprocal identification and containment, for the experiences of thinking and coming to knowledge that she seeks. The reciprocity of identification is a major problem, as she explains when (after a brief digression on cinema, which I will return to) the lecture continues its phenomenological analysis of excitement. Stein poses the question of how one makes acquaintance with actors in books, in real life, and on the stage ("how are the actors introduced to the sight, hearing and consciousness of the person having the emotion about them" [105]), and after some meditation and analysis arrives at what I think is the crux of her understanding:

> In ordinary life one has known pretty well the people with whom one is having the exciting scene before the exciting scene takes place and one of the most exciting elements in the excitement be it love or a quarrel or a struggle is that, that having been well known that is familiarly known, they all act in acting violently act in the same way as they always did of course only the same way has become so completely different that from the standpoint of familiar acquaintance there is none there is complete familiarity but there is no proportion that has hitherto been known, and it is this which makes the scene really exciting, and it is this that leads to completion, the proportion achieves in your emotion the new proportion therefore it is completion but not relief. A new proportion cannot be a relief. (108)

While relief accompanies a return to some prior emotional state or equilibrium, the feeling of completion indexes a new emotional proportion, that is to say, a new ratio or experience of knowing. Such knowing can take place only when one is familiar with those involved: "generally speaking it is the contradiction between the way you know the people you know including yourself act and the way they are acting or feeling or talking that makes of any scene that is an exciting scene an exciting scene" (106). With familiarity comes acquaintance, and with acquaintance comes the possibility of learning, that is, becoming reacquainted both with others and with one's changing self in reciprocal identification with these others. Completion, then, names the feeling of what happens when one learns from experience.

For both Bion and Stein, learning or knowing requires the to-and-fro of emotional coordination, whether in the context of theatrical performance or that of the analytic session. Both of these contexts, theater and analysis, require gradual or incremental familiarity. In Stein's understanding, the nervous excitements or anticipations of theater are too sudden, the emotional syncopations too coarse: "It is not possible in the theater to produce familiarity which is of the essence of acquaintance because, in the first place when the actors are there they are there and they are there right away" (109). This difficulty with acquaintance requires Stein to split her attention, as when, for example, reading a Shakespeare play "it was always necessary to keep one's finger in the list of characters for at least the whole first act" (109), or to keep glancing at the program during a play's performance. Stein must have been aware that her lecture audiences would experience a similar difficulty: she could not expect them to be familiar with her work or her person except through their reading of *The Autobiography of Alice B. Toklas* and its rather full cast of characters. This may explain why, at this point in the lecture, she begins a long review of her experiences of theater from childhood on. Her recollections of San Francisco theater and spectacle of the 1870s and 1880s, from twenty-five-cent opera and Buffalo Bill to Shakespeare and Sarah Bernhardt, would likely have charmed her American audiences, serving to introduce her to them gradually. At the same time, these recollections recontextualize her analysis of theater by giving the audience specific material to think with. For example, she describes the actor Edwin Booth in the role of Hamlet "lying at the Queen's feet during the play. One would suppose that a child would notice other things in the play than that but that is what I remember and I noticed him there more than I did the play he saw, although I knew that there was a play going on, the little play" (114). Stein here recalls the Mousetrap scene, the play-within-a-play that Hamlet produces to trick Claudius into confessing his guilt through emotional response. In this scene Hamlet's asides direct the audience's attention to the king's and queen's reactions. When Stein remembers the actor's body (in the wrong place, perhaps, for in Shakespeare's play Hamlet lies at Ophelia's feet), she is noticing Booth's efforts to coordinate the emotion on the stage with audience attention.

Stein's autobiographical review leads her to recall instances of drama that solved the particular theatrical problems of acquaintance and emotional syncopation, and may also have offered opportunities for varieties of reverie. For example, Sarah Bernhardt's performances, in which "[t]he manners and customs of the french theater created a thing in itself," offered Stein "a very simple direct and moving pleasure"; and because, in American melodrama, plot and character are less important than highly stylized gesture and affect, "there again everything happened so quietly one did not have to get acquainted" (116). Stein refers specifically to a new technique developed by the actor William Gillette, "silence stillness and quick movement" (116), perfected in his successful Civil War melodrama *Secret Service*. In this play Gillette (who became famous in the role of Sherlock Holmes) plays a witty, resourceful, nonchalant Northern spy under cover in the South; most of his characters were similarly dashing men, making it easy to get acquainted with any of them. We can gather from a particularly detailed set of stage directions what Stein means by Gillette's technique: "Picks up cigar with left hand. Puts revolver at right end of table with right hand, and gets a match with that hand. Stands an instant looking left. Strikes match and is about to relight cigar. Pause—eyes front. Match burning. Listening. Looks left—lights cigar—as he is lighting cigar thinks of gas being out, and steps to right, turns it on and lights it."[22] Many "quick springs," "dashes," and "instantaneous turns" sharply contrast with silent, motionless pauses precisely to telegraph every thought ("thinks of gas being out") and emotion to a concentrated audience's attention. This telegraphic effect is in part due to the abundance and precision of the stage directions, but it is also due to the fact that, in this scene, Gillette's character is being spied upon by other characters. Just as in *Hamlet*'s play-within-a-play, in *Secret Service* the audience's role is itself doubled or thematized on stage, actively directing and concentrating audience attention. "One was no longer bothered by the theater," states Stein, "you had to get acquainted of course but that was quickly over and after that nothing bothered" (116–17).

In the last part of the lecture Stein finally turns to her own playwriting and explains her solution to the problem of emotional syncopation. As in melodrama and Bernhardt, Stein too subordinates narrative to other dramatic elements: "What is the use of telling a story since there are so many and everybody knows so many" (118–19). Her first experiments (written around 1913) were efforts to "make a play the essence of what happened" (119) without actually telling what happened. These plays pose considerable challenges to a reader in that they regularly do not distinguish between various formal, conventional theatrical elements, such as dialogue, stage direction, setting, character, or even titles. Take, for example, *An Exercise in Analysis* (1917), which consists of a large number of act and part divisions followed by one or more sentences, and begins this way:

A PLAY
I have given up analysis.
Act II
Splendid profit.
Act III
I have paid my debt to humanity.
Act III
Hurry.
Act IV
Climb. In climbing do not be contented.
Part II
Run ahead.
Run on ahead.²³

A reader used to longer acts that group a handful of scenes, each of which contains characters and dialogue, may initially be confused by the logic of Stein's text. But the play becomes surprisingly readable (and amusing) with the decision or realization that the act and part divisions can be read as names of characters. This play can be cast for four voices: Act II, Act III, Act IV, and one whose name begins as A Play and becomes Part x (where x is a roman numeral from II to LX). Differentiating the voices lets a reader explore a play that has the feel of a gossip session; when four readers get together to read the play (as I have done and have had students do), it becomes precisely a skewed exercise in analysis of their own competitive and collaborative relations.

In the 1920s Stein began to model her playwriting on the experience of landscape: "I felt that if a play was exactly like a landscape then there would be no difficulty about the emotion of the person looking on at the play being behind or ahead of the play because the landscape does not have to make acquaintance. You may have to make acquaintance with it, but it does not with you, it is there."²⁴ If melodrama solves the problem of emotional syncopation by tightly constraining audience attention to the emotion on the stage through highly artificial or stylized techniques,

Stein's landscape drama unconstrains audience attention and aims for much looser affective coordinations: "the landscape not moving but being always in relation, the trees to the hills the hills to the fields the trees to each other any piece of it to any sky and then any detail to any other detail, the story is only of importance if you like to tell or like to hear a story but the relation is there anyway" (125). De-emphasizing plot and the closure of narrative, Stein's plays open up the relational space of the stage itself by focusing on other theatrical elements, including linguistic play, bodily movement or gesture, sound, sets, lighting, costume, all of which come to have equivalent value. For example, Stein's late retelling of the Faust myth in *Doctor Faustus Lights the Lights* (1938) includes a ballet that begins this way:

> Doctor Faustus sitting alone surrounded by electric lights.
> His dog comes in and says
> Thank you.
> One of the electric lights goes out again the dog says
> Thank you.
> The electric light that went out is replaced by a glow.
> The dog murmurs.
> My my what a sky.
> And then he says
> Thank you.[25]

The theater director Robert Wilson staged this play in the 1990s with an acrobatic troupe and a light show illuminating the audience as often as the actors on the stage. Its effect was to re-create the theatrical space in such a way that it could permit what Stein calls "a movement in and out with which anybody looking on can keep time."[26] Rather than insisting on one-way audience identification with the actors on the stage, Stein's landscape plays generally aim for experiences of reverie and reversibility; they let audiences and actors take part in, both to contain and to be contained by, a set of loosely coordinated relations among multiple theatrical elements, including the audience members themselves.

For Stein, it turns out, the representation of coordinated relations among a number of individuals defines theatrical form itself. Consider, in the last section of her lecture, her seemingly simple remarks on the difference between what motivates her portraits and her plays:

> I had before I began writing plays written many portraits. I had been enormously interested all my life in finding out what made each one that one and so I had written a great many portraits.

> I came to think that since each one is that one and that there are a number of them each one being that one, the only way to express this thing each one being that one and there being a number of them knowing each other was in a play. (119)

If portraiture is a genre for knowing individuals, then plays, as Stein understands the genre, are representations of a number of individuals in relation. This description fits well with the changes that took place during a key transition between what is usually called the first and second phase of Stein's writing, a change from the repetitious prose style of *The Making of Americans* to the lucidly opaque poetic style of *Tender Buttons*. Stein wrote her first play, *What Happened. A Play in Five Acts*, in 1913, not long after completing *A Long Gay Book* and *Many Many Women*, works that attempt depictions of small numbers of persons, mostly couples and triples. She took up the project of investigating aggregates of individuals in the plays that she began writing in the second decade of the twentieth century; her plays can generally be read as they stage relations of dynamic knowing among a number of people. The specific question they pose is How can one know these aggregate relations of knowing? How can one possibly know, and depict or represent, the complexity of group relations?

It is of more than passing interest, then, that Bion developed his theory of thinking alongside (or not long after) his explorations of group psychology. Bion coined the term *group therapy* in the first of a series of articles on the subject published between 1943 and 1952 (collected in *Experiences in Groups and Other Papers* [1961]), by which term he meant not primarily the therapy of the individual in the group but the therapy of the group as such, or the attempt "to make the study of their tensions a group task."[27] Bion's basic methodological question is similar to Stein's: How can one know and experience aggregates of individuals using analytic, transferential methods, based as they are on an exchange between two people? That is, how can one identify with groups for the purposes of studying them? In *Learning from Experience* (1962) Bion develops and revises his thinking on groups in the more general terms of container and contained. In the context of this work I conclude that the problem of the theater, as Stein's lecture understands it, is the problem of thinking, knowing, and making emotional contact with groups. It follows that the particular challenges of Stein's plays emerge from her epistemic ambitions for them: they offer a literary form for representing a group's dynamics to itself.

These conclusions support and extend my argument that Henry James used theatrical devices in his later novels as a way to investigate group psychology. They also offer a way to understand Stein's choice of James as her immediate literary ancestor, as she puts it in *The Autobiography*, and her use of James in *Four in America* (1947) to explore the difference between Shakespeare's sonnets and plays. I will conclude this chapter in a manner that resembles my chapter on James, with some remarks about Stein's writing in its technological and media contexts, focusing especially on television.

Stein's plays pose questions about the dynamics of transferential relations and the technical—that is to say, emotional and sensational—nature of identification. These questions are difficult enough to pose when the object of knowledge is one individual, such as a patient who comes for analysis or a friend who sits for a portrait. They become much more difficult when what is being investigated is groups or numbers of persons. And the epistemological situation becomes yet more complex when group transferential procedures take place in the environment of technologies that, as Stein points out in the middle of her lecture, shape the modernist moment. As it turns out, the lecture's technical questions are not only her own:

> I may say that as a matter of fact the thing which has induced a person like myself to constantly think about the theater from the standpoint of sight and sound and its relation to emotion and time, rather than in relation to story and action is the same as you may say general form of conception as the inevitable experiments made by the cinema although the method of doing so has naturally nothing to do with the other. . . . The fact remains that there is the same impulse to solve the problem of time in relation to emotion and the relation of the scene to the emotion of the audience in the one case as in the other. (104)

The same day that she arrived in the United States for her lecture tour, Stein was filmed in a newsreel that was released to cinemas across North America; a week after "Plays" was first given, she was interviewed live on NBC radio coast-to-coast. On her American tour she encountered the media machines that were to create the fame she was seeking, thereby encountering, at first hand, those powerful sociopolitical institutions that had cornered the market on precisely the same task she thought plays were best suited for: to represent a group's dynamics to itself. Radio, film, and television are precisely theatrical technologies, not only in the sense that they borrowed and integrated the forms and techniques of live theater (what current media studies calls "remediation") but also in that they take on the function of representing groups to themselves.

Stein's blustery emphasis on facticity in the passage above marks her attempt to bring her writing into relation with the most prestigious theatrical technology of modernism and at the same time to deny its priority, and while she is right to insist that her experimental method "has naturally nothing to do with" cinema, it does closely resemble the technical operations of a different medium emerging in the 1930s: television. It is indeed a strange "matter of fact" that one can imagine Gertrude Stein writing to be analogous to the televisual process of scanning and synchronizing images, those operations fundamental to the working of live television: for an image to be transmitted, "it is crucial that it be analysed, point by point by a scanning beam, and for the received image to be synthesized by another scanning beam synchronized to that at the transmitter."[28] Consider the description Stein gives of her portraiture method in the lecture "Portraits and Repetition":

> I began writing the portraits of any one by saying what I knew of that one as I talked and listened that one, and each time that I talked and listened that one I said what I knew they were then.... Every time I said what they were I said it so that they were this thing, and each time I said what they were as they were, as I was, naturally more or less but never the same thing each time that I said what they were I said what they were, not that they were different nor that I was different but as it was not the same moment which I said I said it with a difference. So finally I was emptied of saying this thing, and so no longer said what they were.[29]

Unlike a photographic portrait, which captures a subject at a moment in time, Stein aims to communicate a given individual's peculiar intensity, liveliness, or rhythm over time. Her method aims to represent duration and the reciprocal relations of observation that take place between portraitist and subject; indeed Stein began writing portraits only after she had sat as subject, over several months, for Picasso's famous portrait of her. Rather than film, the more accurate analogy for her writing technique is the decomposition and recomposition of a televisual image.

Like televisual scanning, Stein's method of "talking and listening" a person is synchronized. Talking, or sending out language and gesture, and listening, or taking in language and gesture: the possibilities of accurate portraiture depend on talking and listening at the same time, one of Stein's definitions of genius. Think of talking and listening as the operations of two scanning beams. One beam reads an image by analyzing points of light registered on a photoconductive surface; it encodes the differences between these points as electrical signals, while the other beam writes the image nearly instantaneously by decoding and reproducing these same differences on another surface at a distant location. If these operations are synchronized, then an image can be accurately reproduced. While televisual scanning shares with photography the need for a photosensitive surface, that surface never acts as a storage medium—there is no moment at which the image is iconically preserved (or remembered) so that it can be reproduced later. In this way a television image is more like a telegraphic communication than a film still, always in process of being deconstituted and reconstituted by the scanning beams. What we see when we watch television is writing in process, not the reproduction of what has been remembered or stored but the recreation of a present moment. There is something fundamentally antimimetic about both television scanning and Stein writing. As she puts it in "Poetry and Grammar," "Language as a real thing is not imitation either of sounds or colors or emotions it is an intellectual recreation."[30] In making portraits of individuals Stein re-creates the movement inside her as it may coordinate with the movement inside another. At once transmitter and receiver, writing takes in and sends out those movements that communicate the rhythms of Stein's subject. In writing landscape plays she brings this technique of coordination to depict groups.

In the Derridean terms that I sketched in my introduction, the strange resemblance between Stein's writing and televisual scanning techniques can be read as an index to the new role for affect in a rapidly changing scene of writing, one transformed by broadcasting and other graphic technologies of reproduction. This reading offers a way to approach the contemporariness of Stein's writing, in particular the remarkable influence of her landscape poetics on a variety of nonnaturalist twentieth- and twenty-first-century performance practices (including Andy Warhol's, as I discuss in the next chapter). Arguably no other modernist writer in the literary canon (in English) has exercised as strong a gravitational pull on the (especially but by no means exclusively American) performance avant-garde, beginning with John Cage and other New York artists of the 1940s and 1950s (groups such as the Living Theater and the Judson Poets Theatre) and extending through the second half of the twentieth-century (Richard Foreman, Robert Wilson, Anne Bogart).[31] This impact shows no sign of abating, as Stein's plays and other texts continue to be taken up in contemporary multimedia performance; as the editors of the collection *Land/Scape/Theater* (2002) put it, "Landscape names the modern theater's new spatial paradigm."[32] Stein's poetics have made their mark because of how they address fundamental questions of identification in the context of the displacement and integration of theater, and theatrical technique, into newer media, especially televisual forms. If playgoing could serve earlier writers (such as Adam Smith and Rousseau) as a general figure for relations of social spectatorship and affective exchange within the state, for Stein and other twentieth-century writers, the figure of the theater was inflected by the techniques and technologies that reproduce and distribute to great numbers the face and the voice. How can one think, know, and make contact with groups in the environment of such technologies? This is the contemporary version of the problem of the theater, as Stein's lecture permits it to be reposed.

5 / Vis-à-vis Television: Andy Warhol's Therapeutics

Here's an observation: the most common twentieth-century North American slang words for *television* were names for genitalia and other intimate body parts. The box, the tube, the boob tube—how to understand this sexualization of television? How better to understand it than in terms of what Melanie Klein called part-objects, those elements of infantile phantasy that refer, in the first instance, to the breast? "The part-object," as Robert Hinshelwood explains, "is firstly an emotional object, having a function rather than a material existence"; it is, for the infant, what "touches his cheek, intrudes a nipple into his mouth for good or bad purposes. In spite of having only these ephemeral qualities it is completely real for the infant."[1] From the perspective of object-relations theory, these slang words point less to a material object than to a sensual, emotional, and intentional one: a part-object that functions to contain (box) and deliver (tube) nourishment and poison, love and hate, idiocy and entertainment. The boob tube may be part of larger objects such as networks or nations that intrude, with mixed purposes, into the lives of viewers, but these whole objects are often difficult to perceive. "From the infant's point of view," as Hinshelwood puts it, "the part is all there is to the object" (379). Television, it can seem, is all that we can touch, see, or hear.

No longer a tube but a flat display, television now appears on any number of portable devices that we have, if anything, an even more explicitly infantile relation to; we keep these devices close, fingering or manipulating them to ensure a constant flow of communication through umbilical connections to mouth or ear. I begin with the somewhat familiar figure of TV-as-breast from the less familiar vantage of object-relations theory not to denounce or disdain television (as maternal, infantilizing, feminizing) but to begin thinking about our powerful *because* fundamentally infantile relations to it. From a Kleinian perspective, denunciations of television would appear to come from the paranoid-schizoid position, that early state of mind characterized by the strict separation of what is good (in other words, what supports life) from what is bad (what threatens to destroy it). For example, take the slogan, printed on many thousands of bumper stickers and T-shirts, "Kill Your TV"—presumably before it kills you by draining your life force, turning you into a zombified consumer. Or consider the opposite response, the boosterist window-on-the-world perspective from which television appears to educate and inform, creating conditions for global democracy and so on. Neither of these attitudes toward television is entirely wrong, but they are split, partial, unintegrated. I would like to approach television from the perspective of that other infantile state of mind, what Klein called the depressive position, to perceive television as a whole object, an irremediably mixed, contaminated, or damaged object that invites reparation. To put it another way, how can we think of television as the form of theater that mass democratic cultures deserve?

I believe that this is how Andy Warhol watched and thought of television: he not only accepted it, consuming large amounts (like most other North Americans of his time and ours); he also avidly made use of our infantile relations to television in much of his work. Warhol's poetics, as I understand them, adopt a televisual perspective on emotion, and in the first part of this chapter I explore these poetics in readings of some of his early film and video work. These televisual poetics closely resemble Gertrude Stein's landscape poetics. Consider the terms in which Warhol explains the appeal of his early films, such as *Sleep* (1963) and *Empire* (1964), in which very little seems to happen:

> My first films using the stationary objects were also made to help the audiences get more acquainted with themselves. Usually when you go to the movies, you sit in a fantasy world, but when you see something that disturbs you, you get a little more involved with the people next to you. Movies are doing a little more than you can do with plays and concerts where you just have to sit there and I think television will do more than the movies. You could do more things watching my movies than with other kinds of movies: you could eat and drink and smoke and cough and look away and then look back and they'd still be there. It's not the ideal movie, it's just my kind of movie.[2]

Warhol's contrast between the "fantasy world" that audiences enter when they watch most movies (or other staged performances) and the more engaged social spaces created by watching his films would initially seem to invite a Brechtian reading in terms of disturbance, defamiliarization, or modernist shock of some kind. But the qualities of audience experience that he describes ("You could do more things watching my movies") can be specifically understood in terms of increased capacities, possibilities, or (in the terms of my previous chapter) those loose affective coordinations that permit a reversible relation of containment between audience and screen. Like Stein's plays, Warhol's early films turn away from the pressures of one-way identification with character and anticipation of plot and toward the infantile intensities of reverie, as Wilfred Bion understands it. Warhol suggests that something about the reliability or dependability of his films ("they'd still be there") helps audiences "get more acquainted with themselves" and that this therapeutic object stability is even more pronounced when we watch television.

It is this unusual approach to television as an instrument for self-acquaintance that I pursue in the second half of this chapter, where I argue that Warhol adopts a televisual perspective in developing the celebrated self that emerged during the 1960s as the emblem of Pop Art. In addition to Kleinian and other affect theory, I turn to Michel Foucault's late lectures on ancient therapeutics to offer a reading of *The Philosophy of Andy Warhol (From A to B and Back Again)* (1975). Here Warhol figures television as a therapeutic device, a figure specifically for conversion and control; it is one among several devices that offer him the technical means to become himself, Andy Warhol, by regulating or tuning emotional perspective and distance. In its theatrical capacity to frame affect by reproducing the face or the voice, television resembles some of the other instruments in Warhol's bag of tricks, such as the screen print, the tape recorder, the camera, and even the mirror. But unlike these other devices, television names both an instrument of graphic reproduction and an entire industry that permits viewers from home to enter imaginary relations with a mass audience. Warhol identified with television along these lines, aiming to mimic its position as culture industry, as instrument of emotional feedback, and as agent of transference. His so-called passivity and affectlessness should be viewed, in this context, as a highly engaged response to televised emotion, his impassive face the expression of an analytic stance that was, in principle, shareable. If, as he famously put it, "I think everybody should be a machine," the machine that Warhol most wanted everyone to be was television.[3]

I begin with the recent scholarship that has demonstrated the central place of television in Warhol's art practices. By the time the *Philosophy* was published in 1975, Warhol had been experimenting with video technology and television's forms and genres for more than a decade. The film *Soap Opera* (1964) spliced together footage from producer Lester Persky's television commercials with scenes of superstar Baby Jane Holzer and others. In the summer of 1965 Warhol received promotional use of a Norelco video camera and monitor and made several hours' worth of video tapes at the Factory, using two of these tapes in a complex film portrait of Edie Sedgwick called *Outer and Inner Space* (1965; more on this below). Callie Angell, the Warhol archivist and historian, points out that these experiments with video predate Nam June Paik's, marking him as a very early video artist; but as Lynn Spigel notes in her exploration of Warhol's uses of television, "Warhol TV was not counter-TV in the video-art sense."[4] Rather Warhol evolved an attitude toward television that did not oppose commercial aims and sensibilities to modernist or experimental ones. For example, in 1968 he directed a one-minute television advertisement for Shrafft's restaurants called "Underground Sundae" (1968) in which a red dot turns into a swirl of color, out of which emerges an ice-cream sundae with a cherry on top. In 1971 he set up Andy Warhol Studio with Vincent Fremont and continued experimenting with television genres, eventually producing three series for cable television. Through the 1970s and 1980s Warhol appeared in TV commercials and in 1985 on an episode of *The Love Boat*.[5]

As this brief, highly selective survey indicates, Warhol worked with television in a variety of ways throughout his career. Graig Uhlin has convincingly argued that even Warhol's early films should be understood by way of the televisual "elements of indefinite duration, liveness, and a spectatorial experience defined by 'waiting.'"[6] In a discussion of *Empire*, Warhol's eight-hour film portrait of the Empire State Building, Uhlin observes that the film's subject houses one of the most powerful television transmitters in the world and reads the film as "a sort of staring contest between the two media ... and it is no question for Warhol which one will blink first" (5). Relatedly, but along different lines, J. Hoberman has suggested that *Empire* and *Sleep* "might be considered the original video installations" and that generally "Warhol used 16mm film as if it *were* videotape."[7] Refreshingly the scholars who focus on television tend to avoid the standard art historical narrative that insists that Warhol's career declined after he turned to what he called Business Art (the commissioned portraits and bigger budget films) in the 1970s. As Spigel puts it, "This way of understanding Warhol winds up returning him to the modernist—and masculinist—embrace of irony and distance from all things kitsch—in effect erasing Warhol's queerness and denying or at least bypassing pop's more complicated and integral relations to domesticity, everydayness, femininity, and consumerism."[8] Like Spigel, I find it difficult to imagine any convincing account of Warhol's career that discounts these relations, as well as his remarkable celebrity and strategies for remaking his queer self in the context of the media-saturated postwar culture.[9]

But Spigel does not always acknowledge Warhol's use of some form of ironic distance, what permits him to represent the kitsch or popular, its beauty and his desire for it, so directly. Television, I suggest, offers Warhol just this form of direct distance and perspective. Consider, as primary examples of this televisual perspective, the *Screen Tests*, a series of over four hundred short, silent black-and-white film portraits that Warhol and his assistants (most often Gerard Malanga and Billy Linich) made at the Silver Factory between 1964 and 1966. Certainly Uhlin's televisual elements of duration, liveness, and waiting characterize the *Screen Tests*, what Warhol and company called, by contrast with movies, the "stillies." Here is Callie Angell's precise descriptive summary:

> Warhol provided himself with a set of simple rules to follow, rules similar to those required for passport photographs: the camera should not move; the background should be as plain as possible; subjects must be well lit and centered in the frame; each poser should face forward, hold as still as possible, refrain from talking or smiling, and try not to blink. By transposing the conventions of the formal or institutional photographic portrait into the time-based medium of film, he created a set of diabolically challenging performance instructions for his sitters, who, suddenly finding themselves up against the wall and face-to-face with Warhol's Bolex, struggled to hold a pose while their brief moment of exposure was prolonged into a nearly unendurable three minutes. The subject's emotional and physiological responses to this ordeal are often the most riveting aspect of the *Screen Tests*, adding complex layers of psychological meaning to the visual images structured by the artist. The films' silent projection speed further exaggerates these behaviors, revealing each involuntary tremor or flutter of an eyelid in clinical slow motion.[10]

Warhol's filming conditions can be understood by way of what Laplanche and Pontalis, in their dictionary of psychoanalytic terms, call neutrality, "one of the defining characteristics of the attitude of the analyst during the treatment": the analyst's neutrality consists of a refusal "to direct the treatment according to some ideal," a lack of immediate response to the patient's emotional provocations, and a suspension of the analyst's own "theoretical preconceptions" when listening to the patient's discourse.[11] In the *Screen Tests* analytic neutrality is an effect of the combined stillness of the camera and a minimal directing style, so minimal that Warhol would sometimes walk away, leaving the subject to contend with the camera alone. Warhol's unwillingness to let his subject's discomfort interrupt the filming process, a basic part of his filming technique, makes actors (and often viewers) uncomfortable—one reason why his filmmaking is so often described as sadistic. But this neutrality is precisely what enables the transference to take place, both the positive and especially the negative transference, that is, the expression of aggression, hate, and envy toward Warhol or his camera.

Not that these feelings are what we see expressed, not directly; rather all of the *Screen Tests* show the portrait subjects' different strategies for coping with the posing conditions. For example, Ann Buchanan's first portrait shows a young woman who keeps extremely still (fig. 6). As Angell puts it, "apparently under instructions not to blink, she heroically holds her eyes wide open while they slowly well up with glistening tears."[12] A glimmer of a smile crosses her face toward the end of the film as Buchanan expresses some pride at having managed to follow Warhol's instructions to the letter. In a film taken right after, "she fixes the camera with a moist, wide-eyed gaze and then very slowly crosses her eyes" (45). Other subjects show different strategies: Paul America chews gum and smirks; Billy Linich (aka Billy Name), in charge of setting up lighting for the stillies, wears sunglasses that reflect the studio lights back at the viewer; Nico glances at a magazine and performs utter boredom; and Ingrid Superstar consciously imitates Warhol's hand gestures and facial expressions.[13] Warhol's neutrality lets viewers pay close attention to the subtle dynamics of facial expression, and the less the subject does, the more interesting the portrait becomes. Buchanan is one of the few who managed to follow Warhol's instructions, and as a consequence of her extreme stillness, it becomes difficult to distinguish between minute facial movements and the movement of the film projection itself. This indistinction makes the expressiveness of face and film continuous: her tears may express distress, but at the same time they are a physiological consequence of her unblinking gaze into bright lights. In these films, then, affect takes place on the surface of the skin as a consequence of the filming process, its expression an index to the transferential relation between subject and camera.

FIGURE 6. Andy Warhol, *Screen Test: Ann Buchanan*, 1964. 16mm film, black and white, silent, 4.5 minutes at 16fps. ©2014 The Andy Warhol Museum, Pittsburgh, a museum of Carnegie Institute. All rights reserved. Film still courtesy of The Andy Warhol Museum.

Warhol's analytic neutrality is less in the service of diagnosing his subjects than of displaying them, permitting the performance of idiosyncratic facial styles, and watching this bare-bones theatricality can be a psychedelic experience: the silent, slowed-down film projection gives us the unusual experience of paying extremely close attention to strangers' (mostly young and beautiful) faces close up, without being directed by discourse or language. In chapter 2, on expression and faces in Poe's short stories, I discussed what Silvan Tomkins calls "the taboos on looking," in which the affect of shame-humiliation inhibits and underlines experiences of looking and being looked at. There I suggested that theater suspends these taboos on looking: audiences are permitted to stare at the faces of actors on the stage without the shame of being caught in the act of looking. While film and television certainly offer these pleasures of looking and are forms of theater in this sense, in most cases our visual attention is guided (and sometimes overwhelmed) by language or by the requirements of narrative. This is why, according to Tomkins, watching television with the sound turned down may be useful for "the student of affect":

> Language interaction is usually so demanding and obtrusive that few individuals may penetrate the linguistic envelope to isolate the idiosyncratic style of the face of the other during conversation. For the student of affect, however, if he will turn off the flow of information from linguistic interaction and attend simply to the face of the other, there is immediately revealed an astonishingly personal and simple style of affective facial behavior. This can easily be done by turning off the sound of any unrehearsed television program. (*AIC* 1: 143)

Television offers one of the few opportunities to stare at a stranger's face in silence, something we might otherwise do with someone we know and love, without risking the humiliation of breaking the taboos on looking.[14] Elsewhere Tomkins remarks that in watching television talk shows "much of what appeared on the face became ground to speech as figure. One had to turn down the speech to see the face."[15] In the *Screen Tests* Warhol finds a comparably simple and powerful way to reverse the figure-ground relations between language and facial affect, and, like Tomkins, he makes spaces of social exchange (a living room, a night club) into laboratory settings in order to experience something other than strictly verbal meaning. "When I read magazines," asserts Warhol in one of his most cited interviews, "I just look at the pictures and the words, I don't usually read it. There's no meaning to the words, I just feel the shapes with my eye and if you look at something long enough, I've discovered, the meaning goes away."[16] Warhol's *Screen Tests* let propositional or verbal meaning subside so as to allow other kinds of meaning, affective ones, to surface.

I'm suggesting that in the *Screen Tests* Warhol uses the medium of film televisually to represent facial affect or behavior and that this televisual perspective, in making affect figural, enables transferential movements of emotion to take place between viewer and screen. I turn now to a more complex set of transferential dynamics in a film that represents the television set itself. In the black-and-white sound film *Outer and Inner Space*, Edie Sedgwick is seated in front of a television set on which her prerecorded image plays back (fig. 7). The televised image (Warhol used the videotapes he shot of her) is in full profile facing right, while Sedgwick is filmed in three-quarter profile looking left, her head framed by the television behind her while she addresses someone off-screen. Once again I use Angell's apt description of the mise-en-scène: "On the left, a brightly glowing video image transforms Sedgwick's profile into a flattened, glamorous mask which seems almost vapid in its graphic

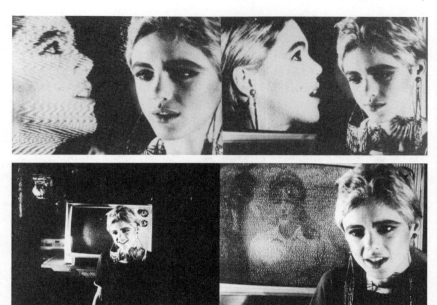

FIGURE 7. Andy Warhol, *Outer and Inner Space*, 1965. 16mm film, black and white, sound, 66 minutes or 33 minutes in double screen. ©2014 The Andy Warhol Museum, Pittsburgh, a museum of Carnegie Institute. All rights reserved. Film still courtesy of The Andy Warhol Museum.

simplicity; on the right, the filmed face of the 'real' Edie, shadowed and expressively modeled by the glow of her own video image, exposes every detail of her increasingly unhappy subjectivity as she endured the ordeal of this face-off with her televised self."[17] Warhol filmed two thirty-three-minute reels and projected them simultaneously to create four images of Sedgwick across the screen in a manner that recalls earlier screen prints. The first reel (projected on the left) begins with a tight close-up, making it difficult to see the television at first, then eventually zooms out; the second reel (projected on the right) begins from the longer shot, eventually returning to a tighter close-up of the two faces. The audio veers in and out of intelligibility, each reel recording the voices of both Sedgwicks, along with ambient sounds of the Factory setting.

These attempts simply to describe Warhol's portrait trip over some basic representational and media paradoxes, as when Angell calls the filmed Sedgwick "real" (in scare quotes) or when Uhlin contrasts the "live" Sedgwick with the televised image. Warhol's arrangement, as Uhlin points out, reverses the usual associations of television and film: the filmed Sedgwick is lively, animated, and expressive (like a talk-show guest), while the televised Sedgwick is larger than life, iconic, still, and glamorous.[18] This reversal accords well with what Warhol says in contrasting movies and television in the *Philosophy*: "People sometimes say that the way things happen in the movies is unreal, but actually it's the way things happen to you in life that's unreal. The movies make emotions look so strong and real, whereas when things really do happen to you, it's like watching television—you don't feel anything."[19] Warhol understands that "the movies" (classic Hollywood film), in representing faces and voices on the big screen, delineate emotions more clearly and, often, more simply than in ordinary life, largely an effect of the sutured, single point of identification with the camera (as psychoanalytic film theory has it). Television, on the other hand, offers viewers multiple points of view simultaneously, whether within a program (switching between multiple cameras), or between program and commercials, or as a result of the viewer's own ability to switch channels; these all contribute to the fundamental televisual experiences of fragmentation and flow. Integrated into ordinary domestic routines and living spaces, television offers multiplicity, simultaneity, and emotional complexity, the terms in which Warhol casts his own psychic experience: "Right when I was shot and ever since, I knew that I was watching television. The channels switch, but it's all television. When you're really involved with something, you're usually thinking about something else. When something's happening, you fantasize about other things" (91). David Joselit, in his discussion of these passages, suggests that for Warhol, "'TV' and 'life' mutually de-realize one another."[20] But I read it another way: for Warhol, affective life is like television in being multiple, complex, volatile, and suffused with phantasy; emotionally there are always several things happening at the same time.

Outer and Inner Space makes film televisual not simply by including television as its subject but by conveying its multiple perspectives: each of the four images of Sedgwick is, as it were, a different channel, a different angle (in time or space) on Warhol's subject, the relatively small size of each projection analogous to a television screen. Here the transferential relations are enacted primarily between Sedgwick and her televised image, which, as Uhlin puts it, "seems to be whispering into the 'live' superstar's ear."[21] Uhlin goes on to suggest that, "Like a vampire draining its victim of her life, TV-Edie hovers menacingly near film-Edie's neck" (18), identifying Warhol (some of his associates called him "Drella," a combination of Dracula and Cinderella) with the TV set. But the television, just behind her and to one side, is also in the analyst's position. As much as it appears to drain or mortify Sedgwick, her televised image also irritates, provokes, or animates her in a manner that both Hoberman and Uhlin describe in psychoanalytic terms: Hoberman describes her schizoid attention and hysteria, while Uhlin describes her tendency to free-associate.[22] Here the basic transference of the *Screen Tests* is layered and multiplied: Sedgwick, initially in front of the video camera, is now between film camera and television set. For a viewer, these multiple transferential relations are then doubled by the two reels being projected simultaneously to maximal psychedelic effect, as we scan back and forth across the four Sedgwicks' similar voices and facial expressions as they resonate and echo with and against one another.[23]

Watching *Outer and Inner Space* can be a strange and delirious experience, made even more so by the fact that Warhol and Sedgwick were themselves media and psychic projections of one another. Warhol describes Sedgwick in the *Philosophy* (where he calls her Taxi) this way: "She had a poignantly vacant, vulnerable quality that made her the reflection of everybody's private fantasies.... She was a wonderful, beautiful blank."[24] Warhol cultivated his own version of vulnerable blankness or nothingness, in part as a response to becoming an object of mass-media attention in the early 1960s, and *Outer and Inner Space* exemplifies the kind of dizzying mirror show that he excelled at setting in motion. The film ends with the four images of Sedgwick disappearing one by one: first, her televised image on the left projection disappears, then her televised image on the right; the film on the left ends, leaving a white screen as the reel runs out; meanwhile the television set on the right tunes into broadcast TV, briefly showing static-filled images of a cowboy. These classic western images connoting outside space break the closed loop of Warhol's video camera and monitor, but only to invoke the inside space of a studio other than Warhol's, a television studio somewhere in Hollywood. Consider Warhol's definition of Pop Art, from the first paragraph of *POPism: The Warhol Sixties* (1980): "Pop Art took the inside and put it outside, took the outside and put it inside."[25] Television is key in permitting these postwar reversals, bringing outside spaces (baseball fields, western landscapes) into living rooms and broadcasting interior spaces (studios, newsrooms) out. *Outer and Inner Space* ends with the television set turned off but still offering Sedgwick's image: a reflection of her dangling earring and white neck remains on the screen behind her while the lights flash and the film reel runs out. Television, in Warhol's work, has become, like film, a medium that reflects light, just as film has become multiple, emotionally layered, and dependent on visual scanning, like television.

I would like to move now from the televisual poetics of Warhol's early films to the role of television in his therapeutics. Or, to put this somewhat differently, I would like to offer a reading of *The Philosophy of Andy Warhol (From A to B and Back Again)* as philosophy. This may seem an unlikely approach, especially if one reads the title of this book as a spoof of philosophy in its claims to theoretical definitiveness (*the* philosophy), authority (of Andy Warhol, by Andy Warhol), and systematic coverage. All we're getting is one step forward, one step back, not the "A to Z" of everything. But Warhol's book offers readers sharp insights and brilliant observations in the mode of philosophy as Pierre Hadot understands this term. For Hadot, a historian of ancient philosophy, philosophical discourse should be viewed not as theory or system but "from the perspective of the way of life of which it is both the expression and the means" and as it emerges from an existential choice that is "never made in solitude. There can never be a philosophy or philosophers outside a group, a community—in a word, a philosophical 'school.'"[26] From this ancient and colloquial perspective Warhol's *Philosophy* resembles books associated with, for example, the Hellenistic schools: it gathers years of accumulated wisdom under a single title, is based on oral teachings (that is, recorded interviews) on a variety of time-honored subjects (love, beauty, time, art, money), and is collected and organized by someone other than the philosopher, in this case Pat Hackett, an associate of that 1960s and 1970s school of philosophy called the Factory.

Ancient philosophy, Hadot argues, is essentially therapeutic and involves work on or with one's self, especially one's problematic emotions, by way of the disciplined practice of spiritual exercises. Warhol's book qualifies as philosophy in exactly this sense, page after page demonstrating its baseline concern for and work on the self that goes by the name Andy Warhol. Consider this useful exercise:

> Sometimes people let the same problem make them miserable for years when they could just say, "So what." That's one of my favorite things to say. "So what."
> "My mother didn't love me." So what.
> "My husband won't ball me." So what.
> "I'm a success but I'm still alone." So what.
> I don't know how I made it through all the years before I learned how to do that trick. It took a long time for me to learn it, but once you do, you never forget.[27]

Is this not Warhol's version of that ancient spiritual exercise that Hadot calls "indifference to indifferent things," part of the therapeutic practice of distinguishing what depends upon you from what does not?[28] There are other examples in Warhol's book, recommendations for daily living taken from his own practice ("What you should do is get a box for a month, and drop everything in it and at the end of the month lock it up. Then date it and send it over to Jersey") and slogans that he finds useful to repeat under certain social circumstances (for example, "I'm not the type").[29] I find these slogans and practices both funny and serious. They seem to work, at least for Warhol, although it's not always clear how, or exactly what work they do. Warhol's abiding attitude of and ideas about self-care mark his book as a work of philosophy; later I will relate his therapeutics specifically to those of the ancient Cynics.

But my primary goal is less to bring Warhol in line with the ancients than to understand the role of television in his philosophy, and for this purpose I make less use of Hadot's work than Foucault's, in particular the two late courses collected under the titles *The Hermeneutics of the Subject* (2005) and *The Courage of Truth* (2011). In these lectures Foucault, informed by Hadot's understanding of philosophy, examines the theme of "care of oneself" across a variety of ancient Greek, Roman, and early Christian writing. Foucault's lectures, I should note, also count as philosophy, primarily oral teachings on the subject of self-care that were recorded and edited by his students and associates. Given the marked differences from his earlier work—the genealogies of apparatuses of modern state power and criticism of discourses of truth—one might wonder whether the later work on ancient therapeutics properly belongs to that school of philosophy called Foucauldian. It is clear, however, that a career-long concern with power and the relations between subjectivity and truth remain a pressing motive for his thinking. Foucault puts it this way: "I think we may have to suspect that we find it impossible today to constitute an ethic of self, even though it may be an urgent, fundamental, and politically indispensable task, if it is true after all that there is no first or final point of resistance to political power other than in the relationship one has to oneself."[30] I bring Warhol together with Foucault (rather than with Hadot, who does not appear to share these critical commitments) because they were both concerned to develop an "aesthetics of the self" (251) adequate to twentieth-century modes of governance and self-relation.[31] Foucault and Warhol, an unlikely pairing, have a surprising amount in common: almost identical life spans (Foucault 1926–84, Warhol 1928–87), queer sexualities formed in transgressive relation to postwar consolidations, and radical work that veered sharply away from both Marxist revolutionary politics and the interiorizing aspects of psychology and psychoanalysis.

Warhol and Foucault, perhaps also surprisingly, share an underexamined set of relations to mid-twentieth-century cybernetics. I cannot offer a full exposition of these historical and conceptual relations here, but I would like briefly to indicate the role of some key cybernetic ideas for these thinkers; this will help me to unfold the connections between television and therapeutics that I see in Warhol's work. The term *cybernetics* was coined by the mathematician Norbert Wiener and disseminated in his influential book *Cybernetics, or Control and Communication in the Animal and the Machine* (1948). Its title pointed to the central idea that control is a function of communication, as well as to its unusual disciplinary mix: studies of humans and other animals in a variety of life sciences with studies of machines in physics and engineering. Television was a technology of considerable interest to cyberneticians, appearing in the introductory pages of Wiener's book as a device that can assist in transforming perception. For Wiener, the technology of television works as a prosthesis (for example, in "designing an apparatus to enable the blind to read the printed page by ear")[32] that can amplify sensory experience because of its scanning capacity, its real-time analysis and synthesis of vast amounts of data. As I explained in the previous chapter, scanning names the process by which an image is "read," decomposed point by point into electrical signals, and "written," or recomposed nearly instantaneously. From a cybernetic perspective, television is a powerful device for analysis and synthesis, for reading and writing, a perspective that Warhol takes when he defines television, in one of his later interviews, as "just moveable print."[33] I wouldn't be the first critic to suggest that Warhol's remarks about wanting to be a machine should be read in relation to the popularization of cybernetics during the 1950s and 1960s.[34] In this context the parenthetical subtitle of Warhol's *Philosophy* offers more than simply a joke about philosophy: it offers a succinct definition of circular causality, one of the most important concepts to emerge from (first-order) cybernetic theory. Steve Heims summarizes this idea in *The Cybernetics Group*: "In traditional thinking since the ancient Greeks a cause A results in an effect B. With circular causality A and B are mutually cause and effect of each other. Moreover, not only does A affect B but through B acts back on itself. The circular causality concept seemed appropriate for much in the human sciences. It meant that A cannot do things to B without being itself effected."[35] Both Warhol's poetics and his therapeutics, as we shall see, are partly defined by circular causality and feedback relations, key ingredients in the cybernetic recipe for control.

The significance of cybernetic theory and practice to postwar thinking on both sides of the Atlantic has been emerging more clearly as histories of this complex transdisciplinary research program are being written.[36] While Foucault has not often been included in these histories (several of which track the importance of cybernetic ideas for French intellectuals), echoes of the cybernetic notion of control can be heard clearly in his writings on power of the mid- to late 1970s.[37] I could turn to *The History of Sexuality: An Introduction* (1976) to support this observation, or more briefly to the set of "hypotheses" about power in the interview "Power and Strategies" (1977): "that power is co-extensive with the social body; there are no spaces of primal liberty between the meshes of its network"; "that relations of power are interwoven with other kinds of relations"; that "one should not assume a massive and primal condition of domination, a binary structure with 'dominators' on one side and 'dominated' on the other"; "that there are no relations of power without resistances; the latter are all the more real and effective because they are formed right at the point where relations of power are exercised."[38] The metaphor of network and weave in these hypotheses emerges most influentially from a cybernetic-engineering perspective on control as a function of networks of communication, or what Foucault calls systems of discourse. Wiener defined control as "nothing but the sending of messages which effectively change the behavior of the recipient."[39] His recurring example of a control system that operates on the principle of negative feedback is a room whose temperature is maintained by a thermostat: control is located not only at the thermostat where the desired temperature is set but anywhere along the loop of communication. Gregory Bateson put it this way: "In the steam engine with a 'governor,' the very word 'governor' is a misnomer if it be taken to mean that this part of the system has unilateral control. . . . The behavior of the governor is determined . . . by the behavior of other parts of the system, and indirectly by its own behavior at a previous time."[40] Foucault's fundamental ideas about power—that it should not be understood in binary terms of dominator/dominated and that resistance always accompanies power in place and time—are mapped by the cybernetic understanding of control as never unilateral, or even bilateral, but always a function of the temporal and spatial dynamics of communication in a system or network.

Foucault's discussions of the government of self and others in his later work on ancient therapeutics exploit the shared etymological root of the words *govern* and *cybernetics*, from ancient Greek for "steersman." Indeed, according to the *OED*, the French word *cybernétique* is both a mid-twentieth-century translation from Wiener's book and has the earlier nineteenth-century sense "art of governing" from ancient Greek "pilot's art." Foucault discusses the metaphor of navigation or steering at an important moment in *The Hermeneutics of the Subject* (2005) in the context of his lectures on conversion, just after he summarizes what he calls the Hellenistic model of "conversion to oneself" this way:

> It involves a real shift, a certain movement of the subject with regard to himself, whose nature we will have to investigate. The subject must advance towards something that is himself. Shift, trajectory, effort, and movement: all of this must be retained in the idea of a conversion to self. Second, in this idea of a conversion to self there is the important, difficult, not very clear, and ambiguous theme of return. What does it mean to return to the self? What is this circle, this loop, this falling back that we must carry out with regard to something, yet something that is not given to us, since at best we are promised it at the end of our life?[41]

While the concepts of conversion and control initially seem to have little to do with one another, perhaps even opposing one another (fundamental change versus stasis), these terms are based on similar circular movements: *conversion* is literally a "turning around," while *control* depends on the circular, causal, self-correcting relations of negative feedback (the word comes from a medieval bookkeeping method for checking accounts back and forth "against the roll"). Foucault notes the frequent appearance of the metaphor of navigation or piloting in the ancient writings on conversion, observing that "the idea of piloting as an art, as a theoretical and practical technique necessary to existence" (249) consistently shows up in discussions of medicine, political government (the ship of state), and the direction of oneself (navigating one's life journey). For the ancient Greeks and Romans, Foucault suggests, these three seemingly distinct activities and domains share a kind of knowledge: the thematics of conversion (to self) are linked with those of control (of one's body, of others).

Foucault pursues the connections between the therapeutic turn toward the self and questions of power by way of the notion of governmentality: "If we understand by governmentality a strategic field of power relations in their mobility, transformability, and reversibility, then I do not think that reflection on this notion of governmentality can avoid passing through, theoretically and practically, the element of a subject defined by the relationship of self to self" (252). While it is not exactly clear how this "passing through" takes place, how governmentality and self-relation are connected, he appears to be offering an implicit critique and revision of Louis Althusser's notion of interpellation: those moments when the networks of control and dependence that characterize any sociopolitical organization are realized in intersubjective relation. Whereas Althusser's famous example is being hailed on the street by a police officer—the moment I turn around to answer the call is the moment of my becoming, as he would put it, the subject of ideology—Foucault seeks to prioritize self-relation ("the relationship of self to self") rather than the relation of self to other, or in the Lacanian terms that Althusser's notion of interpellation depends on, Self to Other. Frédéric Gros offers a helpful frame for thinking about Foucault's focus on ethics and intersubjectivity in a discussion of the kind of self-division that accompanies the ancient Greek idea of the *daimon*: "The ethical dimension is not then the effect of an internalization of the other's gaze. We should say, rather, that the *daimon* is like the mythical figure of a first, irreducible caesura: that of self to self. And the Other takes up its place within this relationship, because there is first of all this relationship. It is the Other who is a projection of the Self, and if we must really tremble, it is before the Self rather than before this Other who is only its emblem."[42] Put differently, we might say that Foucault chooses Melanie Klein over Jacques Lacan: he focuses on the primacy (or inevitability) of self-splitting or self-differentiation, the way others and otherness can be experienced only by way of the complex and confusing movements of projective and introjective identification (object relations emerge only as a consequence of self-differentiation). We might say this, but Foucault certainly wouldn't. There's no reason to believe that he wouldn't have distrusted Kleinian theory along with the rest of psychoanalysis (despite what I see as a potentially productive conceptual alliance). Psychoanalysis, for Foucault, was the most significant of those modern disciplines that subordinated techniques of self-care to the (scientific) project of self-knowledge, of telling the truth of the subject in the medium of language at the cost of other, ethical or political aims.[43]

It is no accident, then, that Foucault's remarks on governmentality take place in the middle of his two lectures on conversion, or what he calls "the great image of turning around towards oneself":[44] his concern is to explore the dynamics of turning toward one's self (in the world), in the therapeutic mode of self-care, rather than only toward the other, or even one's self as an other, in the epistemic mode of knowledge or belief. His specific goal in these lectures is to unearth a Hellenistic model of conversion that was overwritten by or assimilated to the "two great models in Western culture" (216) that Hadot identified: Platonic *epistrophe* and Christian *metanoia*. The Hellenistic model of conversion contrasts with the Platonic model in that it "does not function on the axis opposing this world here to the other world" and "does not take place then in the break with my body" (210). And whereas "a fundamental element of Christian conversion is renunciation of oneself, dying to oneself, and being reborn in a different self and a new form" (211), Foucault argues that the Hellenistic model requires a break, not within the self but with what surrounds the self, "so that it is no longer enslaved, dependent, and constrained" (212). Foucault wants to recover a this-worldly form of conversion, a "self-subjectivation" that contrasts with Platonic and Christian models of "trans-subjectivation" (214); the stakes are to find practices of self-care that do not take one out of the world but locate one firmly in it, for better and for worse. His most powerful statement of these stakes comes at the end of the lectures on conversion in a discussion of the Stoic spiritual exercise of the "view from above." The person who undertakes this exercise, says Foucault, "must understand that all the wonders to be found in heaven, in the stars and meteors, in the beauty of the earth, in the plains, in the sea and the mountains, are all inextricably bound up with the thousand plagues of the body and soul, with wars, robbery, death, and suffering. . . . He is shown the world precisely so that he clearly understands that there is no choice, that nothing can be chosen without choosing the rest, that there is only one possible world, and that we are bound to this world" (284). To my Kleinian ears, this sounds very much like the insight of the depressive position, the perception of a mixed or contaminated whole, and the place of the self in the networks of dependency that embed it. This form of perception aims to distinguish between what is necessary for that self and what may not be necessary, what can be changed and what (at a given time) cannot.

Warhol's *Philosophy*, as I understand it, is thoroughly concerned with the dynamics of conversion and control that I have begun to unfold here: "from A to B and back again" names both the control relations of circular causality or feedback as well as the circle or loop, the shifts and returns of Warhol's conversion to self. These movements take place primarily by way of dialogue between A and B, that is, between Andy and (in the first instance) Brigid Berlin (aka Brigid Polk), one of Warhol's longtime telephone confidantes. Pat Hackett wrote or "redacted" the *Philosophy* based on recordings of telephone calls with Berlin, as well as her own interviews with Warhol. More generally B names any of Andy's associates, assistants, or worker bees, and dialogue between A and B serves as the book's central formal and thematic device. Almost every chapter begins with an epigraph, a (sometimes implied) dialogue that illustrates the relevant theme; most chapters contain dialogues or narratives featuring A and B as well. In *POPism* Warhol explains the importance of this kind of dialogue to his working method: "I was never embarrassed about asking someone, literally, 'What should I paint?' Because Pop comes from the outside, and how is asking someone for ideas any different from looking for them in a magazine?"⁴⁵ From A to B and back again describes Warhol's poetics, his use of others in his artistic practices and his basic connection to the "outside" as creative source. And as the chapter "Work" makes clear, A and B also stand for Art and Business: Warhol, a successful commercial artist turned fine artist, helped to upset the myth of art's autonomy from the market (especially the market in images) by showing their reciprocal interdependence. Finally, as an edited, redacted assemblage the *Philosophy* consists of conversations with Warhol, made available to his readers who then become implicated in or part of the loop.

The book's prologue, titled "B and I: How Andy Puts His Warhol On," jumps right into the self-constituting (and deconstituting) dynamics of A's conversion to self with a telephone conversation.

> I wake up and call B.
> B is anybody who helps me kill time.
> B is anybody and I'm nobody. B and I.
> I need B because I can't be alone. Except when I sleep. Then I can't be with anybody.
> I wake up and call B.⁴⁶

The conversation that follows, a hilarious and often vulgar sequence of seeming non sequiturs, offers a camp mix of irony and existentialism as a way to introduce readers to A, our narrator, at once utterly dependent ("I need B because I can't be alone") and aloof ("Except when I sleep"). Over the course of the telephone call A is transformed from "nobody" to that media somebody called Andy Warhol, an image, however, that never replaces the narrator's "nobody." Quite the opposite: what emerges from this opening chapter is an image that constantly turns on the idea of nobody or nothing: "I'm sure I'm going to look in the mirror and see nothing. People are always calling me a mirror and if a mirror looks into a mirror, what is there to see?" (7). With its allusion to Emily Dickinson (poem 260 begins, "I'm Nobody! Who are you? / Are you—Nobody— too? / Then there's a pair of us! / Don't tell! they'd advertise—you know!"), Warhol's book begins by staging a basic problem that accompanies any act of publication, print or otherwise: how to navigate between the self of everyday emotional experience and the self that is imaged or viewed from the perspective of another. Warhol refuses to maintain an absolute difference between these selves—inside and outside are reversible, as in *Outer and Inner Space*—but neither does he entirely collapse them. Rather his strategy is to identify precisely with those technologies that introduce the gaps or shifts in perspective in the first place: mirror, telephone, and television.

Consider this opening chapter's telephonic perspective. While A and B describe their morning rituals and dreams from the night before, a reader is kept constantly aware of the medium, a transcribed telephone call: twice B interrupts the conversation to go pee ("I took a dehydration pill and they make me pee every fifteen minutes" [5]), and once B yells, "I CAN'T HEAR YOU. I CAN'T UNDERSTAND WHAT YOU'RE SAYING" (7). This telephonic perspective becomes the reader's, who may also find it hard to follow the conversation since it's not always clear who is speaking. A reader becomes even more implicated in the dynamics of A's conversion to self when, in the middle of the chapter, the narrator offers a long, comic-virtuoso description of what he sees in the mirror when he puts himself together in the morning: "Nothing is missing. It's all there. The affectless gaze. The diffracted grace. . . . The bored languor, the wasted pallor. . . . The chic freakiness, the basically passive astonishment, the enthralling secret knowledge. . . . The glamour rooted in despair" (10). The list goes on and on, a collage of descriptions of Warhol taken from journalistic and other accounts.[47] "It's all there, B. Nothing is missing. I'm everything my scrapbook says I am" (10): the highly cultivated, and (I will return to this) entirely swish persona of Andy Warhol makes its familiar visual appearance to a reader who, the writing can assume, has seen this image many times before in magazines and on television.

Television is the primary technology in these dynamics of A's conversion to self. Not only is B watching television when he calls ("A? Wait and I'll turn off the TV" [5]), but she is also literally identified with television as "anybody who helps me kill time." A's first bit of philosophical meditation offers up his own identification with television—"A whole day of life is like a whole day of television. TV never goes off the air once it starts for the day, and I don't either" (5)—and he goes on to admit to "the great unfulfilled ambition of my life: my own regular TV show. I'm going to call it *Nothing Special*" (6). Andy Warhol's *Nothing Special*: in much the same way that commercial television juxtaposes news reports of mass death with advertisements for orange juice, the flat, even tone of the *Philosophy* weaves together meditations on life and death with descriptions of going to the bathroom. For example, a discussion of their scars segues quickly into B's account of A's shooting: "You were in a room in the intensive care unit, getting all these cards and presents from everybody, including me, but you wouldn't let me come and visit you because you thought I'd steal your pills. And you said you thought that coming so close to death was really like coming so close to life, because life is nothing" (12). Certainly the thematics of nothingness in this chapter could be read in relation to Warhol's near-death experience in the late spring of 1968. But I read nothingness in these pages primarily as an index to theatricality, to the defining, structural hollowness or void of the stage, the page, the screen, the canvas, and especially the tube.[48]

One way to redescribe Warhol's minimalism is in terms of his alignment with or his attempt to embody the hollowness of theatricality. His blankness and pallor, his white wig, the silver Factory are all images of this hollowness, the distance between feeling and image introduced by technologies of reproduction. I have shown how television in particular offered this distance, a shift in perspective on emotion that guided Warhol's art practices. Here I suggest that television guided his practices of self-conversion as well, eliciting his infamous "affectless gaze" that empties out expressiveness to make room for performance. As Warhol explains in *POPism*, "David [Bourdon] tells me that I used to be much friendlier, more open and ingenuous—right through to '64. 'You didn't have that cool, eyeball-through-the-wall, spaced look that you developed later on.' But I didn't *need* it then like I would later on."[49] Warhol develops his look (in both senses) only when he becomes a celebrated object of media attention, and his skill, in part, was in transforming (what he calls transmuting) this mass attention into a set of performance practices. Rather than affectless, I would characterize Warhol's look as casual or cool, and the flat or even tone of the *Philosophy* as its print equivalent: a cool look and tone that invite a minimum of judgment and a maximum of interest. Warhol describes this casual style later in the *Philosophy* as a way to keep in time: "Then there's that time on the street, when you run into somebody you haven't seen in, say, five years, and you play it all on one level.... Just a casual check-in. Very light, cool, off-hand, very American. Nobody's fazed, nobody's thrown out of time, nobody gets hysterical, nobody loses a beat.... Just play it all on one level, like everything was yesterday" (111). Warhol's cool style, keeping it all on one level, orients him to the present of experience. This is a version of an American poetics of the contemporary that connects him to John Cage, Gertrude Stein, and their predecessors, Emerson and William James. In Stein's poetics the space of psychic experience itself becomes theatricalized, creating an empty space that can accommodate the back-and-forth movements of proximity and distance in experiences of coming to new knowledge. For Warhol, the hollowness of theatricality serves a somewhat different therapeutic project, his conversion to self. "I have to go and dye. I haven't done it yet today," A says toward the end of the chapter, to which B replies, "Sometimes I'd like to pull your wig off but somehow I can't ever do it. I know how it would hurt you" (16).

Television is A's best B: it offers the most effective means for creating the protective, theatrical space that lets Warhol's self-conversion take place. Consider a story about television that takes place in the next chapter, titled "Love (Puberty)," which replays the dynamics of A's conversion to self in the register of memoir rather than seriocomic dialogue. The chapter begins with Warhol narrating his decision to seek psychiatric treatment: "At a certain point in my life, in the late 50s, I began to feel that I was picking up problems from the people I knew" (21). After a couple of pages of extraordinarily compressed life narrative Warhol describes how he bought his first television set on his way home from a session with a Greenwich Village psychiatrist, who, it turns out, never called him back to make another appointment: "Right away I forgot all about the psychiatrist. I kept the TV on all the time, especially when people were telling me their problems, and the television I found to be just diverting enough so the problems people told me didn't really affect me any more. It was like some kind of magic" (24). The reader is given the chance to identify with television precisely in this protective, therapeutic role. The compressed narration introduces readers to a younger Andy, inviting us to settle comfortably into our armchairs to make sense of the life of the artist. The *Reader's Digest* version of his past includes the three nervous breakdowns he had as a child, his immigrant father's absence and his mother's love, his sexual naïveté, move to New York City, gradual entry into commercial art, and frustrated desires for intimacy with many roommates. But our comfort (and superiority) is quickly disrupted by the story about television as the more reliable therapist that somehow offers him magical protection or a second skin to layer on his own famously sensitive skin; as he puts it toward the end of the chapter, "When I got my first TV set, I stopped caring so much about having close relationships with other people" (26). While the chapter tempts a reader to take up a diagnostic position—nothing would be easier than to point to Warhol's "problems" (his ironic code word for homosexuality)—it also lets us know that we don't have to practice such a version of pop psychiatry. Rather we can work our own televisual magic by accepting the Pop perspective offered by the tone of the writing, becoming one of Andy's Bs and protecting him from our own impingement on him (that is, our own envious desires, the very ones he elicits).

I find Warhol's story about television-as-therapist both funny and provocative: what could he possibly mean by television's magic? What's so funny (and is it discomfort or relief?) in the image of television as a successful rival to psychiatry in mid-twentieth-century America? Postwar medicalized psychiatry, with all its damaging homophobic and heteronormative authority over sexuality, was clearly not going to guide him through his process of conversion to self.[50] Television, on the other hand, just might. Young Andy's main professed problem is his susceptibility to vicarious identification, a theme that reappears later in the *Philosophy* when he describes losing his skin pigmentation as a child: "I saw a girl walking down the street and she was two-toned and I was so fascinated I kept following her. Within two months I was two-toned myself" (64). Two become one (becomes two again); this is a kind of love story, as indicated by the word *fascination*. (The end of the chapter "Love [Puberty]" introduces Warhol's interest in Edie Sedgwick by asserting, "The fascination I experienced was probably very close to a certain kind of love" [27].) Television lets Warhol cultivate intimacy as fascination. Not that his desire for intimacy ever diminishes. Consider that, in yet another reference to television in the *Philosophy*, he describes the pleasure of watching talk shows this way: "I'd love to be able to know everything about a person from watching them on television—to be able to tell *what their problem is*" (80). But television resists this diagnostic form of intimacy: "I would also be thrilled to be able to know what color eyes a person has just from looking at them, because color TV still can't help you too much there" (80). Rather than giving him knowledge of the problems of others, as psychiatry claims to do, television diverts his attention ("The television I found to be just diverting enough so the problems people told me didn't really affect me any more" [24]), converting intimacy to fascination. Warhol's vicariousness can then become a promiscuous relationship with television itself—"So in the late 50s I started an affair with my television which has continued to the present, when I play around in my bedroom with as many as four at a time" (26)—one of several tools for self-care. And he goes on: "But I didn't get married until 1964 when I got my first tape recorder. My wife" (26). Warhol explains the tape recorder's therapeutic power: "Nothing was ever a problem again, because a problem just meant a good tape, and when a problem transforms itself into a good tape it's not a problem anymore. An interesting problem was an interesting tape. Everybody knew that and performed for the tape. You couldn't tell which problems were real and which were exaggerated for the tape. Better yet, the people telling you the problems couldn't decide any more if they were really having the problems or if they were just performing" (26–27). If we remember the role of the tape recorder in the creation of the book we are reading, then this chapter about Warhol's problems is itself transformed and becomes a good (transcribed) tape, that is to say, an interesting performance.

Television's magic, like the tape recorder's, is the perspective it offers on emotion: its capacity to change problems into performances. The *Screen Tests* exemplify this kind of magic, offering an analytic perspective on his Bs that Warhol used both in his artwork (his poetics) and in his work on himself (his therapeutics). To cast my reading in the terms that Foucault offers, television permits Warhol to practice the therapeutic technique of converting one's vision in Hellenistic philosophy, a technique that is not in the service of knowing oneself, as it were, objectively, "not a movement of the mind or of attention that would lead us to detect everything bad in ourselves"; it permits us instead "to concentrate on keeping to the straight line we must follow in heading to our destination.... It is an exercise of the subject's concentration."[51] According to Foucault, the Hellenistic technique of vision offers an athletic discipline that permits us to "clear a space around the self, to think of the aim, or rather of the relation between yourself and the aim" (223). Television helps the workaholic Warhol convert his gaze toward his self, not to define and understand his own problems (as a normative psychiatry might) but to convert these problems into performances in the service of his primary aim or goal, as he gives it to readers in the opening chapter of the *Philosophy*: "I wish I could invent something like bluejeans. Something to be remembered for. Something mass" (13). The fundamental wish for what is mass—to turn himself into a mass object, like Levis—motivates Warhol's performance practices, and the televisual perspective lets him attend to this aim directly. In the late 1950s, Warhol tells us, he begins a process of conversion to self by way of television; by 1960 he is painting in his new Pop style; and by 1962 the Campbell's Soup cans introduce Warhol to a level of celebrity that no other postwar artist would receive. Television serves Warhol's practices of self-conversion: watching TV becomes a therapeutic technique for focusing his gaze on the mass.

It may help to clarify my reading here by comparing it with the only other in-depth reading of the figure of television in the *Philosophy* that I have seen, Steven Shaviro's essay "The Life, after Death, of Postmodern Emotions." Shaviro takes up a commonplace of recent and still contemporary discussions that casts postmodern emotion in terms of a combination of "terminal irony" and political helplessness, most famously captured by Fredric Jameson's phrase "the waning of affect."[52] This commonplace is structured by a set of oppositions that one could summarize as follows: Warhol chooses postmodern, posthuman surfaces over the depth orientation of an earlier modernist, humanist psychology. Shaviro reads Warhol's *Philosophy* in order to fill out the details that might make the commonplace convincing, noting that "Warhol credits the technologies of mass reproduction, the very ones that form the basis of his art, for killing off his emotions" (127) and emphasizing the role of television in this process: unlike movies (which, as we have seen, "make emotions look so strong and real"), television, due to its intimacy, its proximity to us, and the continuity of scale between us and it becomes the primary agent of postmodern simulation. Shaviro focuses on Warhol's camp irony as it becomes mainstreamed and co-opted by an overarching self-conscious, smug popular culture. His argument here resembles that of David Foster Wallace, who, in the essay "e unibus plurum: Television and U.S. Fiction," argues that what was once, in the 1960s, a politicized, critical ironic response to television was co-opted by television itself. Wallace goes on to diagnose the failure of writers of the 1980s to develop any alternatives to ironic detachment toward mass culture.[53] Unlike Wallace, Shaviro refuses nostalgia for modernist critique, embracing Warhol as "an exemplary postmodern aesthete" whose "self-described 'affectless gaze' of 'basically passive astonishment' is his updated version of Kantian disinterest."[54]

These descriptions of Warhol, as I pointed out earlier, are not Warhol's own but come from journalistic and other accounts. Shaviro accepts these as self-descriptions because they support the Christian model of conversion he is proposing: Warhol's emotions die to be reborn under the Enlightenment rubric of Kantian aesthetics and the disinterested contemplation of beauty. I have turned to Foucault's Hellenistic model of conversion as it offers an alternative precisely to such models of death and rebirth, especially as these tend to disembody or depoliticize by way of a decontaminating renunciation. It's worth observing that Warhol never describes his emotions as having been killed off. Rather he explains television's magic as a form of protection that offers a fascinated, analytic perspective on emotion: "During the 60s, I think, people forgot what emotions were supposed to be. And I don't think they ever remembered. I think that once you see emotions from a certain angle you can never think of them as real again."[55] Rather than killing off emotions, television's therapeutic angle lets Warhol see them not as marks of authenticity but as performance: emotion becomes theatricalized, the medium for the transferential relations between selves and technologies of reproduction. As I have demonstrated, this change in the status of emotion has a longer history than the twentieth-century transition from modernism to postmodernism: Warhol completes a trajectory from a Romantic to a post-Romantic theatricalization of writing and affect, from Poe via Stein to the postwar moment.

In my reading of the *Philosophy* television works as a therapeutic device that converts Warhol to a canny perspective on his self in a world of complex and ever-shifting relations of dependency, the mass consumer culture of postwar America that is governed, in part, by television itself. Warhol never disavowed his dependence on mass consumer culture and never stopped being the successful commercial artist he had become during the 1950s. Quite the opposite: after his success in fine art in the 1960s he sought ways to pursue what he called Business Art in the 1970s and 1980s, including the lucrative portrait projects, less commercially successful film and television productions, and *Interview* magazine. His full acknowledgment of mass consumer culture has proven difficult for critics to assess, more difficult, in some ways, than his sexuality. That these are related to one another is evident from a well-known story that Warhol tells in *POPism*: when he asks his friend Emile de Antonio why Jasper Johns and Robert Rauschenberg (homosexual artists who did commercial art pseudonymously) didn't like him, de Antonio says, "You're too swish, that's what upsets them."[56] De Antonio goes on to list Warhol's success as a commercial artist and his habit of collecting other artists' work ("Traditionally artists don't buy the work of other artists, it just isn't done" [14]) as strikes against Warhol, concluding, "The *major painters* [of Pop Art] try to look straight; you play up the swish—it's like an armor with you" (15). Warhol writes, "It was all too true. So I decided I just wasn't going to care, because those were all things that I didn't want to change anyway, that I didn't think I *should* want to change" (15). Warhol's therapeutics or care of self involved both an embrace of the New York gay and queer undergrounds and his own obsessive habits as a collector, as well as a refusal to give up his commercial art ambitions. His swishness, a key aspect of his self-presentation, can be read as a marker of sexuality and also an investment in elegance, fashion, style, smartness, the cutting edge.

Warhol's politics (in the conventional sense) may not have been radical (as Pat Hackett puts it, "Philosophically, Andy Warhol was a liberal Democrat, although he never voted because, he said, he didn't want to get called up for jury duty"),[57] but his therapeutic practices were: his powerful indifference ("I decided I just wasn't going to care") let him reject norms of sexual and artistic behavior. In the concluding pages of this chapter I briefly consider this indifference, and Warhol's therapeutics more generally, by way of Foucault's lectures on the ancient Cynics. At least three aspects of Warhol's self-presentations accord well with Cynic therapeutics: his outness, or his impulse to demystify, that is, to represent the scandal of the ordinary; his commitment to mistake, transmutation, or what I would call bad performance as a way of life; and a strategy of amplification or positive feedback. These are all related to one another as well as to basic Cynic principles, as Foucault explained them in his last course of lectures, *The Courage of Truth* (2011). Foucault argues that Cynicism is "the broken mirror, as it were, for ancient philosophy"; while Cynicism shares a number of basic principles with other schools of ancient Greek philosophy (the principles of care of self, of philosophy as preparation for life, and others), it differs in its direct and immediate linking of truth-telling to mode of life: "This is the kernel of Cynicism; practicing the scandal of truth in and through one's life."[58]

One main source of Cynic difference is the slogan or principle, given to Diogenes of Sinope by the Delphic oracle, to "alter the value of the currency" (238–39), an oracular pronouncement that, as Louisa Shea explains, can be read as "You must deface the social norms, you must alter the moral currency."[59] Foucault contrasts the Cynic slogan with the basic principle of Socratic philosophy, "Know yourself," and sketches two lines that develop from the philosophical principle of care of the self: the first leads by way of Plato and Western metaphysics to the contemplation of the soul and the "other world," the second to a radically "other life" (246) by way of Cynicism and its inheritors, a distinctively antitheoretical development that "gives rise to nothing more, in a sense, than Cynic crudeness" (247). Foucault offers a broad survey of this second line of Cynic development, not in philosophy itself so much as in anti-institutional forms of Christian asceticism, in militant revolutionary politics, and in European culture and art; describing what he calls the anti-Platonism and anti-Aristotelianism of modern art, he concludes that "modern art is Cynicism in culture" (189). Certainly Warhol can be located in this line of modern art, from Symbolism to Surrealism, Dada to Pop and punk, each of which might productively be read along the lines of the Cynic principle "Give a new stamp to the common currency."

A primary technique for achieving this goal was the Cynic practice of shamelessness and exposure described as living a dog's life. Foucault points out that the dog's life takes to its logical extreme the Stoic ideal of the unconcealed life, "no longer an ideal principle of conduct ... [but] the staging of life in its material and everyday reality under the real gaze of others, of everyone else, or at any rate of the greatest possible number of others" (253). For the Cynic who masturbates in the marketplace (as Diogenes was said to do), nonconcealment is "the blaze of the human being's naturalness in full view of all" (254). Warhol's films operate with this logic of letting it all hang out, a demystifying or deflating of conventions and norms of behavior that he describes in the *Philosophy* this way: "I love every 'lib' movement there is, because after the 'lib' the things that were always a mystique become understandable and boring, and then nobody has to feel left out if they're not part of what is happening" (45). In much of his film and video work Warhol stages the unconcealed life in its everydayness, making the improper into something ordinary or banal.[60] Television, in the genre of reality TV, has become central to the practice of depicting versions of the unconcealed life, but in the *Philosophy* such televised self-exposures and shameless performances appear as part of an explicitly political discourse. In the opening chapter, B presents a fantasy of Warhol's presidency, which involves "a nightly talk show— your own talk show as President. You'd have somebody else come on, the other President that's the President for you, and he would talk your diary out to the people, every night for half an hour" (13). This version of Andy Warhol's Nothing Special offers a pastiche of Roosevelt's Fireside Chats, but rather than exploiting the intimacy of broadcasting for the purposes of political governance, Warhol offers up the diary genre only to delink it from confession and authenticity. (Indeed *Andy Warhol's Diaries* reveals not Warhol's thoughts and feelings but the amount of money he spends on taxis, dinners, parties, and the general comings and goings of a complex network of acquaintances.)

Warhol's ideas about what we now call reality TV are politically inflected throughout the *Philosophy*. For example, after noting a basic contradiction in the American ideal of classlessness—"Somebody still has to do it" (99)—Warhol pitches the following television show: "If the President would go into a public bathroom in the Capitol, and have the TV camera film him cleaning the toilets and saying 'Why not? Somebody's got to do it!' then that would do so much for the morale of the people who do the wonderful job of keeping the toilets clean" (100). In his persona of ingénue, he goes on to elaborate the show's premise: the president "should just sit down one day and make a list of all the things that people are embarrassed to do that they shouldn't be embarrassed to do, and then do them all on television" (100). As faux-naïve as this sounds, Warhol still offers a Cynic use of television that presents the performance of normatively shameful activities in front of as many people as possible as a form of public therapeutics.[61] By contrast with Warhol's show idea, consider the game shows that Chuck Barris began inventing in the 1960s (*The Dating Game*, *The Newlywed Game*) and brought to perfected form with *The Gong Show* (1976): like the more recent reality programs that descend from them, these game shows demand that their viewers experience all the shame or embarrassment that contestants don't. (In other words, the audience gets cast as at once naïve and knowing.) Warhol's program reverses this premise, accommodating rather than projecting shame. And while Barris and Warhol share a keen interest in bad performance, Barris's shows aim to elicit Schadenfreude in viewers, whereas Warhol looks for a very different pleasure: "I can only understand really amateur performers or really bad performers, because whatever they do never really comes off, so therefore it can't be phoney" (82). For Warhol, bad performance has the advantage of relieving epistemological pressures on authenticity, something that reality TV, with its generic insistence on "reality," never manages to do.

Bad performance also makes available the experience of surprise: "What I like are things that are different every time. That's why I like amateur performers and bad performers—you can never tell what they'll do next" (82). This interest in the surprises of bad performance is closely related to Warhol's preference for misunderstandings: "Something that I look for in an associate is a certain amount of misunderstanding of what I'm trying to do. Not a fundamental misunderstanding; just minor misunderstandings here and there.... When you work with people who misunderstand you, instead of getting *transmissions* you get *transmutations*, and that's much more interesting in the long run" (99). Like Gertrude Stein, who values words to the degree that they can be mistaken, Warhol enjoys the noisy, positive feedback and lively surprises that accompany a good compositional game of broken telephone.

I have read Warhol's "from A to B and back again" in terms of a cybernetic definition of circular causality, and now I would like to modify this reading: whereas most cyberneticians focus on negative feedback, crucial for establishing stability or equilibrium (in homeostatic systems, say), Warhol sought out a certain amount of positive feedback for the purposes of transmutation. I mean positive feedback in the colloquial sense as well as the technical one, Warhol's consistent exclamations of pleasure ("Gee! That's fantastic!") working to amplify the activities of his associates or assistants rather than subduing or correcting them. Not that Warhol wasn't capable of subduing his associates, but he seemed to prefer to use positive feedback as a technique. Hackett describes Warhol's "three ways of dealing with employee incompetence," one of which was to "break into an impromptu imitation of the person—never a literal one, but rather *his* interpretation of *their* vision of themselves—and it was always funny."[62] The technique of noisy or positive feedback serves Warhol (paradoxically perhaps) as a control strategy, for example when he gives out different stories about his childhood in interviews, as he explains in the *Philosophy*: "I used to like to give different information to different magazines because it was like putting a tracer on where people get their information. That way I could always tell when I met people what newspapers and magazines they were reading by the things they would tell me I had said" (79). Rather than playing into mass journalism's efforts to establish stability and consensus through the correction of mistake, Warhol destabilizes the directional flows of communication to bring information about readers to him.

Such reversals accompany what Foucault describes as "the systematic practice of dishonor" in Cynic philosophy: "Dishonor is actually sought after by the Cynics who actively look for humiliating situations which are valuable because they train the Cynic in resistance to everything to do with opinions, beliefs, and conventions."[63] Foucault suggests another reason for the Cynic's interest in seeking out such situations: "Within the accepted humiliation, one is able to turn the situation around, as it were, to take back control of it" (261). He tells the story of a dinner at which Diogenes, called the Dog, was thrown a bone—which he accepted only to lift his leg and piss on the guests. Warhol's many interviews exemplify this kind of amplification and redirection, a reversal of control that brings the interviewers' assumptions and the norms and conventions of the interview genre itself into question. Similarly his seeking out of embarrassing moments in his films and other performances serves as a strategy that aims to discover or uncover both what is present and what is actually necessary, the amplification of convention until its contingency or gratuity can be perceived. This strategy offers one way to understand the last chapter of Warhol's *Philosophy*, "Underwear Power" or "What I Do on Saturday When My Philosophy Runs Out," in which he shops for underwear at Macy's with one of his Bs. This would initially appear to be as un-Cynical an activity as possible, especially given Foucault's discussion of the Cynic "conduct of poverty" as the limit case of philosophical indifference to material goods.[64] In late twentieth-century America, however, buying takes on a different set of meanings than in ancient Athens: "Buying is much more American than thinking and I'm as American as they come" (229).

Consider the fact that through the 1970s and 1980s Warhol went shopping for several hours every day before going to his office, eventually accumulating more than $25 million worth of consumer goods, most of which were boxed up and put into storage; these more than six hundred boxes have come to be understood as an extensive art-and-collecting project, Warhol's Time Capsules.[65] The everyday objects in these boxes range from financial papers to newspaper clippings, photobooth strips that Warhol would use as the basis for portraits, postcards, letters, other people's manuscripts, food, toys, and more. Taken out of circulation and use, these objects become (more or less enigmatic) indexes to Warhol's life, and at the same time art objects of a kind: Warhol wanted to offer the sealed boxes for sale at a gallery show, all at the same price (initially $100, but later in his life $4,000 to $5,000). His extraordinary amplification of U.S. habits of consumption both exaggerated his responsibility as an American to be a consumer of global commodities in his historical moment and cannily repackaged the everyday objects that gave him the idea for many of his Pop artworks. Here again are Warhol's Bs, ideas from the outside that, boxed and put into storage, reemerge later (from B to A and back again) with a different value. And how much of a stretch would it be to think of these boxes as Warhol's televisions, his boxes that contain, and later deliver, the detritus of a Cynic mode of life, so many episodes of nothing special? Give a new stamp to the common currency indeed, for better and for worse.

Out and Across

Morton Feldman, the great mid-twentieth-century American (Brooklyn-born, Russian Jewish) composer whose music is as lush, spare, and quiet as his person was large, brash, and obnoxious, liked to tell a story about what he learned from the transplanted French composer Edgard Varèse. I take this story from a transcription of a seminar Feldman gave in Frankfurt in 1984:

> I had one lesson on the street with Varèse, one lesson on the street, it lasted half a minute, it made me an orchestrator. He said, "What are you writing now, Morton?" I told him. He says, "Make sure you think about the time it takes from the stage to go out there into the audience. Let me know when you get a performance, I'd like to hear it." And he walked away. That was my one lesson, it took an instant, one lesson and I started out, I was about seventeen when I knew him, and from then on, I started to listen.[1]

I would like to end my study with a little reading of this story so that I can sketch, quickly and with a few broad strokes, several key aspects of the poetics that I have called *transferential*. I might just as well have called these poetics *out there* since the work of all the thinkers, writers, and artists I have discussed can be characterized as *out there* or, more simply, *out*. I am using this term primarily in a musical rather than a sexual sense. I first encountered this musical meaning about fifteen years ago in a New York record store that used the term *out* to name a kind of music that was otherwise difficult or impossible to classify. Unlike the categories of experimental, avant-garde, or contemporary, which it closely resembles, the idea of out music comes (as far as I can tell) from jazz improvisation and the practice of playing out: playing outside the melody or rhythm, and ultimately playing out at the very edge of the performer's abilities to make musical sense. Even when it owes little or nothing to jazz sounds or idioms (as in Feldman's work), out music gets way out there in its expressive means and commitments. These are the meanings of *out* that I want meditate on briefly by way of conclusion.

In the story that Feldman tells, Varèse directs the younger composer to pay attention not primarily to a composition's structure or musical form but to "the time it takes from the stage to go out there into the audience." This is not the conventional emphasis on temporality in composition (time signature) or even performance (tempo) but something else: the temporality of audience reception. What could this mean? One clue lies in Feldman's statement that Varèse's lesson made him into "an orchestrator," that is, the person responsible for instrumentation and musical arrangement. An orchestrator knows the distinctive characteristics of musical instruments and, often, performers and deals in dynamics, tonal registers, timbres, how notes vary depending on acoustic source and performance technique. Composition-as-orchestration, Feldman's story suggests, should include thinking about the pragmatics of instrumentation and arrangement, not only musical form but also force: the physical properties of instruments, the specific qualities of the players, those elements that somehow affect listeners most directly. Here is one important aspect of the work of the writers and thinkers that I have studied in this book: an attention, in aesthetic composition, to the idiosyncrasies of materials in performance as it conditions the movement *out there* from composition to audience and back again.

Feldman tends to compose with a few notes spaced out over great (sometimes extreme) lengths of time. As Alex Ross describes it, "In confining himself to so little material, Feldman releases the expressive power of the space around the notes. The sounds animate the surrounding silence."[2] Feldman's use of expressive silences in his compositions brings me to another and related aspect of *out there* poetics: the quality of listening or receptiveness. Both heroes in his story, Varèse the teacher ("I'd like to hear it") and Feldman the student ("I started to listen"), take up the role of careful and interested listener. Feldman's work tries to induce this attitude of receptiveness in performers as well as audiences. In a set of liner notes for the album *New Directions in Music 2* (1959) the poet Frank O'Hara described the role of unpredictability in Feldman's early piano works, written using a graphic notation that required a performer to choose which specific notes to play (within given ranges) during a performance. "In Feldman's work unpredictability involves the performer and audience much in the same way it does the composer, inviting an increase of sensitivity and intensity," O'Hara writes. "What Feldman is assuming, and it is a courageous assumption, is that the performer is a sensitive and inspired musician who has the best interests of the work at heart."[3] In Feldman's musical compositions receptiveness involves listening in a way that is potentially contagious: if the performer listens to the demands of the composition, then the audience may find itself doing something similar. This is another aspect of *out there* poetics: reception, or the act of listening, can re-create the space of composition.

Such receptiveness can have dramatic consequences. In Feldman's story young Morton is, in an "instant," transformed and launched into lifelong listening and composing habits. The drama of receptiveness and sudden change can take place anywhere, anytime, in a concert hall audience paying to listen to contemporary music or as a result of a chance encounter on the street. The high theatricality of this drama is communicated through Feldman's rhythmic, repetitive style: "one lesson on the street with Varèse, one lesson on the street, it lasted half a minute." About half a minute is as long as this story takes to tell. One way that Feldman transfers his exchange from street to seminar room is by reproducing the temporal frame of the experience, with its dramatic structure of endings ("And he walked away") leading to new beginnings ("I started out"). Street theater can become pedagogy because Feldman's style reflexively insists on the performativity of everyday conversation in which verbal instruction takes instant effect as an act of almost magical transformation.

These are some of the key characteristics of the *out there* or transferential poetics that I have discussed in this book: a close attention to the materialities of compositional force, a commitment to listening as it re-creates the space of composition, and a keen interest in the transforming possibilities of theatricality and the theatricalization of writing. My work in this book has banked on a nervy commitment to paying attention to affective responses as they can make us acquainted with what motivates composition. In an earlier, twentieth-century moment indebted to classical Freudian theory, this kind of inquiry into motivation would have been characterized as trying to go deep. But the works of Poe, James, Klein, Stein, Tomkins, Bion, Warhol, Feldman, and others invite critics to describe and understand the phenomena of feeling and thinking as they go out and across.

Notes

Introduction: Affect in the Scene of Writing

1. Sedgwick and Frank, "Shame in the Cybernetic Fold." This essay, lightly revised, became the introduction to Tomkins, *Shame and Its Sisters*.

2. Tomkins, *Affect Imagery Consciousness*, 2: 230. Unless otherwise noted, citations of Tomkins's work will be to *Affect Imagery Consciousness*, hereafter *AIC*.

3. Sedgwick, "Paranoid Reading and Reparative Reading," in *Touching Feeling*, 133. More extensive discussions of Tomkins's notion of theory appear in Sedgwick and Frank, "Shame in the Cybernetic Fold" as well as in Frank, "Phantoms Limn."

4. The phrase *affective turn* is from the title of a book edited by Patricia Clough, one among many publications that mark this moment in literary and cultural criticism. A very short, selected list of such publications might include Terada, *Feeling in Theory*; Massumi, *Parables for the Virtual*; Cvetkovich, *An Archive of Feelings*; Ngai, *Ugly Feelings*; Thrailkill, *Affecting Fictions*; Clough, *The Affective Turn*; Gregg and Seigworth, *The Affect Theory Reader*; Wilson, *Affect and Artificial Intelligence*. For an essay review of some earlier work in this field that considers the motivation for the turn to affect, see Frank, "Some Avenues for Feeling." For critiques of this turn, see Hemmings, "Invoking Affect"; Papoulias and Callard, "Biology's Gift"; Leys, "The Turn to Affect." For a response to Leys, see Frank and Wilson, "Like-minded." The interest in affect and emotion crosses disciplinary boundaries, reaching across philosophy, social theory, geography, psychology, and neuroscience. There is no current consensus in the sciences or humanities on a theory of affect or emotion.

5. Winter, *Freud and the Institution of Psychoanalytic Knowledge*; Felman, "To Open the Question."

6. For a useful historical approach to the idea of medium and the possibility of criticism across mediums, see Guillory, "Genesis of the Media Concept."

7. See especially works by Massumi and Clough. For exceptions, see Cartwright, *Moral Spectatorship*; Lane, *Feeling Cinema*; Gibbs, "Panic!"

8. See the chapter "Freedom of the Will and the Structure of the Affect System" in *AIC* volume 1 for Tomkins's emendation of Freud's drive theory. For a comparative discussion of Freud and Tomkins, especially with regard to the ideas of repression and civilization, see Frank, "Some Affective Bases for Guilt."

9. I emphasize that Tomkins's writing offers affect as an object of and for understanding. Brian Massumi offers a very different approach in *Parables for the Virtual*, where he defines affect as unqualified intensity in sharp contrast to emotion: "An emotion is a subjective content, the sociolinguistic fixing of the quality of an experience which is from that point onward defined as personal. Emotion is qualified intensity, the conventional, consensual point of insertion of intensity into semantically and semiotically formed progressions, into narrativizable action-reaction circuits, into function and meaning. It is intensity owned and recognized. It is crucial to theorize the difference between affect and emotion.... Affect is unqualified. As such, it is not ownable or recognizable and is thus resistant to critique" (28). Where affect, in Massumi's understanding, is presubjective and nonlinguistic, taking place in the half-second before representation and ideology have intervened, emotion is affect temporalized and domesticated by discourse and language. This emotion/affect distinction, which echoes a certain modernist rejection of emotion or sentiment in favor of an aestheticized sensation that grounds response, has the (to my mind) unfortunate consequence of making affect unavailable to qualitative criticism. By defining affect as unqualified intensity—an arousal that discourse must interpret if it is to be given quality—Massumi reintroduces the language/body opposition that the category of affect promised to suspend or complicate. Tomkins's distinction between affect and emotion, in which affects are like basic atoms and emotions complex molecules, requires no such rigid opposition.

10. Tomkins, "Inverse Archaeology: Facial Affect and the Interfaces of Scripts within and between Persons," in *Exploring Affect*, 285.

11. Tomkins's cybernetic approach to the faciality of affect should be contrasted with approaches to the face as a display of internal states. For Tomkins, the information that the face offers is complex and difficult to assess because of our tendency to experience multiple affects simultaneously, assembled with one another and with cognitions and drive states, all embedded in complex theories and scripts. For an engaging discussion of the face as the site of affect, see Cole, *About Face*.

12. For Tomkins's discussions of ideology and affect, see the chapter "Ideology and Anger" in *AIC*, volume 3 and the section "Affect and Ideology," in *Exploring Affect*.

13. Freud, "Fragment of an Analysis of Hysteria (Dora)," 534.

14. Klein, "The Origins of Transference," in *Envy and Gratitude*, 48.

15. Hinshelwood, *A Dictionary of Kleinian Thought*, 465.

16. Klein, "Origins of Transference," 54.

17. In this respect I follow Sedgwick's use of both these theorists in her writing. See, for example, her essays "Paranoid Reading and Reparative Reading," and "Melanie Klein and the Difference Affect Makes," in *The Weather in Proust*.

18. On Descartes, see Roach, *The Player's Passion*, 60–65. On Smith, see Marshall, *The Figure of Theater*; Agnew, *Worlds Apart*. On Darwin, see Prodger, *Darwin's Camera*.

19. Unless otherwise specified, my citations to this essay are to Derrida, *Writing and Difference*. The quotation about affectivity is from "Force and Signification" in the same work: "The will and the attempt to write are not the desire to write, for it is

a question here not of affectivity but of freedom and duty. In its relationship to Being, the attempt-to-write poses itself as the only way out of affectivity" (13). To my mind, such moral-ontological questions of freedom and duty are built out of affective elements or primitive object relations, even when they are subsequently opposed to them.

20. Johnson, *System and Writing*, 67. I have also found Elizabeth Wilson's work helpful for understanding Derrida's essay. See Wilson, *Neural Geographies*. Both Wilson and Johnson link Derrida's thinking with work in the fields of cybernetics, systems theory, and connectionism in cognitive science, giving context for the transdisciplinary nature of his work.

21. Derrida, *Of Grammatology*, 84, 85.

22. For a different approach to Derrida and emotion, one that pursues the consequences of accepting the affect/emotion distinction and is primarily concerned with emotion as representation of self in a Cartesian theater of mind, see Terada, *Feeling in Theory*. For another exploration of Derrida's use of the theatrical metaphor, see Ross, "Derrida's Writing-Theatre."

23. Artaud, "The Theatre of Cruelty," 59.

24. Johnson, *System and Writing*, 211.

25. Artaud, "Theatre of Cruelty," 61.

26. See Wilden, "Analog and Digital Communication."

27. For a similar approach to the relations between on stage and off, see Güçbilmez, "An Uncanny Theatricality."

28. I emphasize that affect is only one form of this relation to the other, a form this relation takes especially in humans and other animals with affect systems, that is, motile animals. The question of whether affect should also name this relation to the other in living organisms that do not move, or in inanimate objects, is beyond the scope of this discussion.

29. Goldberg, *Writing Matter*, 24.

30. Ibid., 310.

31. For an example of this earlier approach, see Frank, "Valdemar's Tongue, Poe's Telegraphy."

32. For an approach to Derrida's essay that arrives at a similar conclusion about the importance of television, although along very different argumentative lines, see Clough, "The Technical Substrates of Unconscious Memory," in *Autoaffection*. See too Elsaesser, "Freud as Media Theorist."

33. Bateson, "A Theory of Play and Fantasy," in *Steps to an Ecology of Mind*, 177–93. This essay first appeared in *A.P.A. Psychiatric Research Reports* 2 (1955). In *System and Writing*, Christopher Johnson notes several conceptual similarities between Bateson and Derrida.

34. Bateson, "A Theory of Play," 180. Bateson argues that the nip is of a higher logical type than the bite that is being simulated; translated into speech, the playful nip is saying something like "This is not a bite," which is a higher order message than the bite itself. He then theorizes that "every metacommunicative message"—that is, every communication about communication—"is or defines a psychological frame" (188). This frame determines the interpretive relations within it since everything that takes place within the frame is supposed to be of the same logical type. Bateson insists that these metacommunicative frames are necessarily labile and can disappear: the nip can suddenly become a bite, or love in the psychoanalytic transference can become realized.

35. Here's another example of affective metacommunication: if a child falls, and the fall is not too painful, the child will often look at his or her parent or guardian to find out how to interpret the experience. Is it an injury or simply an accident? If an accident, is it funny, distressing, or angering? Any significant pain will tend to determine the experience in favor of injury and distress, but often the parent's expression can trigger the frame in which the child will then interpret his or her experience. Here the parent's affect acts as a metacommunication that informs the child about how to interpret.

36. Williams, "Drama in a Dramatised Society," 4.

37. Sedgwick, *Touching Feeling*, 8.

1 / Thinking Confusion: On the Compositional Aspect of Affect

1. Laplanche and Pontalis, *The Language of Psycho-Analysis*, 14.

2. Stein added the title when Leonard Woolf of the Hogarth Press agreed to publish the lecture in June 1926, just after it was delivered. The version I am using appears in *A Stein Reader*, 493–503. For detailed context on the lecture's writing, delivery, and publication, see Dydo and Rice, *Gertrude Stein*, 77–132.

3. Stein, "Poetry and Grammar," in *Lectures in America*, 209.

4. Meyer, *Irresistible Dictation*, 105.

5. As an ontological aside, I would speculate that Stein's commitment to the liveliness of words can be read as part of a long history of nonreductive materialist theories of nature, examples of which can be seen in traditions of Epicurean atomism; in Spinoza's monist thinking, in which all things are animate to different degrees; in some eighteenth-century vitalism; in the early Derrida's understanding of a generalized notion of writing; and in notions of autopoiesis or self-generation as theorized by later twentieth-century biology and informed by complexity theory. Here I will simply point to research that explores such theories and their relations more fully, such as Jonathan Goldberg's *The Seeds of Things* and Jessica Riskin's recent work on Leibniz. I also observe in many of these philosophies a central concern with affect and feeling as these index a fundamental continuity between self and world. Stein's emphasis on enjoyment, activity, and complexity recalls some central propositions and attitudes in Spinoza's *Ethics* (123–31): his emphasis on joy as a mark of activity of the mind and his discussion of the composite nature of bodies and minds insofar as they take such composite bodies as objects of ideas (2: P13–P18).

6. Stein, "Poetry and Grammar," 211.

7. James had been a reader for Singer's dissertation, submitted to the Philosophy Department at Penn in 1894, titled "On the Composite Nature of Consciousness." The term *composite* appears to be linked to a turn-of-the-century problem in the philosophy and psychology in which James trained all his students, "the self-compounding of consciousness." One analysis of this technical metaphysical problem suggests that it was also a social and political problem: how to theorize relations between individual and group consciousness. According to Francesca Bordogna, James gave up the logical principle of identity in committing to a notion of "flux," flow, or stream, in which no boundaries separate any bit of experience from another. Stein, in her approach to composition, does not take this route; if she gives up any of the primary logical principles, it is the law of the excluded middle. See Bordogna, "Inner Division and Uncertain Contours," 532.

Singer is best known as one of the founders of the journal *Philosophy of Science* (started January 1934); he was an influential teacher for later participants in the field of operations research. (Two of his students, C. West Churchman and Russell Ackoff, went on to management studies and social science work in operations research.) Thanks to my colleague Alan Richardson at the University of British Columbia for information about Edgar Singer and his context.

8. Sedgwick, *Touching Feeling*, 13.
9. Stein, "Portraits and Repetition," in *Lectures in America*, 173.
10. Stein, "Paintings," in *Lectures in America*, 87.
11. Arguably some key elements of Clement Greenberg's aesthetic writings (especially his early work) are interpretations of Stein's published lectures and her book on Picasso. I have made this argument in "Two Fat Jews: Morton Feldman and Gertrude Stein," given at the conference Queer Performance in the Americas: 1945–1954 at Yale University, April 4, 2004.
12. Stein, "Portraits and Repetition," 173.
13. Hinshelwood, Robinson, and Zarate, *Introducing Melanie Klein*, 88.
14. Stein, *The Autobiography of Alice B. Toklas*, 79.
15. Despite her public rejection of psychoanalysis, as Brenda Wineapple notes, privately Stein considered Freud "a stage one must go through." Wineapple, *Sister Brother*, 316.
16. Hejinian, "Three Lives," 286, emphasis in the original.
17. Stein, "Poetry and Grammar," 238.
18. Howe, *My Emily Dickinson*, 13.
19. Stein, *Tender Buttons*, 461.
20. Stein, "Poetry and Grammar," 235.
21. Ibid., 236–37.
22. Stein, *Tender Buttons*, 470.
23. Ibid., 496.
24. Hinshelwood, *A Dictionary of Kleinian Thought*, 32. See Hinshelwood's essay on unconscious phantasy.
25. Ibid., 37.
26. Isaacs's paper was first published in 1948.
27. Likierman, *Melanie Klein*, 139.
28. Ibid.; Isaacs, "The Nature and Function of Phantasy," 277.
29. Hinshelwood, *Dictionary of Kleinian Thought*, 34.
30. Likierman, *Melanie Klein*, 140.
31. Isaacs, "The Nature and Function of Phantasy," 274, 283, 284, emphasis in the original.
32. Glover in ibid., 326, 327.
33. Hinshelwood, *Dictionary of Kleinian Thought*, 440.
34. Klein, "Envy and Gratitude," in *Envy and Gratitude*, 184.
35. Laplanche and Pontalis, *Language of Psycho-Analysis*, 101.
36. Interestingly the negative affect of shame is not observable at birth but, according to Tomkins, appears some time between the third and seventh month of the first year of life, around the time the infant comes to recognize the mother's face. Also unlike what I am proposing that we think of as the "death-instinct" affects, shame works to help compose a sense of self even while it renders that self unbearably visible

or exposed. For more on the compatibilities between Tomkins's theory of shame and Klein's depressive position, see Frank, "Some Affective Bases for Guilt."

37. Stein, *Picasso*, 14–15.
38. Stein, "Portraits and Repetition," 174.

2 / Expression and Theatricality, or Medium Poe

1. Spiegelman and Kidd, *Jack Cole and Plastic Man*.
2. Ellison, *Cato's Tears and the Making of Anglo-American Emotion*.
3. Smith, *The Theory of Moral Sentiments*, 9.
4. See the section titled "Restrictions of Freedom Inherent in the Affect System," in *AIC* 1: 143–49.
5. Borch-Jacobsen, *The Emotional Tie*. For a related argument, see Chertok and Stengers, *A Critique of Psychoanalytic Reason*.
6. Poe, "Letter to B—," in *Edgar Allan Poe: Essays and Reviews*, 11. The emphasis is Poe's here and in all subsequent quotations.
7. Poe, "The Philosophy of Composition," in *Edgar Allan Poe: Essays and Reviews*, 16.
8. Poe, *Edgar Allan Poe: Tales and Sketches*, 1: 310, 1: 378. The citations are to "Ligeia" and "The Man That Was Used Up." All subsequent references to Poe's tales are from these volumes. Because these are paginated sequentially, I omit the volume number.
9. Silverman, *Edgar A. Poe*.
10. See Meredith McGill's discussion of Poe's techniques of deracination in *American Literature and the Culture of Reprinting*, 155–164.
11. Muller and Richardson, *The Purloined Poe*.
12. For a reading of the facial dynamics in "The Purloined Letter" that uses Tomkins's affect theory to locate the specific role for contempt in the dynamics of analysis, see Frank, "The Letter of the Laugh."
13. Elmer, *Reading at the Social Limit*, 50.
14. For more on how Poe's writing allegorizes and manipulates serial readers, as well as on the specifically telegraphic nature of Poe's tales of mesmerism, see Frank, "Valdemar's Tongue, Poe's Telegraphy."
15. McMaster, *The Index of the Mind*. Poe was likely familiar with materialist theories of expression based on physiological theories of function and potentially more integrated mind-body relations. These emerged, in part, from physiognomic theory but came to compete with the forms of theological explanation on offer, often substituting functionalist explanations for expression. See Hartley, *Physiognomy and the Meaning of Expression in Nineteenth-Century Culture*.
16. Ginzburg, "Clues." See also Benjamin, "On Some Motifs in Baudelaire."
17. More precisely, what so excited Tomkins and others taken by the theoretical power of cybernetics was "the capacity of certain complex physical systems, through their behavior, to mimic—to *simulate*—the manifestations of what in everyday language, unpurified by scientific rigor, we call purposes and ends, even intention and finality." Dupuy, *The Mechanization of the Mind*, 9. The cybernetic simulation of purposive behavior seemed to obviate the need to posit mystified or reified notions of will or intention.
18. See "The Dynamics of Enjoyment-Joy: The Social Bond," in *AIC* 1: 419 and following.

19. In this context see Tomkins's corrective of the psychoanalytic use of the term *anxiety* to name psychic suffering generally and his proposal that "the intense form of fear now known as anxiety be replaced by the word *terror*, which has not yet lost its affective connotation" (*AIC* 3: 494). However, I suggest that the term *anxiety* might still be useful to describe the effect of suppression: anxiety takes place when any affect inhibits any other. This suggestion attempts to bridge Tomkins's affect theory with various psychoanalytic definitions of anxiety in terms of internal conflict between instincts.

20. One answer to this question would characterize the tale as a case study in over-the-top Oedipal paranoia: the narrator, wracked with guilt for the crime of murder, and for whatever imagined or real transgressions preceded the murder, confesses in order to create the conditions for his own punishment. The eye, in a classical psychoanalytic reading, would stand in for the authoritative, punitive superego (or ego ideal) that the narrator projects outward and seeks to destroy. The tale's attractions involve both the narrator's marked success and his equally marked failure, his successful destruction of the eye followed by his confession to the crime, which ensures his own punishment. This reading, convincing as far as it goes, unproblematically accepts the Romantic equivalence of the eye and the I without explaining the substitution; it leaves out the variety of affects that the tale puts into circulation in favor of an analysis solely in terms of guilt; most important, it leaves out the reader, who, I have been arguing, is the primary object of Poe's stories.

For readings of this tale in relation to mid-nineteenth-century psychology and notions of paranoia, see Bynum, "'Observe How Healthily—How Calmly I Can Tell You the Whole Story'"; Zimmerman, "'Moral Insanity' or Paranoid Schizophrenia."

21. See Tomkins's discussion "Shame-Humiliation and the Taboos on Looking," in *AIC* 2: 157–83. These taboos supplement those of psychoanalysis—on incest and homosexuality, or sex with the self-same, however that gets defined—with a set of taboos that do not begin with or assume a notion of sameness. For a reading of these taboos vis-à-vis Freud's essay on the uncanny, see Frank, "Phantoms Limn."

22. For a somewhat different approach to the question of audience embarrassment, see Ridout, *Stage Fright, Animals, and Other Theatrical Problems*.

23. Smith, *Theory of Moral Sentiments*, 21–22.

24. The model for Smith's scenes of sympathy or imaginative identification and judgment is the "attentive spectator" at the theater. His general definition of sympathy as "our fellow-feeling with any passion whatever" assumes that imaginative identification takes place in an interior space figured by the theater, where passions can be properly situated. See Marshall, "Adam Smith and the Theatricality of Moral Sentiments," in *The Figure of Theater*. I return to Smith's theory in relation to theatricality in chapter 4.

25. For Smith, the visual sense acts to control or regulate emotion, otherwise potentially unregulated by the communication of sound. Contemporary with Smith's writing on sympathy were J. J. Quantz's careful and complicated instructions for using pulsations of the heart to measure musical tempo (adagio, andante, etc.), which were initially introduced to indicate the mood or character of music but acquired meanings associated with measured time. Chronometers and metronomes using clockwork mechanisms became popular for keeping musical time in the early nineteenth century: Maelzel is the name most associated with the metronome, the same who appears in Poe's article "Maelzel's Chess Player." Regulating emotion by mechanizing musical

tempo becomes thinkable through these texts and machines. See Harding, *The Metronome and It's* [sic] *Precursors*.

26. A more historicist reading of this tale could understand Poe to be exaggerating and exploding Smith's theory of sympathy and offering a burlesque of the liberal national politics subtended by it. See Agnew, *World's Apart* for Smith's psychological system's "resemblance to the market imperatives from which it presumably stood apart" (186). See too Jones, "The Danger of Sympathy."

27. Warhol, *Having a Good Cry*.

28. This image originally appeared as a cover of the March/April 1996 issue of the comics anthology *Zero Zero*, ed. Kim Thompson (Seattle: Fantagraphics Books, 1996).

29. See Smith, *The Poe Cinema*; Smith, *Poe in the Media*.

30. See Elmer, *Reading at the Social Limit* for a theorization of Poe's writing as exemplary of mass culture.

3 / Maisie's Spasms: Transferential Poetics in Henry James and Wilfred Bion

1. James, *What Maisie Knew*, 22.

2. On this projection of gender and other questions of the ethics of reading, see Miller, "Reading, Doing," 72.

3. Bion, *Experiences in Groups and Other Papers*, 25. The "Committee" here is the Professional Committee of the Tavistock Clinic that encouraged Bion to explore his techniques of group therapy.

4. Hinshelwood, *Dictionary of Kleinian Thought*, 235.

5. For a discussion of a transpersonal space of thinking in James, see Sharon Cameron, *Thinking in Henry James*, especially 63–76 on *Maisie*. Cameron's concern here is with "tension arising from the shifting barrier between consciousness and repression" (64), whereas my reading orients not toward a classical psychoanalytic understanding of repression but toward an object-relations approach to phantasies of the group.

6. These observations arose in the graduate seminar Affect, Print and Film held at the University of British Columbia in the fall of 2005. I am grateful to the seminar participants: Kate Hallemeier, Matt Hiebert, Matthew Kennedy, Victoria Killington, Rachel Kruger, and Peter Sun.

7. Harvey, "Kleinian Developmental Narrative and James' *What Maisie Knew*."

8. James, *The Complete Notebooks*, 161–62.

9. See Novick, "Henry James on Stage" for a useful alternative to Leon Edel's version in *Henry James: A Life*.

10. For an example of a reading that proposes that James rejected the theater for the novel's more intimate one-to-one relation to audience or reader, see Rosenbaum, "'The Stuff of Poetry and Tragedy and Art.'" But see David Kurnick's much different and, to my mind, more interesting way of accounting for James's relations to theatricality in "'Horrible Impossible." Kurnick argues that *The Awkward Age* (1899) should be read as "a sustained exploration of the possibilities of resisting" the form of the novel of psychological depth and suggests that James "demur[s] from the idea of interiority in favor of a model of group consciousness" (110). I am exploring one such model here, although not one that is opposed to interiority. I will return to Kurnick's argument about Jamesian theatricality and his late style at the end of the chapter.

11. Brooks, *The Melodramatic Imagination*, 5. See also Levy, *Versions of Melodrama*.

12. See Eric Bentley's discussion of melodrama as "the quintessence of drama" in *The Life of Drama*, 195–218.
13. Thanks to Michael Moon for this observation.
14. Litvak, *Caught in the Act*, 214. For another assessment of the central place of both shame and theatricality in James, see Sedgwick, "Shame, Theatricality, and Queer Performativity: Henry James's *The Art of the Novel*," in *Touching Feeling*.
15. Bion, *Attention and Interpretation*, 73.
16. Kurnick, *Empty Houses*, 112. The chapter titled "Henry James's Awkward Stage" includes material from an essay on *The Awkward Age* (previously cited) as well as Kurnick, "What Does Jamesian Style Want?"
17. *The Golden Bowl* was directed by James Cellan Jones and dramatized by Jack Pulman.
18. Barry, "Enduring Ephemera," 122.
19. James, *The Complete Plays*, 94.
20. Kurnick also explores James's stage directions (specifically in the play *The Other House* [1909]) to make a related point: that they refer to "a reality conscious of its status as performatively constituted, a space in which the boundary between actress and character recedes into indistinction." Kurnick, *Empty Houses*, 124. In this way James's stage directions anticipate televisual reality, which works precisely to render indistinct the difference between actors and characters (as in the genre of reality television, itself based on the earlier game show genre). In my understanding this is primarily a consequence of the peculiar spatial scale of James's stage directions.
21. While the recent film adaptation *What Maisie Knew* (2012), directed by Scott McGehee and David Siegel, succeeds in capturing aspects of James's experiments with a child's perspective (especially by using complex sound spaces to offer unusual angles on adult conversations), it leaves out those aspects of the novel that address Maisie's changing relations to the adults around her over time. It would be challenging for film to span the six or eight years of the novel. I have not seen either the 1968 BBC television adaptation or Babette Mangolte's 1976 art film adaptation of James's novel.

4 / Loose Coordinations: Theater and Thinking in Gertrude Stein

1. Quoted in Rice, "Gertrude Stein's American Lecture Tour," 335.
2. Stein, "Plays," *Lectures in America*, 93. Unless otherwise noted, all citations of Stein's writing are to this work.
3. By the time of her lecture tour Stein had been writing for more than three decades and, while she had achieved significant recognition, was looking for a wider audience. When the Plain Edition, a small press set up with Toklas as publisher, was not the commercial success they had hoped for, Stein wrote *The Autobiography of Alice B. Toklas*. This was serialized in the *Atlantic Monthly* and published by Harper Collins in the spring and summer of 1933, and its success rapidly created the audience they had been seeking, established Stein's popularity, and prompted the American tour.
4. Stein, *Painted Lace and Other Pieces*, 255.
5. Quoted in Rice, "Stein's American Lecture Tour," 335.
6. Rousseau, *Letter to D'Alembert*, 263.
7. Marshall, "Rousseau and the State of Theater," in *The Surprising Effects of Sympathy*.

8. Benjamin, "What Is the Epic Theater? (II)," 304. See also Brecht, *Brecht on Theatre*.
9. Meyer, *Irresistible Dictation*.
10. James, *Principles of Psychology*, 2: 451.
11. Meyer, *Irresistible Dictation*, 23.
12. Stein, *The Making of Americans*, 180. For discussions of this distinction, see James, *Principles of Psychology*; Meyer, *Irresistible Dictation*; Steiner, *Exact Resemblance to Exact Resemblance*.
13. Stein, *Lectures in America*, 181.
14. Aristotle, *Poetics*, 10.
15. Ford, "*Katharsis*," 120.
16. Bion, "Attacks on Linking," in *Second Thoughts*, 93.
17. Klein, "Notes on Some Schizoid Mechanisms (1946)," in *Envy and Gratitude*.
18. Hinshelwood, *Dictionary of Kleinian Thought*, 235.
19. Bion, *Learning from Experience*, 28–29, emphasis in original.
20. My summary is necessarily simplified, as these terms (*preconception, realization*) indicate. According to Bion, a thought results from the "mating" of a preconception—modeled on the infant's inborn disposition to expect a breast—with either a positive or a negative realization, in other words, with an awareness of either the breast's presence or its absence. Bion calls the mating of a preconception with a positive realization a "conception," which is accompanied by a feeling of satisfaction. He calls the mating of a preconception with a negative realization a "thought," which is accompanied by frustration. See Bion, "A Theory of Thinking" in *Second Thoughts*, 112. This essay was first published in the *International Journal of Psycho-Analysis* 43 (1962).

I would note that some of Bion's fundamental ideas have recently been synthesized, along with insights from a handful of other areas of study (especially attachment theory, empirical studies of infants, and neurophysiology), and reconsidered under the umbrella term *affect regulation*. Peter Fonagy and his colleagues suggest that "a dyadic regulatory system evolves where the infant's signals of moment-to-moment changes in his state are understood and responded to by the caregiver, thereby achieving their regulation." This mother-child system for regulating affects becomes the basis for the development of what these writers call "reflective function" as well as "mentalization," the foundations for what developmental psychology currently calls theory of mind. See Fonagy et al., *Affect Regulation, Mentalization, and the Development of Self*, 37. For a valuable critique of theory of mind from the perspective of affect theory, see Sedgwick, "Affect Theory and Theory of Mind," in *The Weather in Proust*.

21. Bion, *Learning from Experience*, 47.
22. Gillette, "Secret Service," 162–63.
23. Stein, *Last Operas and Plays*, 119.
24. Stein, *Lectures in America*, 122.
25. Stein, *Last Operas and Plays*, 91.
26. Stein, *Lectures in America*, 131.
27. Bion, *Experiences in Groups*, 29.
28. Burns, *Television*, 4.
29. Stein, *Lectures in America*, 185.
30. Ibid., 238.
31. Robinson, *The Other American Drama*.
32. Fuchs and Chaudhuri, *Land/Scape/Theater*, 2.

5 / Vis-à-vis Television: Andy Warhol's Therapeutics

1. Hinshelwood, *A Dictionary of Kleinian Thought*, 378, 379.
2. Warhol, *I'll Be Your Mirror*, 92.
3. Warhol, "What Is Pop Art? Answers from 8 Painters, Part I," interview with G. R. Swenson (1963), in *I'll Be Your Mirror*, 16.
4. Angell, "Andy Warhol," 16; Spigel, "Warhol TV," 260.
5. Warhol's cable series were the interview/variety shows *Fashion* (1979), *Andy Warhol's T.V.* (1980–83), and *Andy Warhol's Fifteen Minutes* (1986–87). Two exhibition catalogues offer helpful overviews of Warhol's use of television throughout his career: *Andy Warhol's Film and Television* and *Warhol TV*. See the former for a selected videography (including episode lists for Warhol's shows) and the latter for an eclectic collection of writing about Warhol and television.
6. Uhlin, "TV, Time, and the Films of Andy Warhol," 22, 5.
7. Hoberman, "Nobody's Land," 22, 21.
8. Spigel, "Warhol TV," 253.
9. On Warhol's queerness, see the essays collected in Doyle, Flatley, and Muñoz, *Pop Out*, especially Michael Moon's "Screen Memories, or, Pop Comes from the Outside," which offers a compelling reading of Warhol's early Pop cartoon paintings in terms of infantile sexuality that has informed my Kleinian approach here. Other works that I have found helpful include Wollen, "Notes from the Underground"; Mattick, "The Andy Warhol of Philosophy and the Philosophy of Andy Warhol." For an approach to Warhol and television that shares this chapter's concerns, although in a different idiom, see Joselit, *Feedback*.
10. Angell, *Andy Warhol Screen Tests*, 14.
11. Laplanche and Pontalis, "Neutrality," in *The Language of Psycho-Analysis*, 271.
12. Angell, *Andy Warhol Screen Tests*, 45.
13. Warhol, *13 Most Beautiful*.
14. For a video art piece that explores these opportunities in the public space of the subway station, see Nina Toft's "The One I Think I Am," http://presentationhousegallery.org/exhibition/nina-toft-the-one-i-think-i-am/.
15. Tomkins, "The Phantasy behind the Face," in *Exploring Affect*, 267–68.
16. Warhol, "My True Story," an interview with Gretchen Berg, in *I'll Be Your Mirror*, 95.
17. Angell, "Andy Warhol," 16.
18. Uhlin, "TV, Time, and the Films of Andy Warhol," 17.
19. Warhol, *The Philosophy of Andy Warhol*, 91.
20. Joselit, *Feedback*, 116–17.
21. Uhlin, "TV, Time, and the Films of Andy Warhol," 18.
22. Hoberman, "Nobody's Land," 23; Uhlin, "TV, Time, and the Films of Andy Warhol," 18.
23. One example of this echoing: late in the film we see the televised Sedgwick on the right sneeze, then explain that she just faked a sneeze, and repeats it; meanwhile the "live" Sedgwick also sneezes, initiating an exchange between them. The film Sedgwick then goes on to talk about blinking and the feeling of "pay[ing] attention to the little muscles" of the face and eyes. See Edgett, "What Edie Said in *Outer and Inner Space*," 27–39.
24. Warhol, *Philosophy*, 33.

25. Warhol and Hackett. *POPism*, 3.
26. Hadot, *What Is Ancient Philosophy?*, 3, 4.
27. Warhol, *Philosophy*, 112. Unless otherwise noted, all subsequent citations of Warhol are to this work.
28. Hadot, *Philosophy as a Way of Life*, 84.
29. Warhol, *Philosophy*, 145, 154.
30. Foucault, *The Hermeneutics of the Subject*, 252. In the same work, see Gros's "Course Context" for helpful ways of situating Foucault's late lectures in relation to his previous work.
31. Hadot's work tends much more quickly and easily toward the universalizing, cosmic dimensions of ancient philosophical thinking. He distinguishes his own work from Foucault's along these lines: "In this way, one identifies oneself with an 'Other': nature, or universal reason, as it is present within each individual. This implies a radical transformation of perspective, and contains a universalist, cosmic dimension, upon which, it seems to me, M. Foucault did not sufficiently insist." Hadot, "Reflections on the Idea of the 'Cultivation of the Self,'" in *Philosophy as a Way of Life*, 211.
32. Wiener, *Cybernetics*, 22.
33. Jones, "Andy Warhol," 41.
34. Reva Wolf suggests this in a footnote to her introduction to *I'll Be Your Mirror*, 408. A fuller exposition of Warhol and cybernetics would track his relations to Marshall McLuhan's media theory (in *Understanding Media* [1964] and elsewhere). McLuhan's idea that technologies are "extensions of man," prosthetic devices that amplify human capacities in the external environment and reciprocally modify the "sense-ratios" of human bodies, depends on a cybernetic understanding of the continuities between animal bodies and machines. Warhol was familiar with McLuhan's ideas. In several interviews he describes his films as permitting viewers to become more "involved," a form of attention he associates with television and a term that echoes (if not quotes) McLuhan's assessment of television as a participant medium that involves its viewers (see, for example, *I'll Be Your Mirror*, 92; McLuhan, *Understanding Media*, 113). Two essays that address the role of machines in Warhol's aesthetics are Tata, "Warholian Machinehood I" and Otty, "*The No Man Show*."
35. Heims, *The Cybernetics Group*, 23.
36. The impact of cybernetics on postwar European thinking has been the subject of a number of studies. See especially those by Christopher Johnson, *System and Writing* and "Derrida." See also Lafontaine, *L'Empire cybernetique* and "The Cybernetic Matrix of 'French Theory'"; Liu, "The Cybernetic Unconscious"; Geoghegan, "From Information Theory to French Theory." For the German context, see Winthrop-Young, "Silicon Sociology." For the British context, see Pickering, *The Cybernetic Brain*.
37. Céline Lafontaine makes a similar point in "The Cybernetic Matrix of 'French Theory,'" 36.
38. Foucault, *Power/Knowledge*, 142.
39. Wiener, *The Human Use of Human Beings*, 8.
40. Bateson, "The Cybernetics of 'Self': A Theory of Alcoholism," in *Steps to an Ecology of Mind*, 315–16.
41. Foucault, *Hermeneutics of the Subject*, 248.
42. Gros, "Course Context," in ibid., 542–43.
43. For a critical discussion of the relations between Foucault and psychoanalysis, see Whitebook, "Against Interiority."

44. Foucault, *Hermeneutics of the Subject*, 207.
45. Warhol and Hackett, *POPism*, 20.
46. Warhol, *Philosophy*, 5.
47. See, for example, Koch, *Stargazer*, 12.
48. For an interesting discussion of the space of the stage and the structural void of theatricality, see Weber, *Theatricality as Medium*, 9.
49. Warhol and Hackett, *POPism*, 25.
50. Psychiatry shows up several times in *POPism* as a rival to queer performance practices. Consider, for example, the party Warhol was invited to attend (he brought the Velvet Underground) at the New York Society for Clinical Psychiatry (183), or his quotation of underground filmmaker Jack Smith, who acted in other people's films for this reason: "He said that he did it for the therapy, because he couldn't afford 'professional help,' and that wasn't it brave of him to take psychoanalysis in such a public way" (40).
51. Foucault, *Hermeneutics of the Subject*, 221, 221–22.
52. Shaviro, "The Life, after Death, of Postmodern Emotions," 126.
53. Wallace, *A Supposedly Fun Thing I'll Never Do Again*.
54. Shaviro, "The Life, after Death, of Postmodern Emotions," 138, 138.
55. Warhol, *Philosophy*, 27.
56. Warhol and Hackett, *POPism*, 14.
57. Warhol, *The Andy Warhol Diaries*, xvi.
58. Foucault, *The Courage of Truth*, 232, 174.
59. Shea, *The Cynic Enlightenment*, 9.
60. Lynn Spigel makes this point when she describes Warhol's television productions: they "deflated the scandal of homosexuality by rendering it ordinary." "Warhol TV," 270.
61. For a reading of this passage in relation to race and shame, see Sedgwick, "Queer Performativity."
62. Warhol, *Andy Warhol Diaries*, x.
63. Foucault, *Courage of Truth*, 260, 261.
64. Ibid., 258.
65. Warhol, *Andy Warhol's Time Capsule 21*.

Out and Across

1. Feldman, "The Future of Local Music," 170.
2. Ross, *The Rest Is Noise*, 486.
3. O'Hara, "New Directions in Music," 217. For a discussion of the difference between Feldman's use of indeterminacy with regard to the performance and John Cage's use of chance in composition, see Nyman, *Experimental Music*.

Bibliography

Agnew, Jean-Christophe. *Worlds Apart: The Market and the Theater in Anglo-American Thought, 1550–1750.* Cambridge: Cambridge University Press, 1986.
Angell, Callie. "Andy Warhol: *Outer and Inner Space.*" In *From Stills to Motion and Back Again: Texts on Andy Warhol's Screen Tests and Outer and Inner Space.* Vancouver: Presentation House Gallery, 2003.
——— . *Andy Warhol Screen Tests: The Films of Andy Warhol Catalogue Raisonné.* Vol. 1. New York: Abrams, Whitney Museum of American Art, 2006.
Aristotle, *Poetics.* Translated by Malcolm Heath. London: Penguin Books, 1996.
Artaud, Antonin. "The Theatre of Cruelty." Translated by Mary Caroline Richards. In *The Theory of the Modern Stage: An Introduction to Modern Theatre and Drama,* edited by Eric Bentley. London: Penguin Books, 1976.
Barry, Neil. "Enduring Ephemera: James Cellan Jones, Henry James, and the BBC." In *Henry James on Stage and Screen,* edited by John R. Bradley. New York: Palgrave, 2000.
Bateson, Gregory. *Steps to an Ecology of Mind.* San Francisco: Chandler, 1972.
Benjamin, Walter. "On Some Motifs in Baudelaire." In *Illuminations,* edited by Hannah Arendt. Translated by Harry Zohn. New York: Harcourt, Brace & World, 1968.
——— . "What Is the Epic Theater? (II)." In *Walter Benjamin: Selected Writings. Volume 4, 1938–1940,* edited by Howard Eiland and Michael W. Jennings. Translated by Edmund Jephcott and others. Cambridge, MA: Harvard University Press, 2003.
Bentley, Eric. *The Life of Drama.* New York: Atheneum, 1964.
Bion, Wilfred R. *Attention and Interpretation.* Lanham, MD: Rowman & Littlefield, 2004.
——— . *Experiences in Groups and Other Papers.* London: Tavistock, 1961.

———. *Learning from Experience*. 1962. London: H. Karnac Books, 1991.
———. *Second Thoughts: Selected Papers on Psycho-Analysis*. 1967. London: H. Karnac Books, 2005.
Brecht, Bertolt. *Brecht on Theatre: The Development of an Aesthetic*. Edited and translated by John Willett. New York: Hill and Wang, 1964.
Borch-Jacobsen, Mikkel. *The Emotional Tie: Psychoanalysis, Mimesis, Affect*. Translated by Angela Brewer and X. P. Callahan. Stanford: Stanford University Press, 1992.
Bordogna, Francesca. "Inner Division and Uncertain Contours: William James and the Politics of the Modern Self." *British Journal of the History of Science* 40, no. 4 (2007): 505–36.
Brooks, Peter. *The Melodramatic Imagination: Balzac, James, Melodrama, and the Mode of Excess*. New Haven, CT: Yale University Press, 1976.
Burns, R. W. *Television: An International History of the Formative Years*. IEE History of Technology Series 22. London: Institution of Electrical Engineers, 1998.
Byford, Andy. "The Figure of the 'Spectator' in the Theoretical Writings of Brecht, Diderot, and Rousseau." *Symposium: A Journal in Modern Literatures* 56, no. 1 (2002): 25–42.
Bynum, Paige Matthey. "'Observe How Healthily—How Calmly I Can Tell You the Whole Story': Moral Insanity and Edgar Allan Poe's 'The Tell-Tale Heart,.'" In *Literature and Science as Modes of Expression*, edited by Frederick Amrine. Dordrecht: Kluwer Academic, 1989.
Cameron, Sharon. *Thinking in Henry James*. Chicago: University of Chicago Press, 1989.
Cartwright, Lisa. *Moral Spectatorship: Technologies of Voice and Affect in Postwar Representations of the Child*. Durham, NC: Duke University Press, 2008.
Chertok, Léon, and Isabelle Stengers. *A Critique of Psychoanalytic Reason: Hypnosis as a Scientific Problem from Lavoisier to Lacan*. Translated by Martha Noel Evans. Stanford: Stanford University Press, 1992.
Clough, Patricia, ed. *The Affective Turn: Theorizing the Social*. Durham, NC: Duke University Press, 2007.
———. *Autoaffection: Unconscious Thought in the Age of Teletechnology*. Minneapolis: University of Minnesota Press, 2000.
Cole, Jonathan. *About Face*. Cambridge, MA: MIT Press, 1998.
Côté, Jean-François. *Le Triangle D'Hermès. Poe, Stein, Warhol: Figures de la Modernité Esthétique*. Brussels: La Lettre Volée, 2003.
Cvetkovich, Ann. *An Archive of Feelings: Trauma, Sexuality, and Lesbian Public Cultures*. Durham, NC: Duke University Press, 2003.
Darwin, Charles. *The Expression of the Emotions in Man and Animals*. Edited and with Notes by Paul Ekman. Oxford: Oxford University Press, 2009.
Derrida, Jacques. *Ecriture et la différance*. Paris: Editions du Seuil, 1967.
———. *Of Grammatology*. Translated by Gayatri Chakravorty Spivak. Baltimore: Johns Hopkins University Press, 1976.

---. *Writing and Difference*. Translated by Alan Bass. Chicago: University of Chicago Press, 1978.
Descartes, René. *The Passions of the Soul*. Translated and Annotated by Stephen Voss. Indianapolis: Hackett, 1989.
Doyle, Jennifer, Jonathan Flatley, and José Esteban Muñoz, eds. *Pop Out: Queer Warhol*. Durham, NC: Duke University Press, 1996.
Dupuy, Jean-Pierre. *The Mechanization of the Mind: On the Origins of Cognitive Science*. Translated by M. B. DeBevoise. Princeton, NJ: Princeton University Press, 2000.
Dydo, Ulla, with William Rice. *Gertrude Stein: The Language That Rises, 1923–1934*. Evanston, IL: Northwestern University Press, 2003.
Edel, Leon. *Henry James: A Life*. New York: Harper & Row, 1985.
Edgett, Lisa Dillon. "What Edie Said in *Outer and Inner Space*." In *From Stills to Motion and Back Again: Texts on Andy Warhol's Screen Tests and Outer and Inner Space*. Vancouver: Presentation House Gallery, 2003.
Ellison, Julie. *Cato's Tears and the Making of Anglo-American Emotion*. Chicago: University of Chicago Press, 1999.
Elmer, Jonathan. *Reading at the Social Limit: Affect, Mass Culture, and Edgar Allan Poe*. Stanford: Stanford University Press, 1995.
Elsaesser, Thomas. "Freud as Media Theorist: Mystic Writing-Pads and the Matter of Memory." *Screen* 50, no. 1 (2009): 100–113.
Feldman, Morton. "The Future of Local Music." In *Give My Regards to Eighth Street: Collected Writings of Morton Feldman*, edited and with an introduction by B. H. Friedman. Cambridge, MA: Exact Change, 2000.
Felman, Shoshana. "To Open the Question." In *Literature and Psychoanalysis: The Question of Reading: Otherwise*. Baltimore: Johns Hopkins University Press, 1982.
Fonagy, Peter, Gyorgy Gergely, Eliot Jurist, and Mary Target. *Affect Regulation, Mentalization, and the Development of Self*. New York: Other Press, 2002.
Ford, Andrew. "*Katharsis*: The Ancient Problem." In *Performativity and Performance*, edited by Andrew Parker and Eve Kosofsky Sedgwick. New York: Routledge, 1995.
Foucault, Michel. *The Courage of Truth: The Government of Self and Others II. Lectures at the Collège de France, 1981–82*. Edited by Frédéric Gros. Translated by Graham Burchell. New York: Palgrave Macmillan, 2011.
---. *The Hermeneutics of the Subject: Lectures at the Collège de France, 1981–82*. Edited by Frédéric Gros. Translated by Graham Burchell. New York: Picador, 2005.
---. *Power/Knowledge: Selected Interviews and Other Writings 1972–1977*. Edited by Colin Gordon. Translated by Colin Gordon, Leo Marshall, John Mepham, and Kate Soper. New York: Pantheon Books, 1980.
Frank, Adam. "The Letter of the Laugh." *Poe Studies* 33, nos. 1–2 (2000): 29–32.
---. "Phantoms Limn: Silvan Tomkins and Affective Prosthetics." *Theory & Psychology* 17, no. 4 (2007): 515–28.

———. "Some Affective Bases for Guilt: Tomkins, Freud, Object Relations." *English Studies in Canada* 32, no. 1 (2006): 13–29.
———. "Some Avenues for Feeling." *Criticism* 46, no. 3 (2004): 511–24.
———. "Valdemar's Tongue, Poe's Telegraphy." *ELH* 72, no. 3 (2005): 635–62.
Frank, Adam, and Elizabeth Wilson. "Like-minded: A Reply to Ruth Leys." *Critical Inquiry* 38, no. 4 (2012): 870–77.
Freud, Sigmund. *Civilization and Its Discontents*. Translated and edited by James Strachey. With a biographical introduction by Peter Gay. New York: Norton, 1961.
———. "Fragment of an Analysis of Hysteria (Dora)." In *The Penguin Freud Reader*, selected and introduced by Adam Phillips. London: Penguin, 2006.
———. *Group Psychology and the Analysis of the Ego*. Translated and edited by James Strachey. With a biographical introduction by Peter Gay. New York: Norton, 1959.
Fuchs, Elinor, and Una Chaudhuri, eds. *Land/Scape/Theater*. Ann Arbor: University of Michigan Press, 2002,
Geoghegan, Bernard Dionysius. "From Information Theory to French Theory: Jakobson, Levi-Strauss, and the Cybernetic Apparatus." *Critical Inquiry* 38, no. 1 (2011): 96–126.
Gibbs, Anna. "Panic! Affect Contagion, Mimesis and Suggestion in the Social Field." *Cultural Studies Review* 14, no. 2 (2008): 130–45.
Gillette, William H. "Secret Service." In *Plays by William Hooker Gillette*. Edited by Rosemary Cullen and Don B. Wilmeth. Cambridge: Cambridge University Press, 1983.
Ginzburg, Carlo. "Clues." In *Myths, Emblems, Clues*. Translated by John Tedeschi and Anne C. Tedeschi. London: Hutchinson Radius, 1990.
Goldberg, Jonathan. *The Seeds of Things: Theorizing Sexuality and Materiality in Renaissance Representations*. New York: Fordham University Press, 2009.
———. *Writing Matter: From the Hands of the English Renaissance*. Stanford: Stanford University Press, 1990.
Gregg, Melissa, and Gregory J. Seigworth, eds. *The Affect Theory Reader*. Durham, NC: Duke University Press, 2010.
Güçbilmez, Beliz. "An Uncanny Theatricality: The Representation of the Offstage." *New Theatre Quarterly* 23, no. 2 (2007): 152–60.
Guillory, John. "Genesis of the Media Concept." *Critical Inquiry* 36, no. 2 (2010): 321–62.
Hadot, Pierre. *Philosophy as a Way of Life: Spiritual Exercises from Socrates to Foucault*. Edited and with an Introduction by Arnold Davidson. Translated by Michael Chase. New York: Blackwell, 1995.
———. *What Is Ancient Philosophy?* Translated by Michael Chase. Cambridge, MA: Harvard University Press, 2002.
Harding, Rosamond E. M. *The Metronome and It's* [sic] *Precursors*. Henley-on-Thames, Oxfordshire: Gresham Books, 1983.

Hartley, Lucy. *Physiognomy and the Meaning of Expression in Nineteenth-Century Culture.* New York: Cambridge University Press, 2001.
Harvey, Jonathan. "Kleinian Developmental Narrative and James' *What Maisie Knew.*" *University of Hartford Studies in Literature: A Journal of Interdisciplinary Criticism* 23, no. 1 (1991): 34–47.
Heims, Steve Joshua. *The Cybernetics Group.* Cambridge, MA: MIT Press, 1991.
Hejinian, Lyn. "Three Lives." In *The Language of Inquiry.* Berkeley: University of California Press, 2000.
Hemmings, Claire. "Invoking Affect: Cultural Theory and the Ontological Turn." *Cultural Studies* 19, no. 5 (2005): 548–67.
Hinshelwood, Robert. *A Dictionary of Kleinian Thought.* London: Free Association Books, 1991.
Hinshelwood, Robert, Susan Robinson, and Oscar Zarate. *Introducing Melanie Klein.* Cambridge, UK: Icon Books, 1999.
Hoberman, J. "Nobody's Land: Inside *Outer and Inner Space.*" In *From Stills to Motion and Back Again: Texts on Andy Warhol's Screen Tests and Outer and Inner Space.* Vancouver: Presentation House Gallery, 2003.
Horkheimer, Max, and Theodor Adorno. *The Dialectic of Enlightenment: Philosophical Fragments.* Edited by Gunzelin Schmid Noerr. Translated by Edmund Jephcott. Stanford: Stanford University Press, 2002.
Howe, Susan. *My Emily Dickinson.* Berkeley: North Atlantic Books, 1985.
Isaacs, Susan. "The Nature and Function of Phantasy." In *The Freud-Klein Controversies, 1941–45.* Edited by Pearl King and Riccardo Steiner. London: Routledge, 1991.
Jacobus, Mary. *The Poetics of Psychoanalysis: In the Wake of Klein.* Oxford: Oxford University Press, 2005.
James, Henry. *The Awkward Age.* 1899. London: Penguin Books, 1987.
———. *The Complete Notebooks of Henry James.* Edited by Leon Edel and Lyall H. Powers. New York: Oxford University Press, 1987.
———. *The Complete Plays of Henry James.* Edited by Leon Edel. New York: Oxford University Press, 1990.
———. *The Other House.* 1896. New York: New York Review of Books, 1999.
———. *The Spoils of Poynton.* 1897. Oxford: Oxford University Press, 2000.
———. *What Maisie Knew.* 1897. Oxford: Oxford University Press, 1998.
James, William. *Principles of Psychology.* 2 vols. 1890. New York: Dover, 1950.
Johnson, Christopher. "Derrida: The Machine and the Animal." *Paragraph* 28, no. 3 (2005): 102–20.
———. *System and Writing in the Philosophy of Jacques Derrida.* Cambridge: Cambridge University Press, 1993.
Jones, Alan. "Andy Warhol: L'imprimé mobile de la télévision / Television's Movable Print." *Art Press* 199 (1995): 35–41.
Jones, James Cellan, director. *The Golden Bowl.* Dramatized by Jack Pulman. In *The Henry James Collection.* DVD. BBC Video, 2009.

Jones, Paul Christian. "The Danger of Sympathy: Edgar Allan Poe's 'Hop-Frog' and the Abolitionist Rhetoric of Pathos." *Journal of American Studies* 35, no. 2 (2001): 239–54.
Joselit, David. *Feedback: Television against Democracy*. Cambridge, MA: MIT Press, 2007.
Kittler, Friedrich. *Discourse Networks 1800/1900*. Translated by Michael Metteer, with Chris Cullens. Stanford: Stanford University Press, 1990.
———. *Gramophone, Film, Typewriter*. Translated by Geoffrey Winthrop-Young and Michael Wutz. Stanford: Stanford University Press, 1999.
Klein, Melanie. *Envy and Gratitude and Other Works 1946–1963*. 1975. London: Vintage Books, 1997.
Klein, Melanie, and Joan Riviere. *Love, Hate and Reparation*. New York: Norton, 1964.
Koch, Stephen. *Stargazer: Andy Warhol's World and His Films*. New York: Praeger, 1973.
Kurnick. David. *Empty Houses: Theatrical Failure and the Novel*. Princeton, NJ: Princeton University Press, 2012.
———. "'Horrible Impossible': Henry James's Awkward Stage." *Henry James Review* 26, no. 2 (2005): 109–29.
———. "What Does Jamesian Style Want?" *Henry James Review* 28, no. 3 (2007): 213–22.
Lafontaine, Céline. "The Cybernetic Matrix of 'French Theory.'" *Theory, Culture & Society* 24, no. 5 (2007): 27–46.
———. *L'Empire cybernetique: Des machines a penser a la pensée machine*. Paris: Seuil, 2004.
Lane, Tarja. *Feeling Cinema: Emotional Dynamics in Film Studies*. New York: Bloomsbury Academic, 2011.
Laplanche, Jean, and Jean-Bertrand Pontalis. *The Language of Psycho-Analysis*. Translated by Donald Nicholson-Smith. New York: Norton, 1973.
Leroi-Gourhan, André. *Gesture and Speech*. Translated by Anna Bostock Berger. Cambridge, MA: MIT Press, 1993.
Levy, Leo B. *Versions of Melodrama: A Study of the Fiction and Drama of Henry James, 1865–1897*. Berkeley: University of California Press, 1957.
Leys, Ruth. "The Turn to Affect: A Critique." *Critical Inquiry* 37, no. 3 (2011): 434–72.
Likierman, Meira. *Melanie Klein: Her Work in Context*. London: Continuum, 2001.
Litvak, Joseph. *Caught in the Act: Theatricality in the Nineteenth-Century English Novel*. Berkeley: University of California Press, 1992.
Liu, Lydia H. "The Cybernetic Unconscious: Rethinking Lacan, Poe, and French Theory." *Critical Inquiry* 36, no. 2 (2010), 288–320.
Luhmann, Niklas. *The Reality of the Mass Media*. Translated by Kathleen Cross. Stanford: Stanford University Press, 2000.
Marshall, David. *The Figure of Theater: Shaftesbury, Defoe, Adam Smith, and George Eliot*. New York: Columbia University Press, 1986.

———. *The Surprising Effects of Sympathy: Marivaux, Diderot, Rousseau, and Mary Shelley*. Chicago: University of Chicago Press, 1988.
Massumi, Brian. *Parables for the Virtual*. Durham, NC: Duke University Press, 2002.
Mattick, Paul. "The Andy Warhol of Philosophy and the Philosophy of Andy Warhol." *Critical Inquiry* 24, no. 4 (1998): 965–87.
McGehee, Scott, and David Siegel, directors. *What Maisie Knew*. Film. Red Crown Productions, 2012.
McGill, Meredith. *American Literature and the Culture of Reprinting, 1834–1853*. Philadelphia: University of Pennsylvania Press, 2003.
McLuhan, Marshall. *Understanding Media: The Extensions of Man*. 1964. Cambridge, MA: MIT Press, 2001.
McMaster, Juliet. *The Index of the Mind: Physiognomy in the Novel*. Lethbridge, Alberta: University of Lethbridge Press, 1990.
Meyer, Steven. *Irresistible Dictation: Gertrude Stein and the Correlations of Writing and Science*. Stanford: Stanford University Press, 2001.
Miller, J. Hillis. "Reading, Doing: James's *What Maisie Knew*." In *Versions of Pygmalion*. Cambridge, MA: Harvard University Press, 1990.
Moon, Michael. "Screen Memories, or, Pop Comes from the Outside: Warhol and Queer Childhood." In *Pop Out: Queer Warhol*, edited by Jennifer Doyle, Jonathan Flatley, and José Esteban Muñoz. Durham, NC: Duke University Press, 1996.
Muller, John P., and William J. Richardson, eds. *The Purloined Poe: Lacan, Derrida, and Psychoanalytic Reading*. Baltimore: Johns Hopkins University Press, 1987.
Ngai, Sianne. *Ugly Feelings*. Cambridge, MA: Harvard University Press, 2005.
Novick, Sheldon M. "Henry James on Stage." In *Henry James on Stage and Screen*, edited by John R. Bradley. New York: Palgrave, 2000.
Nyman, Michael. *Experimental Music: Cage and Beyond*. Cambridge: Cambridge University Press, 1999.
O'Hara, Frank. "New Directions in Music: Morton Feldman." In *Give My Regards to Eighth Street: Collected Writings of Morton Feldman*, edited and with an introduction by B. H. Friedman. Cambridge, MA: Exact Change, 2000.
Otty, Lisa. "*The No Man Show*: Technology and the Extension of Presence in the Work of Andy Warhol." *Esharp* 5 (2005): 1–13.
Papoulias, Constantina, and Felicity Callard. "Biology's Gift: Interrogating the Turn to Affect." *Body and Society* 16, no. 1 (2010): 29–56.
Pickering, Andrew. *The Cybernetic Brain: Sketches of Another Future*. Chicago: University of Chicago Press, 2010.
Poe, Edgar Allan. *Edgar Allan Poe: Tales and Sketches*. Edited by Thomas Ollive Mabbott. 2 vols. Urbana: University of Illinois Press, 2000.
———. *Edgar Allan Poe: Essays and Reviews*. Notes and selections by G. R. Thompson. New York: Library of America, 1984.

Prodger, Philip. *Darwin's Camera: Art and Photography in the Theory of Evolution*. New York: Oxford University Press, 2009.
Rasch, William, and Cary Wolfe, eds. *Observing Complexity: Systems Theory and Postmodernity*. Minneapolis: University of Minnesota Press, 2000.
Reed, Lou. *The Raven*. CD. Warner Bros. Records, 2003.
Rice, William. "Gertrude Stein's American Lecture Tour." In *The Letters of Gertrude Stein and Thornton Wilder*, edited by Edward Burns and Ulla E. Dydo with William Rice. New Haven, CT: Yale University Press, 1996.
Ridout, Nicholas. *Stage Fright, Animals, and Other Theatrical Problems*. Cambridge: Cambridge University Press, 2006.
Riskin, Jessica. "The Unquiet Clock." Paper presented at the Science and Society Colloquium Series, University of British Columbia, February 4, 2010.
Roach, Joseph R. *The Player's Passion: Studies in the Science of Acting*. Ann Arbor: University of Michigan Press, 1993.
Robinson, Marc. *The Other American Drama*. Cambridge: Cambridge University Press, 1994.
Rose, Phyllis. "Literary Warhol." *Yale Review* 79 (1989): 21–33.
Rosenbaum, Emily. "'The Stuff of Poetry and Tragedy and Art': Henry James, the Theater, and Audience." *American Literary Realism* 38, no. 3 (2006): 203–22.
Ross, Alex. *The Rest Is Noise: Listening to the Twentieth Century*. New York: Farrar, Straus and Giroux, 2007.
Ross, Allison. "Derrida's Writing-Theatre: From the Theatrical Allegory to Political Commitment." *Derrida Today* 1, no. 1 (2008): 76–94.
Rousseau, Jean-Jacques. *Letter to D'Alembert and Writings for the Theater*. Vol. 10: *The Collected Writings of Rousseau*. Edited and translated by Allan Bloom, Charles Butterworth, and Christopher Kelly. Hanover, NH: University Press of New England, 2004.
Sedgwick, Eve Kosofsky. "Queer Performativity: Warhol's Shyness/Warhol's Whiteness." In *Pop Out: Queer Warhol*, edited by Jennifer Doyle, Jonathan Flatley, and José Esteban Muñoz. Durham, NC: Duke University Press, 1996.
———. *Touching Feeling: Affect, Pedagogy, Performativity*. Durham, NC: Duke University Press, 2003.
———. *The Weather in Proust*. Edited by Jonathan Goldberg. Durham, NC: Duke University Press, 2011.
Sedgwick, Eve Kosofsky, and Adam Frank. "Shame in the Cybernetic Fold: Reading Silvan Tomkins." *Critical Inquiry* 21, no. 2 (1995): 496–522.
Shaviro, Steven. "The Life, after Death, of Postmodern Emotions." *Criticism* 46, no. 1 (2004): 125–41.
Shea, Louisa. *The Cynic Enlightenment: Diogenes in the Salon*. Baltimore: Johns Hopkins University Press, 2010.
Silverman, Kenneth. *Edgar A. Poe: Mournful and Never-Ending Remembrance*. New York: HarperCollins, 1991.

Smith, Adam. *The Theory of Moral Sentiments*. Edited by D. D. Raphael and A. L. Macfie. Oxford: Oxford University Press, 1976.
Smith, Don G. *The Poe Cinema: A Critical Filmography*. Jefferson, NC: McFarland, 1999.
Smith, Ronald L. *Poe in the Media: Screen, Songs, and Spoken Word Recordings*. New York: Garland, 1990.
Spiegelman, Art, and Chip Kidd. *Jack Cole and Plastic Man: Forms Stretched to Their Limits!* New York: DC Comics, 2001.
Spigel, Lynn. "Warhol TV." In *TV by Design: Modern Art and the Rise of Network Television*. Chicago: University of Chicago Press, 2008.
Spinoza, Benedict. *The Ethics and Other Works*. Edited and translated by Edwin Curley. Princeton, NJ: Princeton University Press, 1994.
Stein, Gertrude. *The Autobiography of Alice B. Toklas*. 1933. New York: Vintage Books, 1990.
———. *Last Operas and Plays*. 1949. Introduction by Bonnie Marranca. Baltimore: Johns Hopkins University Press, 1995.
———. *Lectures in America*. 1935. Introduction by Wendy Steiner. Boston: Beacon Press, 1985.
———. *The Making of Americans*. 1925. Foreword by William H. Gass. Introduction by Steven Meyer. Normal, IL: Dalkey Archive Press, 1995.
———. *Painted Lace and Other Pieces, 1914–1937*. Vol. 5: *The Yale Edition of the Unpublished Writings of Gertrude Stein*. New Haven, CT: Yale University Press, 1955.
———. *Picasso*. 1938. New York: Dover, 1984.
———. *A Stein Reader*. Edited by Ulla Dydo. Evanston, IL: Northwestern University Press, 1993.
———. *Tender Buttons*. In *Selected Writings of Gertrude Stein*. Edited, with an Introduction and Notes, by Carl Van Vechten. 1946. New York: Vintage Books, 1962.
———. *Three Lives*. New York: Penguin Books, 1990.
Steiner, Wendy. *Exact Resemblance to Exact Resemblance: The Literary Portraiture of Gertrude Stein*. New Haven, CT: Yale University Press, 1978.
Tata, Michael Angelo. "Warholian Machinehood I." *Nebula* 3, no. 1 (2006): 103–21.
Terada, Rei. *Feeling in Theory: Emotion after the "Death of the Subject."* Cambridge, MA: Harvard University Press, 2001.
Thrailkill, Jane. *Affecting Fictions: Mind, Body, and Emotion in American Literary Realism*. Cambridge, MA: Harvard University Press, 2007.
Tomkins, Silvan. *Affect Imagery Consciousness*. 4 vols. New York: Springer, 1962–63, 1991–92.
———. *Exploring Affect: The Selected Writings of Silvan S. Tomkins*. Edited by E. Virginia Demos. Cambridge: Cambridge University Press, 1995.
———. *Shame and Its Sisters: A Silvan Tomkins Reader*. Edited by Eve Kosofsky Sedgwick and Adam Frank. Durham, NC: Duke University Press, 1995

Uhlin, Graig. "TV, Time, and the Films of Andy Warhol." *Cinema Journal* 49, no. 3 (2010): 1–23.

Walker, Julia. "Why Performance? Why Now? Textuality and the Rearticulation of Human Presence." *Yale Journal of Criticism* 16, no. 1 (2003): 149–75.

Wallace, David Foster. *A Supposedly Fun Thing I'll Never Do Again*. Boston: Back Bay Books, 1998.

Warhol, Andy. *The Andy Warhol Diaries*. Edited by Pat Hackett. New York: Warner Books, 1989.

———. *Andy Warhol's Film and Television*. New York: Whitney Museum of American Art, 1991.

———. *Andy Warhol's Time Capsule 21*. Cologne: DuMont Literatur und Kunst Verlag, 2003.

———. *I'll Be Your Mirror: The Selected Andy Warhol Interviews, 1962–1987*. Edited by Kenneth Goldsmith. New York: Carroll & Graf, 2004.

———. *The Philosophy of Andy Warhol (From A to B and Back Again)*. New York: Harcourt Brace Jovanovich, 1975.

———. *13 Most Beautiful . . . Songs for Andy Warhol's Screen Tests*. DVD. Plexifilm, 2009.

———. *Warhol TV*. Paris: La Maison Rouge, 2008.

Warhol, Andy, and Pat Hackett. *POPism: The Warhol Sixties*. New York: Harcourt, Brace, 1980.

Warhol, Robyn. *Having a Good Cry: Effeminate Feelings and Pop-Culture Forms*. Columbus: Ohio State University Press, 2003.

Weber, Samuel. *Theatricality as Medium*. New York: Fordham University Press, 2004.

Whitebook, Joel. "Against Interiority: Foucault's Struggles with Psychoanalysis." In *The Cambridge Companion to Foucault*, edited by Gary Gutting. 2nd edition. Cambridge: Cambridge University Press, 2003.

Wiener, Norbert. *Cybernetics, or Control and Communication in the Animal and the Machine*. Cambridge, MA: MIT Press, 1948.

———. *The Human Use of Human Beings: Cybernetics and Society*. Cambridge, MA: Riverside Press, 1950.

Wilden, Anthony. "Analog and Digital Communication." In *System and Structure: Essays in Communication and Exchange*. London: Tavistock, 1972.

Williams, Raymond. "Drama in a Dramatised Society" In *Raymond Williams on Television: Selected Writings*. Edited by Alan O'Connor. Toronto: Between the Lines, 1989.

———. *Television: Technology and Cultural Form*. London: Fontana, 1974.

Wilson, Elizabeth A. *Affect and Artificial Intelligence*. Seattle: University of Washington Press, 2010.

———. *Neural Geographies: Feminism and the Microstructure of Cognition*. New York: Routledge, 1998.

Wineapple, Brenda. *Sister Brother: Gertrude and Leo Stein*. New York: G. P. Putnam's Sons, 1996.

Winter, Sarah. *Freud and the Institution of Psychoanalytic Knowledge*. Stanford: Stanford University Press, 1999.

Winthrop-Young, Geoffrey. "Silicon Sociology, or, Two Kings on Hegel's Throne? Kittler, Luhmann, and the Posthuman Merger of German Media Theory." *Yale Journal of Criticism* 13, no. 2 (2000): 391–420.

Wollen, Peter. "Notes from the Underground: Andy Warhol." In *Raiding the Icebox: Reflections on Twentieth-Century Culture*. London: Verso, 2008.

Zimmerman, Brett. "'Moral Insanity' or Paranoid Schizophrenia." *Mosaic* 25, no. 2 (1992): 39–48.

Index

abstraction, 25, 33, 36, 42, 46, 91
acting, 88, 111
actor, 10, 13, 90, 92, 94, 98, 101, 103, 109–11, 113, 124, 125, 161n20
affect(s): and acting, 88; co-assemblies, 6, 101; communication of, 7, 10, 17, 19, 22, 48, 49, 51, 52, 55, 59–60, 63, 65, 67, 70, 71, 83, 88, 94, 119; compositional aspect of, 11, 21, 24–46; contagion of, 48–51, 63; and emotion, 101, 154n9, 155n22; and ethics, 81, 135, 154–55n19; freedoms, 5, 8, 31, 50, 82, 101, 103, 154–55n19; as hinge, 7–8, 11, 93; and image, 58–9; inhibition and amplification of, 15, 60–61, 70, 81, 104, 125, 159n19 (*see also* repression; Tomkins, Silvan: and General Images); and language, 12, 18–19, 27, 36, 55, 59–60, 73, 94, 102, 106, 126; location of, 7, 34–35, 50, 58–59 (*see also* face; gesture; voice); and metacommunication, 19, 156n35; movement of, 1, 2, 11, 35, 51, 76, 94, 102, 117, 151 (*see also* identification; transference); and "original relation to the other," 14, 155n28; redundancy, 50; regulation, 23, 52, 66, 121, 159n25, 162n20 (*see also* tempo); and theatricality, 10–11, 18, 81–82, 143; theories of, 1, 31, 97 (*see also* Bion, Wilfred; James, William; Klein, Melanie; object-relations theory; Tomkins, Silvan). *See also entries for specific affects and feelings*
affect theory, 1, 6, 9, 11, 14, 20, 61; definition of, 3; and poetics, 3. *See also* Tomkins, Silvan: and script theory
affective coordination, 98, 102–5, 110–13, 117, 121
"affective turn," 4, 153n4
affectlessness, 3, 121, 138, 139, 143
aggression, 45, 106, 124
analog and digital, 6, 13
analysis. *See* Poe, Edgar Allan: and Angell, Callie, 122, 123, 124, 126–27
anger, 3, 32, 39–40, 41, 43, 45, 50, 64, 65, 67, 68, 79, 81, 91; as basic affect, 5, 6, 101
anticipation, 100–103, 121. *See also* nervousness
anxiety, 38–39, 67, 159n19
Aristotle, 2, 85, 103
Artaud, Antonin, 12–13
astonishment, 81, 98, 138
attention, 1, 21, 25, 26, 42, 46, 72–73, 110, 142, 151; to affect, 1, 8, 29, 33–34, 76, 88, 99–100, 102, 152; analyst's, 9, 36–37; audience, 111–13, 124–5; compassionate, 36; introspective, 6; media, 129, 139.
audience, 1, 9, 15, 25, 111, 150–52; James, Henry: and, 78–79, 91, 94–95, 160n10; and knowledge, 98–99, 108; response, 1, 2, 3, 47, 99–100; and shame, 64, 125,

146, 159n22; Stein, Gertrude: and, 96–99, 110, 161n3; Warhol, Andy: and, 120–21, 147–8. *See also* affective coordination

Bateson, Gregory, 18–19, 92, 133, 155n34
Bion, Wilfred, 1, 10, 33, 77, 82, 93, 95, 97, 98–99, 121, 152; *Experiences in Groups*, 22, 73–76, 83–85, 90, 114; on genius and Establishment, 91–92; *Learning from Experience*, 22, 106–7, 108–9, 114; theory of thinking, 91, 106–9, 110, 114, 162n; writing style, 75–76. *See also* container/contained; group(s); object-relations theory; reverie
boredom, 33, 124, 138
Brecht, Bertolt, 98, 103, 121
Brooks, Peter, 80–82
Burns, Charles, 68–70

Cage, John, 117, 139, 165n3
catharsis, 103
character, 52, 54, 58, 77, 81, 102
childhood, 35, 39, 72, 74, 77, 90, 110, 147
cinema. *See* film
circular causality, 132, 136, 147. *See also* feedback
Cole, Jack, 47–52, 61–62, 70, 71
comedy, 73, 75, 138. *See also* funny
comics, 47–52, 61–62, 68–70
communication, nonverbal, 83, 88. *See also* affect(s): communication of
compassion, 36–37. *See also* sadism
completion, 30, 103–5, 109–10
complexity, 26, 28–29, 102, 132; of affect, 21, 32, 58–61, 81–82, 91, 135; of groups, 114, 115; organized, 5, 30; and television, 128.
composition(al), 1, 2, 3, 6, 8, 11, 20, 24–26, 30, 36, 39, 40, 42, 46, 61, 70, 78, 81, 91, 103, 151, 156n7; differences, 34, 37; force, 1, 2, 152
confession, 65, 75, 146, 159n20
confusion, 9, 11, 21, 25–28, 32–36, 73, 77, 82, 83, 87, 97, 135; and death instinct, 10, 43–44, 60, 76, 81. *See also* envy; muddle
consumer, 120, 123, 144, 148–49
container/contained, 10, 22, 38, 61, 91, 107–8, 109, 113, 114, 121, 129, 137, 149
contempt, 5, 28, 60, 61, 67, 68, 158n12
control, 23, 57, 60, 61, 63, 91, 121, 136, 147–48, 159n25; cybernetic understanding of, 132–34. *See also* affect(s): inhibition and amplification of; feedback
conversion, 23, 121, 133–34, 135–36. *See also* Warhol, Andy: conversion to self criticism, 1, 3–4, 19, 21, 33, 44, 51, 52, 63, 70, 154n9
crowd, 49, 56, 57, 61–62, 74. *See also* multiplicity
cybernetics, 3, 4, 23, 30, 58, 131–34, 147, 154n11, 155n20, 158n17, 164n34, 164n36
Cynics, 23, 131, 144–49

Darwin, Charles, 10, 101
death instinct. *See* Freud, Sigmund: and deconstruction, 11, 16, 19, 51, 55, 81
Deleuze, Gilles, 4
depressive position, 44–46, 120, 136, 157–58n36.
Derrida, Jacques, 2, 55, 104; affect in his general theory, 11, 15, 154–55n19; and cybernetics, 155n20, 164n36; "Freud and the Scene of Writing," 11–18; and materialism, 16, 18, 156n5; metaphor of the stage in, 11–18, 155n22; and structuralism, 13
despair, 57, 84, 90, 138. *See also* distress
destructiveness, 10, 37, 38, 43–45, 61, 63, 84, 91–92, 106, 109. *See also* envy
Diogenes, 145, 148
disgust, 5, 6, 45, 60, 68, 76
distress, 19, 32, 39–40, 41, 47–50, 54, 60, 67, 73, 86, 124, 156n35; as basic affect, 5, 41, 68; cry of, 41, 67, 89–90

embarrassment, 64, 90, 101, 146, 159n22.
emergence, 30, 58, 61, 76, 81, 106
emotion. *See* affect(s): and
emotional syncopation, 96, 96, 99, 110–12
empathy, 98. *See also* identification
enjoyment, 25, 32, 76, 87, 101, 156n5; as basic affect, 5, 31, 49, 50, 61, 63; and communion, 59–60; of excitement, 103; in infant development, 31; of mistake, 27–29, 147; of negative affect, 60
envy, 10, 21, 43–45, 46, 106, 124, 140.
ethics, 80–81, 131, 135, 160n2. *See also* affect(s): and ethics
evil eye. *See* Tomkins, Silvan: and taboos on looking
excitement, 3, 6, 25, 76, 100, 158n17; as basic affect, 5, 31, 101; for grammar, 30; in infant development, 31; nervous, 68–69, 100, 103, 110 (*see also*

nervousness); Poe and, 52, 59, 60; Stein on, 22, 34, 98, 102–5, 109–10; Tomkins on, 22, 32, 60–61, 99, 101
expression, 6, 19, 20, 56, 60, 68, 70, 71, 82, 94, 124, 125, 127, 158n15; of envy, 44; facial, 10, 42, 47, 48, 50, 53, 55, 56, 58, 64–65, 83, 124, 129, 156n35; problem of, 53–55, 63, 68; and repression, 21, 52, 61, 80–81; theory of, 51, 61, 71; verbal, 12, 15, 84. *See also* affect(s): communication of, location of
expressiveness, 10, 18, 51, 52, 57, 58, 60, 65, 66, 68–69, 124, 139, 151

face(s), 11, 47, 94; in comics, 47–50, 68–69; infant perception of, 45, 157n36; as medium of affect, 7, 10, 17–18, 50, 128, 154n11; Poe and, 21, 52–58, 59, 63–65; reproduced and distributed, 118, 121, 128; in Warhol's films, 123–28. *See also* expression, facial; mask(s)
fantasy, 19, 40, 89, 120–21, 128, 129, 146
fear, 37, 41, 45, 50, 55, 68, 77, 85, 89, 103, 104–5, 159n19; as basic affect, 5, 60, 61, 62, 67, 68, 101. *See also* anxiety
feedback, 3, 6, 7, 30, 58, 68, 121, 132, 136; negative, 30, 133, 134, 147; positive, 144, 147
feeling, 1, 6, 8, 9, 21, 25, 26, 28, 29–30, 42, 51, 54, 57, 60, 65, 66–67, 68, 78, 80, 84, 94–95, 99–101, 102, 105, 107, 124, 128, 139, 152, 162n20
Feldman, Morton, 23, 150–52, 157n11, 165n3
film, 17, 18, 20, 22, 66, 67, 71, 109; Henry James and, 161n22; Poe and, 62, 70; psychotronic, 70; Jack Smith and, 165n50; Stein and, 115–16; and theater, 64, 115. *See also* Warhol, Andy: *Empire, Outer and Inner Space, Screen Tests, Sleep*
force, 13, 19, 26, 29, 41, 61, 80–81, 91, 151. *See also* composition(al) force
Foucault, Michel, 20, 23, 121, 164n31; *The Courage of Truth*, 131, 144–45, 148; critique of Althusser, 134–35; and cybernetics, 132–34; *The Hermeneutics of the Subject*, 131, 133–36, 142; on power, 133; and psychoanalysis, 135, 164n; and Warhol, 131–32
frame(s), 2, 10, 18, 19, 47, 48, 52, 121, 123, 152; metacommunicative, 19, 155n34, 156n35

Freud, Sigmund, 3, 4, 12–15, 22, 51, 52; and death instinct, 10, 43, 44–45; differences between Klein and, 8–9, 24, 35, 40, 43; differences between Tomkins and, 4, 5, 24, 41, 67, 154n; and drive theory, 4–5, 41, 45; on group psychology, 74; "Note on the 'Mystic Writing-Pad,'" 13–14; and transference, 8
frustration, 25, 105, 108; and group dynamics, 22, 77, 85; and thinking, 33, 106–7, 162n20
funny, 19, 131, 140, 147, 156n. *See also* comedy

gesture, 11, 14, 35, 42, 49, 56, 80, 94, 111, 113, 116, 124
Goldberg, Jonathan, 16–17, 18, 156n5
governmentality, 23, 131, 133, 134–35, 144, 146
grief, 5, 45, 49. *See also* distress
group(s), 13, 20, 33, 44, 77, 91, 93, 114, 115, 117, 130; basic assumption, 83–85, 90, 93; consciousness, 74, 75, 85, 90, 92, 156n7, 160n10; family, 22, 72, 74; individual and, 7, 15–16, 22, 51, 74, 85, 90, 91–92, 95, 99, 107; leader, 74, 84; psychology, 16, 22, 72–76, 82, 83–85, 93, 95, 99, 114; and technologies of affective communication, 22, 115, 117–18; therapy, 10, 73, 75, 114, 160n3; work group, 74, 83, 85, 90, 93

Hackett, Pat, 130, 136, 144, 147
Hadot, Pierre, 130, 131, 164n31
hand(s), 11, 14, 16, 18
Hejinian, Lyn, 36–37
Hellenistic philosophy, 130, 134, 135–36, 142, 143
here and now, 9, 21, 36–37, 40, 42, 56, 106. *See also* present moment
Hinshelwood, Robert, 9, 35, 40, 41, 75–76, 106, 119
Howe, Susan, 37
humiliation, 67, 76, 79, 126, 148. *See also* shame

identification, 48, 55, 66, 75–76, 90, 97–98, 108–10, 113–18, 121, 159n24; introjective, 8, 9, 74, 107, 109, 128, 135, 137; projective, 8, 9, 10, 67, 74, 85, 106–7, 109, 129, 135
impatience, 6, 94, 100, 101

infantile experience, 8–9, 31, 35, 38, 40, 41, 43–45, 54, 59, 74, 82, 105, 107–8, 109, 119–21, 157n, 162n20
intensity, 5, 6, 35, 50, 51, 58, 60, 81, 102, 116, 152, 154n9
interest, 99, 101, 139. See also excitement
interpretation, 19, 35, 37, 73–74, 76, 95, 108, 147
intersubjectivity, 105, 134–35. See also affect(s): communication of; transference
introjection. See identification, introjective
irony, 19, 73, 75, 77, 83, 86, 123, 137, 140, 143
Isaacs, Susan, 41–43

James, Henry, 1, 3, 19, 20, 29, 72–95, 98, 114–15, 152; *The Golden Bowl*, 93–94; *Guy Domville*, 78, 96; late style, 22, 78, 92–95, 160n10; and melodrama, 80, 82; midcareer novels, 21, 78; notebook, 78–79, 85; preface to New York edition, 73, 77, 90–92; scenic method, 16, 78–79, 81; stage directions, 94, 161n20; and television, 94–95; and theatricality, 78, 79, 82, 90–91, 92, 160n10, 161n14; and transferential poetics, 76; *What Maisie Knew*, 10, 21–22, 72–92.
James, William, 21, 30, 31, 97, 139, 156n7; radical empiricism, 42; theory of emotion, 7, 22, 99–100. See also knowledge, of acquaintance
James-Lange theory of emotion. See James, William

keeping time. See tempo
Klein, Melanie, 1, 8–10, 16, 21, 22, 24, 26, 35–36, 40–45, 55–56, 74, 77, 93, 105–6, 119–20, 135, 152, 163n9; Controversial Discussions, 40–41; and "deep interpretation," 37; "Envy and Gratitude," 43–44; and play technique, 8, 35; and transference, 8–9, 76. See also identification; object-relations theory; phantasy
knowledge, 20, 22, 26, 35, 45, 70, 76–78, 82, 85–88, 96–97, 98–99, 102–3, 108–10, 114, 135, 139, 141, 142; of acquaintance, 102, 106; emotional conditions of, 29, 32, 99, 106, 109
Kurnick, David, 92–93, 160n10, 161n20

language. See affect(s): and

law of the excluded middle, 43, 156n7
leader. See group(s), leader
Likierman, Meira, 41
liveliness, 27–29, 30, 33–4, 38, 44, 46, 78, 100, 104–5, 116, 120, 127–28, 130, 138, 147, 156n5
liveness. See television
logic of noncontradiction, 32. See also law of the excluded middle

mask(s), 52, 70, 126
mass culture, 21, 70, 97, 120, 142–44. See also media, mass
materialism, 16, 18, 156n5, 158n15
materiality of verbal expression, 12, 15. See also writing: material conditions for
media, 1, 4, 18, 20, 50, 70, 115, 118, 122, 123, 127, 129, 137, 139; and affective communication, 17; mass, 10, 17, 19, 22, 129; sociological approaches to, 15–17, 20; studies, 17, 115; and theatricality, 2. See also mass culture; technology
McLuhan, Marshall, 17, 164n34
melodrama, 80–81, 89, 91, 111, 112, 161n12
memory, 13–14, 18, 34, 39, 46, 53, 54, 63, 76, 85, 89, 102, 104, 117
mesmerism, 51, 158n14
metacommunication. See affect(s): and
Meyer, Steven, 29, 99–100
mise-en-scène, 11–12, 13, 101, 126
middle ground, 32, 35, 39. See also law of the excluded middle
"middle ranges of agency," 32
mistake, 58, 100. See also Stein, Gertrude: and poetics of; Warhol, Andy: commitment to
modernism, 21, 26–27, 33, 36–37, 38, 46, 51, 70, 71, 98, 106, 115–17, 121, 122–23, 142, 143, 154n9
Moon, Michael, 161n13, 163n9
motivation, 2, 3, 5, 11, 14–15, 18, 20, 24, 31, 34, 41, 55, 58, 59, 64, 72, 73, 78, 79, 81–83, 102, 105, 113, 152, 153n4
movies. See film
muddle, 73–74, 76, 81, 83, 91. See also confusion
multiplicity, 12, 14, 15–16, 25, 55, 57–58, 59, 61, 81, 105, 113, 128–29, 154n11

nervousness, 22, 63, 68–69, 99–101, 103, 110. See also anticipation

INDEX / 183

object relations, 8, 9, 14, 41, 74, 76, 135, 154–55n19
object-relations theory, 1, 4, 8, 24, 35, 40, 55–56, 99, 105, 119–20, 160n5; compatibility with Tomkins's theory, 41, 45, 157–58n36; relation to Jamesian tradition, 105–6. *See also* Bion; Klein
out there, 23, 62, 150–52. *See also* transferential poetics

paranoia, 75, 159n20
paranoid-schizoid position, 44, 120
part-objects, 8, 43, 44, 82, 107, 119. *See also* object relations
perception, 2, 13–14, 18, 25–26, 33, 38–40, 52, 73–74, 83, 85, 87, 88, 100, 101, 104, 105, 119, 120, 132, 136; *Nachträglich* nature of, 14; role of affect in, 21, 24, 31–32, 42–43, 46. *See also* frame(s); here and now
performance, 1, 10, 15, 18, 64, 82, 88, 89, 94, 96, 99, 100, 101, 110, 117, 121, 123, 125, 139, 141–43, 151–52; bad, 144, 147
performativity, 8, 26, 79, 152, 161n20
phantasy, 2, 9–10, 14, 16, 21, 24, 32, 35, 37, 40–42, 43, 55–56, 59, 74, 85, 90, 93, 106, 119, 128, 160n5
phenomenology, 5, 6, 8, 22, 24, 33, 65, 70, 92, 103, 105, 109
physiognomy, 56–57, 58, 158n15
physiology, 7, 10, 21, 29, 41, 50, 51, 52, 100, 123, 124, 158n15, 163n23. *See also* physiological psychology
physiological psychology, 6, 29–30, 34, 99
Picasso, Pablo, 45–46, 116
play, 13, 18–19, 38, 55–56, 70, 76, 81, 110, 113, 139, 141, 144. *See also* Klein, Melanie: and play technique
pleasure, 28, 47, 51–52, 59, 81, 101, 111, 125, 141, 147
Poe, Edgar Allan, 1, 2, 3, 6, 19, 20, 21, 51–71, 94–95, 97, 143, 152; and analysis, 55, 158n; and character, 52, 54; "Letter to B--," 51–52; "Ligeia," 53–54, 56; "Maelzel's Chess-Player," 159n25; "The Man That Was Used Up," 53–54, 56, 58; "The Man of the Crowd," 56–58, 63; and media, 62–68, 70–71; "The Murders in the Rue Morgue," 55; "The Philosophy of Composition," 2, 52, 54; and poetics of effect 2, 51–52, 67–68; "The Purloined Letter," 55, 158n; "A Tale of the Ragged Mountains," 54, 56; "The Tell-Tale Heart," 6, 21, 52, 60, 62–70
poetics, 1, 2, 3, 17, 19, 22, 25, 33, 51, 52, 59–60, 71, 75, 98, 120, 129, 136, 142, 151; definition of, 2–3; American, of the contemporary, 139; telepoetics, 20. *See also* Aristotle; Poe, Edgar Allan: and poetics of effect; Stein, Gertrude: and poetics of mistake; transferential poetics; Warhol, Andy: televisual
Pop Art, 121, 123, 129, 136, 140, 142, 145, 149
portraiture: Stein and, 34, 102, 113–17; Warhol and, 122–29, 144, 148
present moment, 101–2, 103, 117, 139, 148. *See also* here and now
projection. *See* identification, projective
psychedelia, 125, 129
psychoanalysis, 4, 16, 32, 35, 36, 54, 55, 60, 63, 73, 76, 82, 91, 110, 123, 128, 129, 131, 135, 157n15, 159n19, 164n43, 165n50; and hypnosis, 51; neutrality in, 123–125; and sex drive, 5, 8, 82; total situation, 36. *See also* Bion, Wilfred; Freud, Sigmund; Klein, Melanie

queerness, 36, 48, 70, 91, 123, 131, 144, 163n9, 165n60

radio, 17, 18, 20, 115
rage. 45, 65, 67. *See also* anger
reading, 6, 15, 18, 21, 25–26, 28–29, 39, 56–57, 59, 68, 75–76, 86, 103, 106, 110, 132, 138, 147
Reed, Lou, 70
relief, 103–5, 109
repression, 5, 15, 20, 21, 37, 52, 60, 63, 67–68, 80–81, 154n8. *See also* affect(s): inhibition and amplification of
resentment, 79, 81, 91
reverie, 98, 107–9, 111, 113, 121
Rousseau, Jean-Jacques, 98, 103, 118

sadism, 36–37, 57, 73, 90, 124
sadness, 47–48, 50. *See also* distress; grief
screen, 19, 121, 126–28, 129, 139. *See also* Warhol, Andy: *Screen Tests*
Sedgwick, Edie, 122, 126–29, 141, 163n23
Sedgwick, Eve, 3, 20–21, 32, 154n17, 161n14, 162n20, 165n61
self-care, 20, 131, 135–36, 141. *See also* therapeutics

self-organization, 30. *See also* emergence
sexuality, 8, 16, 51, 77, 78, 82–84, 86–90, 101, 119, 131, 140–41, 144, 159n21, 163n9, 165n60
Shakespeare, William, 110–11, 115
shame, 6, 59, 60–65, 68, 76, 77, 79, 83, 89, 146, 165n61; as basic affect, 5, 6, 60, 61–65, 68–70, 101, 125, 157–58n36; and theatricality, 63–64, 90–91, 159n22, 161n14. *See also* Tomkins, Silvan: and taboos on looking
shamelessness, 3, 6, 21, 52, 62–63, 65, 70–71, 145–46
Shaviro, Steven, 142–43
Smith, Adam, 10, 48–50, 66–67, 97–98, 118, 159–60nn24–26
sociopolitical system, 20, 115, 134
sound, 25, 37, 53–54, 65–66, 113, 125–26, 126, 151, 159n25, 161n21
spectator, 22, 49, 66, 77–78, 82, 83, 85, 87–88, 90, 97, 98, 118, 122, 129, 159n24; "impartial," 66. *See also* audience; viewer
spiritual exercises, 130, 136. *See also* therapeutics
Spinoza, Benedict, 156n5
stage, 11–15, 18, 19, 64, 78, 80, 88, 91, 92, 96, 97, 98, 100–1, 104, 109, 111–13, 125, 139, 150, 165n48; on and off, 13–15, 155n27
Stein, Gertrude, 1, 3, 19, 20, 24–46, 91, 96–118, 120, 121, 139, 143, 152; and audience, 96–97, 161n3; as audience, 99–101; *The Autobiography of Alice B Toklas*, 36, 96, 110, 115, 161n3; "Composition as Explanation," 2, 3, 24–26; and continuous present, 36, 38; *Doctor Faustus Lights the Lights*, 113; and excitement, 101–5 (*see also* nervousness); *An Exercise in Analysis*, 112; *Four in America*, 115; genius, definition of, 34, 116; landscape plays, 10, 12, 22, 91, 97, 99, 112–13, 117, 120; *A Long Gay Book*, 114; *The Making of Americans*, 102, 114; *Many Many Women*, 114; "Meditations on Being about to Visit My Native Land," 97; "Paintings," 33; *Picasso*, 45–46; "Plays," 10, 22, 96–115; poetic project, 25; poetics of mistake, 9, 21, 27–30, 147 (*see also* mistake); "Poetry and Grammar," 26–30, 37, 38, 117; "Portraits and Repetition," 32, 33–35, 102, 116; *Tender Buttons*, 21, 37–40, 114; *Three Lives*, 36; United States lecture tour, 96–97, 115, 161n; *What Happened. A Play*, 114
structuralism, 4, 5, 13, 37
subject/structure, 15–16
sublime, 60, 68
surprise, 35, 37, 76, 81, 89, 98, 138, 147; as basic affect, 5, 68
sympathy, 47–50, 51, 66, 86, 87, 97–98, 159n24, 160n26. *See also* Smith, Adam
system, 11, 15–16, 21, 30, 130, 133
systems theory, 4, 7, 11, 17, 30, 155n20

technology, 1, 2, 4, 16, 19, 28, 34, 115, 122, 132, 137, 139, 143, 164n34; of affective communication, 22, 118; broadcasting, 18, 22; graphic, 16–19, 56, 116–17, 121, 126, 151, 158n14. *See also* film; radio; television; writing
telephone, 136–38, 147
television, 2, 17, 18, 19, 20, 22, 71, 92–95, 115, 116, 118, 119–21, 139, 149, 155n32; as analyst, 128–129; commercials, 122, 123; as culture industry, 121; and cybernetics, 132; as experimental instrument, 125–26, 132; game shows, 146, 161n; intimate scale of, 93–95, 143, 146; liveness, 122, 123, 126; contrast with movies, 120–21, 127–28, 143; reality, 146, 147, 161n20; scanning, 116–17, 129, 132; slang words for, 119; talk shows, 126, 127, 141; as therapeutic device, 23, 121, 129, 137–44. *See also* Warhol, Andy: televisual poetics
televisual perspective (on emotion), 23, 120, 121, 123, 126, 139, 142–43
tempo, 66, 97, 98, 113, 139, 151, 159–60n25
terror, 45, 55, 57, 60, 65–66, 68, 159n19. *See also* fear
theater: metaphor of, 10–15, 118, 159n24; problem of, 22, 100, 103, 109, 111, 114, 118; technologies of, 115
theatricality, 2, 10, 47, 62–63, 64, 71, 77–78, 82, 87–90, 92–93, 121, 125, 139, 140, 143, 152, 160n10; conceptual intimacy with affect, 10, 11, 18–19, 121; definition of, 19; hollowness of, 139, 165n48; and shame, 63–64, 90, 161n14; of social relations, 98, 103; and taboos on looking, 21, 63–64, 71, 125–26; and vindication, 78–81, 91. *See also* stage; theater; writing: theatricalization of

therapeutics, 22, 23, 37, 44, 121, 129–49
thinking, 10, 11, 18, 20, 21, 25, 34, 36, 40, 42, 44, 91, 93, 98, 102, 106, 109, 132, 148, 152, 160n5; apparatus for, 107; as definitively transindividual, 108. *See also* Bion, Wilfred: theory of; frustration, and; group(s), work group
Tomkins, Silvan, 1, 3, 4–8, 20, 21, 22, 24, 26, 30–32, 36, 52, 55, 58, 97, 99; and affect-object reciprocity, 31–32, 35, 40, 101; compatibility with object-relations theory, 10, 41, 45, 154n17, 157–58n36; critique of drive theory, 4–5, 41; and death instinct, 10, 45; and General Images, 21, 52, 58, 59–60, 66, 67–68, 70, 81; and ideology, 7, 8, 154n; "inverse archaeology," 7; and masochistic strategy of affect magnification, 60, 62, 67–70; and role of affect in perception, 31, 32; and script theory, 10–11, 58, 59, 61; and taboos on looking, 21, 52, 63–65, 68, 70, 71, 125–26; and television, 125–26. *See also* affect(s); feedback; phenomenology
tragedy, 4, 103
transference, 1, 2, 7, 8–9, 19, 34, 51, 55, 76, 95, 102, 114, 115, 121, 124, 126, 128, 129, 143, 152
transferential moment, 6–8, 20
transferential poetics, 1, 2, 8, 22, 23, 70, 76, 78, 90, 93, 150–52
translation, 12, 73, 74

uncanny, 3, 52, 54, 67–68, 78, 90, 159n20

verbal behavior. *See* affect(s): and language
vicarious, 64, 77, 78, 86, 89, 141

video, 120, 122, 126–127, 129, 146, 163n14
viewer, 47, 48, 50, 93–94, 95, 119, 121, 124, 126, 128, 129, 146, 147, 148, 164n34
vindication, 78, 90, 91, 92; and theatricality, 78–81; and vindictiveness, 79
voice, 7, 10, 17, 18, 42, 47, 50, 80, 94, 112, 118, 121, 127, 128, 129

Warhol, Andy, 1, 3, 10, 17, 19, 20, 22, 117, 120–49, 152; *Andy Warhol's Diaries*, 146; and cable television, 122, 163n5; commitment to mistake, 144, 147, 148; conversion to self, 136–43; and cybernetics, 132, 164n34; and Cynic philosophy, 144–149; *Empire*, 120, 122; the Factory, 122, 123, 127, 130, 139; *Interview*, 144; as nobody, 137; *Nothing Special*, 138, 146, 149; *Outer and Inner Space*, 122, 126–29, 137; *The Philosophy of Andy Warhol (From A to B and Back Again)*, 23, 121, 122, 128, 129, 130–32, 136–148; and queerness, 123, 138, 144, 163n9; *Screen Tests*, 123–26, 129, 142; *Sleep*, 120, 122; *Soap Opera*, 122; and television, definition of, 132; televisual poetics, 120, 122–29; Time Capsules, 148–49.
Wiener, Norbert, 132, 133
Williams, Raymond, 17, 20
writing: material conditions for, 25, 30, 35, 54, 151, 152; space of, 13–15; theatricalization of, 2, 18–20, 52, 93, 143, 152. *See also* materiality of verbal expression
wonder, 77, 90

Acknowledgments

I experienced many mind-changing transferential relations, with individuals, groups, and institutions, while writing this book. It gives me real pleasure to acknowledge some of them here.

First, Michael Moon read this entire manuscript and offered invaluable feedback, advice, and encouragement along the way. I am deeply grateful to him for his intellectual and emotional support, acuity, practically infinite resources, and the many enjoyable conversations we have had about affect, literature, music, and media over the years. I look forward to many more. Michael, along with Elizabeth Wilson and Jonathan Goldberg, invited me to present parts of this project at Emory University. Thanks to Liz, my main interlocutor on all things Tomkins, and to Jonathan, who read and responded to my last writing for this book, for their love and friendship. Thanks as well to audiences at Emory for helpful questions and suggestions,

Anna Gibbs and Jennifer Biddle gave me the chance to share some of my earliest work on this project at the symposium Affect at the Interface, which took place in Sydney in June 2008. Thanks to the participants in that event as well as its sponsors, the Writing and Society Research Group at the University of Western Sydney and the Center for Contemporary Art and Politics at the College of Fine Arts, Sydney. I am grateful to Fiona Brideoake for arranging my talk on Warhol at the University of Melbourne. And, once again, I am very grateful to Liz Wilson, both for being a great host in Sydney and for taking such good care of me when my back went out.

I am grateful to colleagues for invitations to present talks at various venues: the Science Studies Colloquium at the University of California, San Diego; the symposium Contemporaneities of Gertrude Stein held at the Université du Québec à Montréal; the workshop Varieties of Empathy in Science, Art and Culture held at the University of British Columbia; and others. I am grateful to the audiences who heard and responded to my work, including those at meetings of the Modernist Studies Association, the Society for Literature, Science, and the Arts, and the American Comparative Literature Association.

Thanks to the University of British Columbia for funding the sabbatical leave that let me complete this book and for providing a usable cross-disciplinary environment for intellectual work. In particular, I am grateful to the following colleagues for reading and responding to my writing or otherwise providing vital intellectual and moral support: Robert Brain, Alex Dick, Christina Lupton, Kevin McNeilly, Miguel Mota, Alan Richardson, Sandy Tomc, and Mark Vessey. I would also like to thank those students who were game to think with me about affect theory and literary/media criticism in several courses over the years, especially Natalie Forssman, Aaron Goldsman, Kate Hallemeier, Matt Hiebert, Sean McAlister, Ada Smailbegović, and Kate Stanley.

I wrote the final parts of this book during a sabbatical year in Montréal. I am grateful to Paul Yachnin and the McGill University English Department for providing library use and an office. Ned Schantz made a good year in Montréal even better by providing stimulating conversation (now ongoing) about movies, television, and criticism. I am also grateful to Marcie Frank for inviting me to speak to the English Department at Concordia University.

Jonathan Elmer and Lisa Cartwright read my manuscript for Fordham University Press and offered helpful, generous feedback. I tried to follow the advice of both readers, who suggested that I make more of this project's intervention into media studies. Thanks too to Thomas Lay and the late, grievously missed, Helen Tartar at Fordham for editorial support. Greg Pierce at the Andy Warhol Museum, Gary Groth at Fantagraphics, and the staff at DC Comics helped to secure permissions for reproducing the images in this book. Two journals gave me permission to reprint my earlier writing. Chapter 2 is a revised version of "Medium Poe," which appeared in *Criticism: A Quarterly for Literature and the Arts* 48, no. 2 (2006). Copyright © 2007 Wayne State University Press. Used with the permission of Wayne State University Press. Chapter 4 is a revised version of "Loose Coordinations: Theater and Thinking in Gertrude Stein," which appeared in *Science in Context* 25, no. 3 (2012). Used with the permission of Cambridge University Press.

ACKNOWLEDGMENTS / 189

The thinking that made writing this book possible developed most intensively in the company of a number of individuals and their creative work. Steven Meyer's writing on Gertrude Stein has increased my capacity to enjoy and understand her work, and I have learned enormously from our many conversations about Stein, James, Whitehead, varieties of empiricism, and the history of literary criticism, in coffee shops, restaurants, and museums across North America. Sam Shalabi introduced me to the music and writing of Morton Feldman. I thank him for that and for twenty years (give or take) of conversations about music, politics, philosophy, work and play, ageing, family, and other things. I became thoroughly acquainted with the nitty-gritty of object relations in the company of Dr. Elie Debbané, and for this experience I continue to entertain a complicated feeling of gratitude and chagrin. As for Eve Kosofsky Sedgwick, who passed away in 2009, this book would simply not have taken the shape it has without her presence in my life. I continue to be grateful to Eve for introducing me to Tomkins, Klein, and ways of thinking and feeling that try to make the most of how these are always intertwined. Thanks too to Hal Sedgwick for his unflagging commitment to Eve's work.

My sisters, Marcie and Jill Frank, have always been there with love and advice. In fact Marcie got me into this business in the first place. I doubt she remembers a long conversation we had on an airplane more than twenty-five years ago, but that's what got me started on my gradual slide toward criticism. I am very grateful to her for this conversation and the many others, both personal and professional, we have had since and continue to have.

I am grateful to my parents for so many things, especially for their emotional and financial support over the years and for the value they placed on curiosity, vitality, and emotional honesty. My father, Hershie Frank, passed away after a long illness not long before I completed this book. I have learned to appreciate his directness, stubbornness, considerable mental energy, and what I now think of as his finely tuned bullshit detector; I hope I brought some of these qualities to the writing in this book. I am very grateful to my mother, Esther Frank, for her love, friendship, and open mind.

Finally, Marguerite Pigeon has given me a chance to experience more enjoyment than I ever thought possible. I am most grateful to her, and to the little group that we are making together: Merle, and now the new one, Lewis. To Marguerite, Merle, Michael, Marcie, and my mother (and a few more Ms thrown in beside), I have dedicated this book.

bad dad murder

men of commmunor we was
we critically views
we assess
enjoyment of repairs
of negative aspects